LIFE WITH ROSSETTI

1. Dante Gabriel Rossetti—a portrait by Henry Treffry Dunn.

LIFE WITH ROSSETTI

or

No Peacocks Allowed

GALE PEDRICK

MACDONALD : LONDON

First published in 1964 by
Macdonald & Co. (Publishers) Ltd.,
Gulf House, 2 Portman Street, London, W.1.
Made and printed in Great Britain by
Butler & Tanner Ltd., Frome and London

Thin are the night-skirts left behind
  By daybreak hours that onward creep,
  And thin, alas! the shred of sleep
That wavers with the spirit's wind:
But in half-dreams that shift and roll
  And still remember and forget,
My soul this hour has drawn your soul
  A little nearer yet.

From "Insomnia", a poem by
Dante Gabriel Rossetti.

Acknowledgments

I recall with pleasure a visit to the home in Woodstock, near Oxford, of Helen Rossetti Angeli: and I thank her for the gracious way in which she gave assent to the publication of letters written by her uncle to his friend and companion Henry Treffry Dunn (and of others which passed between Mr. Treffry Dunn and her eminent father).

Most of the correspondence quoted in this book is in the keeping of the Victoria and Albert Museum: and I am most grateful for the co-operation of the Museum and for permission to include so many letters in the following pages. I must mention, too, the generous help given by Mrs. Janet Camp Troxell, of New Haven, Connecticut, U.S.A., who owns the original manuscript of H. T. Dunn's *Recollections of Dante Gabriel Rossetti and His Circle*.

I was courteously assisted by officials of the National Portrait Gallery; the Tate Gallery; the Uffizi Gallery in Florence; the William Morris Gallery; and of The Heatherley School of Fine Art.

Among other kindly-disposed friends whose ready help I acknowledge are Mr. Claude Berry, Editor of the West Briton & Royal Cornwall Gazette; Mr. L. Mason, formerly Editor of the Herne Bay Press; Mr. H. L. Douch, B.A., of the Royal Institution of Cornwall; and surviving members of Harry Treffry Dunn's family. I cannot forget how much this book owes to my father, the late John Gale Pedrick, F.R.Hist.Soc., who edited Dunn's *Recollections* fifty years ago.

G.P.

List of Plates

The author and publishers wish to thank the following for supplying
photographs: *Country Life* for 11, 12; the County Museum and Art Gallery,
Truro, for 6; Merredew for 18; the National Portrait Gallery for 16; the
National Trust, Wightwick Manor, for 13, 14; the Tate Gallery for 9; the
William Morris Gallery, Walthamstow, for 8; and the Uffizi Gallery,
Florence, for 1.

I

You are the best of fellows and my guardian angel.
　　　　　　　　　　　　—Dante Gabriel Rossetti to
　　　　　　　　　"My Dear Dunn", Bognor 1875.

One could spend the leisure of half a lifetime writing a book about the romantically named Dante Gabriel Rossetti who was, as the inscription on his tombstone claims, "honoured among painters as a painter, and among poets as a poet".

Henry Treffry Dunn was Rossetti's art-assistant—which means that for many years he lived under the same roof as Dante Gabriel at 16, Cheyne Walk. One of his tasks was to paint replicas of Rossetti's pictures, and he painted these with such skill that Evelyn Waugh wrote of these facsimiles: "One can only surmise how much of them was the work of Dunn, and how much of the faltering master." This, of course, is a matter of opinion and to be just, Mr. Waugh is referring to a period when Rossetti's brilliance was clouded by illness and the use, in excess, of chloral.

It is true that but for the work he did in Rossetti's studio Dunn's name would long since have been forgotten even by people whose business or pleasure it is to know their history of nineteenth-century art.

I believe Dunn has a claim to be remembered for reasons altogether more genial and intimate. As an artist he was talented, if not outstanding. His portrait in oils of Rossetti is in the Uffizi Gallery in Florence, an unusual distinction for an Englishman. A picture he painted of Rossetti and Theodore Watts-Dunton, seated in a room in Gabriel's Chelsea home, hangs in the National Portrait Gallery in London.

The story of Henry Treffry Dunn's friendship with Rossetti is not widely known. His own brief *Recollections of Dante Gabriel Rossetti*, which I have quoted extensively, had a very limited circulation, although the little book has been a useful, not to say compulsory, reference for the biographers. His style has a naïve and unpretentious charm; which, para-doxically, gives an air of authority to what he has to tell us. When all is said—he was there. If Dunn, as an actor in the play, had merely a walking-on part, he was still a key man in the drama. There are many reasons why his tale is worth the telling.

This book differs from many in which Rossetti plays the leading rôle, because here the bias is towards the domestic rather than the romantic; and I have been able to quote a great many letters, so far unpublished, which were written by Rossetti to my great-uncle Harry.

Harry Dunn was more than an "art-assistant". He was the companion, secretary and unofficial manager who ran Rossetti's chaotic household, paid the bills, hired the models, and sacked the cook. And when the chloral habit began to take its toll of mind and bodily strength, it was to Harry Dunn that Gabriel's devoted brother William turned as an ally.

The letters, these intimate despatches, came into the possession of the kind-hearted Mrs. Clara Watts-Dunton who, as though to harbour indigent artists and men of letters was the most natural thing in the world, gave Harry Dunn in his last years the shelter of her roof. When Mrs. Watts-Dunton died in 1938, these letters were bought on behalf of the Victoria and Albert Museum in whose keeping they remain and with whose permission extracts from them are now printed. I quote from them with the generous approval of Rossetti's niece, Mrs. Helen Rossetti Angeli, whose own picture of her uncle is as brilliantly and poignantly defined as any in existence.

True, Dunn was employed by Rossetti but theirs was a world of ready cash, of paying for goods and service if and when money was to hand. If—as so often happened—"tin" was in short supply, no great bones were made of it.

It is true that in the last years, Dunn became a trifle peeved when his salary was in considerable arrears: but for the greater part of their association the two men were on the best of terms. Gabriel was certainly not a man who would treat a fellow-artist with anything but courtesy.

Sometimes the letters were written with affection, sometimes with impatience, sometimes in ill-health and in the shadow of a nagging anxiety. Of course, there is much in them which is trivial, but the simple explanation for this is that they deal with day-to-day affairs in a carefree and haphazard establishment.

Rossetti in his lifetime and long after his burial in the churchyard of

All Saints', Birchington, was often misunderstood and maligned. Since his death more than eighty years ago, his character has been the target for ill-founded attacks, and for many a callous probing into conduct and motives.

The true Rossetti? I have a feeling that the simple, sometimes commonplace and often gently humorous exchanges between Gabriel and his art-assistant provide a better answer than do the speculations of some who might have been kinder in their assessments.

Mrs. Angeli does not compromise: "It is not excessive to say", she writes, "that no distinguished man of English art or letters of the nineteenth century has been so repeatedly and so unaccountably attacked as Dante Gabriel Rossetti. No poet of the language—not even Edgar Allan Poe—has been more lied about."

Is it not possible that Rossetti was a clever man, a brilliant man, on whom Fate played some devilishly scurvish tricks? The bar-tenders who served him with drinks when he was out for a gay evening with his friends, the cab-drivers and shopkeepers, the florists and the frame-makers, all these must have found him a pleasant and affable man, with a rather more generous allocation of charm than is the general portion. To little Louisa Macdonald, one of the famed Macdonald Sisters who became the mother of Earl Baldwin of Bewdley, Gabriel must have seemed just a jolly, laughing bear of a man who could produce packets of sweets, and tickets for the zoo. The "sly Italian" sneer, much quoted, is unjustified. He was born and brought up as an Englishman.

It is tempting to ask what Rossetti's standing would have been had he lived until broadcasting and television stripped from great men their remoteness, and all the comforting veils of privacy. What would have been his "public image"? That of a genial, portly figure, welcomed in Burlington House for his witty speeches at Royal Academy banquets, and in demand as a speaker on "Round Britain Quiz" or some other amusingly erudite panel?

By 1867 Dunn was living at 16, Cheyne Walk, firmly established as a member of the household. He was then twenty-nine: Rossetti, ten years older. There is some doubt as to the date of their first meeting. The year 1863 has been accepted, but William Michael Rossetti, a stickler for accuracy, thinks Harry Dunn first called on his brother a year or so later than this: at all events, it is certain that Harry Dunn had been introduced to Gabriel some time before he made his home in Chelsea. He had certainly been introduced as an able copyist and had been given a number of commissions.

Harry took up his new duties with zeal and enjoyment.

Gabriel had a host of friends: in his home there was a good deal of entertaining, and plenty of laughter as well as eating and drinking, which often went on far into the night. In spite of this outward show of conviviality Rossetti was often melancholy, often lonely. He needed "looking after". He still felt keenly the loss of his wife a few years earlier and could never forget the tragic circumstances of her death. The household affairs of the big house in Cheyne Walk were conducted in a dilatory and slapdash manner.

Servants came, tarried awhile, and went their ways. As he grew older Gabriel felt less and less inclined to haggle with agents or to cope with their impatience when a deadline was in danger of being dishonoured.

At the time Dunn came on the scene practical help was desperately needed if confusion were not to become worse confounded. Rossetti found it essential to have a buffer between him and the domestic storms which seemed always about to break over his head. In these matters, Gabriel was by nature disposed to take the line of least resistance. Yes, a stand had to be taken—but by whom?

Ostensibly, the young Cornishman was engaged to "assist" in Rossetti's work—to buy brushes, paints and canvases, to attend to the framing of pictures, to engage the lovely, auburn-haired models, to obtain the extraordinary range of objects Rossetti wanted to work upon:

> There is another thing I want—to wit, a dragon-fly or two to paint in my picture, you know they are quite blue and I want one with his wings spread upwards as they do when they fly or sometimes when they stand. You might, if possible, get me 2 or 3 set up in different positions. I am wanting them as soon as possible. Also you might get me a few blue or blue-grey butterflies. These also to be set up in action flying or resting.

Harry was also expected to deal with correspondence, to carry messages, and—most important of all—to help complete commissioned pictures and to paint replicas, an arrangement which was taken as a matter of course in the art world of that time.

Dunn quickly found himself a confidant, a personal bodyguard almost, charged with protecting his employer from ill winds blowing from many quarters. He dealt with persistent callers, shocked himself by the ease with which he manipulated the truth when speaking to tradesmen, took on

cooks and housemaids, dismissed them "with a week's wages", and
attempted with a kind of desperate, if deceptive, efficiency, to preserve
for Rossetti a civilised way of living.

Above all, Dunn contrived to keep at bay the redoubtable Fanny
Cornforth—Fanny the Elephant, as Gabriel called her. Fanny, for years
Rossetti's chief model, whose candid intimacy with him provoked friends
to bewilderment, anxiety, disgust and anger. Fanny, the self-appointed
and non-resident housekeeper, who irritated the staff, grumbled, queened
it, and was not above helping herself to various easily disposable objects
when the fancy took her.

Was Fanny misunderstood? It does seem odd that although she must
have had qualities which endeared her to Rossetti—his loyalty to her
never wavered—few words in her defence have been written. She emerges
as the dark influence upon Rossetti's life—this "Good Elephant" or the
"Dear Good Fan" to whom he addressed so many humorous and affectionate letters. Dunn found it hard to take a charitable view when she
interfered with his efforts to keep the affairs of Number Sixteen from
foundering, and there was little enough love lost between them. He
figures in an impassioned (and unpunctuated) letter from Fanny to
Rossetti which is familiar to most students of Rossetti's life:

> Dunn frequently passed my place on the other side of the way and in the
> middle of the Avenuye with a sneer on his face and concluded that he was
> rejoicing at my downfall.

Dunn's relationship with Rossetti has intrigued me for many years.
First of all, because he was my mother's uncle: and later, because I was
stimulated by the difficulties I encountered when collecting enough information to give even a shadowy picture of the man himself. There was
something of a challenge in the few—but tantalising—glimpses of
Rossetti's "art-assistant". There was Gabriel's own heartfelt tribute,
"You are the best of fellows and my guardian angel." The friend to whom
he wrote that must surely have been a man of some quality.

I found the phrase in one of many letters shown to me by the late Mrs.
Clara Watts-Dunton.

This vivacious and generous little woman, wearing her flaming red hair
as if it were a badge of loyalty to Rossetti and his friends of the Pre-
Raphaelite Brotherhood, had read Violet Hunt's book *The Life of Rossetti*
and was enraged. My father had edited Dunn's all-too-slim volume of

Recollections, and recognising my name in some article I had written she commanded me to call upon her at The Pines.

"That's your Uncle Dunn's corner" were her first words as she showed me into a room overlooking the main road. "I can see him now, sitting there and painting away as happy as a king." She was determined, so she told me, to do everything in her power to clear Rossetti's memory from the slur cast on his private life by recent biographers. As Theodore Watts-Dunton's widow she felt she had a mission to undo some of the hurt which had been done to her husband's friend in these books— especially Miss Hunt's. She was an old lady and far from well, but she was off to Italy to meet some members of the Rossetti family, including his niece, Helen. When she returned she would answer the calumnies in a book of her own, and would be quoting the words of sympathetic friends, my great-uncle Harry among them. Could she count on my help if necessary?

Here surely was a hint that history had done great-uncle Harry less than justice: was his almost total obscurity deserved? All this made me still more eager to discover as much as I could about my elusive relative.

Finally, there appears a description of my great-uncle in a "prefatory note" written by William Michael Rossetti to Dunn's book. I have been unable to trace many letters written by Dunn (Rossetti, I should judge, was not a man to put much value on casual correspondence, and I assume that most of Dunn's letters to him were tossed into the fire in winter or put out with the rubbish in summer). But his *Recollections of Dante Gabriel Rossetti and His Circle* is the only account Dunn left in his own words dealing with the many years he spent as secretary, companion, art-assistant, major domo and jack-of-all-trades at Cheyne Walk. William Michael Rossetti wrote:

> Mr. Dunn saw as much of Dante Rossetti as any other person whatsoever did, or indeed more, if one looks to continuous day-by-day association. He witnessed his comings-out and goings-in, and was highly familiar with his methods of work as a painter. Every look of his countenance, every intonation of his voice, every mood of his temper—sunny, overcast, or variously shifting—was known to him.
>
> I had a very sincere regard for Mr. Dunn, perceiving him to be upright and straightforward in all his dealings, a valuable professional auxiliary for my brother to have secured, and always anxious to serve Rossetti's true interests in matters outside the pictorial range. He did a good deal towards keeping things straight in an establishment where the master's rather unthrifty and negligent habits in household affairs might easily have made them crooked.

Here at least was something to work upon. Firstly, Dante Gabriel Rossetti clearly thought highly enough of my great-uncle to write to him with affection. Secondly, Dunn was obviously an excellent artist as well as a faithful servant. Thirdly, there was a great deal to be read between the lines in the words of William Michael, that man of supreme discretion.

The *Recollections* give an agreeable and sometimes intimate picture of Rossetti and some of his friends. But like Rossetti's brother, Dunn was obviously a man of immense tact and no hint is given that any scandal, anguish or tragedy ever disturbed the distinguished but pleasantly eccentric establishment in Chelsea. There is no printed mention of Fanny, although Mrs. Camp Troxell, now owner of the original manuscript, tells me that when any reference is made to her, Fanny's name is deleted—presumably by William Michael who was invited to "approve" the *Recollections* before publication.

Dunn has nothing to say in his book about the bitter and disastrous attack launched on Rossetti in that notorious article by Robert Buchanan on "The Fleshly School of Poetry" in *The Contemporary Review*. Disastrous because of the effect it had upon the mind of Rossetti. Of the exhumation order to open Mrs. Rossetti's grave in Highgate Cemetery so that the book of poems her husband had buried with her might be recovered, there is no word. This dramatic affair occurred while Dunn was keeping house at 16, Cheyne Walk, but he is exasperatingly reticent. There are no references to Rossetti's enslavement by chloral, his alarming illnesses and the decline of his creative powers. In short, the *Recollections* are tactful to a fault, and I longed to read all that was left out. (And there were many confidences which might, indeed, have given pain to Gabriel's surviving relatives—his brother lived until 1919.) I read the book with sympathetic interest, with exasperation and finally, with a sense of frustration.

There is a whole series of provocative "throw-away" lines in the letters Rossetti wrote to "My dear Dunn", from Scotland, from Oxfordshire, from Bognor, from his Kentish retreat near Herne Bay.

"*The question of Emma must be wound up soon, and I incline strongly to the belief that she will have to go*", is a characteristic comment. More vigorous is the instruction: "*Dear Dunn—it is my express wish and order that Ellen be discharged at once, with a month's board wages and a good character.*"

Fanny prompted this intriguing message, "*My dear Dunn, the Elephant writes in a rage, but I have sent her a settler.*"

B

There is no doubt at all that Rossetti soon leant heavily upon his art-assistant, and not only in matters concerning art. "*My dear Dunn—is the tax-paper a final application? If not, it may stand for awhile. . . .*"

These endearing glimpses of the relationship between the two men made me the more anxious to learn more about the admirable Mr. Dunn. Why, then, should the task present such a problem? Dunn was known to the various eminent visitors who came to Cheyne Walk—Burne-Jones, William Morris, Ford Madox Brown, Whistler, Swinburne, William Bell Scott, Watts-Dunton. No doubt they took the amiable young man for granted. Why indeed should they take any special note of the quiet, efficient "man about the house"? They must have envied Gabriel his luck in having such a willing and agreeable fellow, and were glad there was someone who could control those "unthrifty and negligent habits in household affairs". There was simply no reason why he should impress them enough to mention him in their own diaries, or letters.

Had he, then, no friends, no family from whose records one could learn something of an artist who could certainly not be dismissed as negligible? Well, he was a man who had, I should guess, many friends. There is plenty of evidence, apart from William Michael Rossetti's testimonial, that he was well liked. The Watts-Duntons had no hesitation in being as hospitable to him as they were to Swinburne, and Mrs. Watts-Dunton always spoke of "Treffry" with affection. All the same, except for these eventful years with Rossetti, Dunn seems to have been a true Bohemian. From early manhood he was a rolling stone. When the spirit moved him, he would shut the lid of his paint-box and be off. The few people who knew him in his fifties speak of him as being perfectly in character—with his clock, and his long grey hair glowing frostily beneath a wide-brimmed hat.

He laughed a good deal, and was good company in a world renowned for its boon companions. "Treffry" was popular—but his friends were all of the same kidney, artistic, merry, raffish and amusing. The last thing most of them were inclined to do was to put their thoughts on paper, or even to think of describing their friendship with the easy-going Westcountry-man who would vanish every now and again without even bothering to wave farewell.

There is even less trace of the men and women with whom he gossiped and drank in his favourite haunts than there is of the man himself. The Chelsea of the eighteen-nineties was a rendezvous in which a million happy wanderers touched hands, clinked glasses and were on their way.

His relatives, then? Were there no documents, letters, stories which had been handed down by his contemporaries? Here I came upon the most curious situation. Dunn came of a highly respectable Cornish family. His father owned a tea and spice business in Truro, and a place was found for him in a local bank.

Clearly, this was no life for Harry Dunn. His was not a temperament which could accept a world in which he must keep not only ledgers but regular hours. To quote his own words, he "discharged these duties in a somewhat listless fashion". He saved a few guineas, and when his holiday was due, took himself off to Holland. A sketch-book was the most important item in his luggage.

This, so far as his family life was involved, was his first effective gesture of independence. A year or so later, Harry Dunn had burnt his boats and settled in London, first as an art student, then as a freelance and, finally, as an accepted professional painter.

It would be untrue to say that from that time his family wanted as little to do with him as possible. With one sister, Edith, he formed a strong alliance. Edith, a crisp and self-reliant girl, joined him in London and studied at the same academy. But his father was frankly disappointed. They were never on quite the same terms after Harry had kicked over the traces. His home was elsewhere, his visits unheralded and at long intervals. At times when funds were low or, as Rossetti would have put it, his supply of "the ready" had run out, Harry would arrive in Truro, cutting what his parents must have regarded as a disturbingly picturesque figure, looking as though he had strayed into their lives from some garret under the roofs of Paris.

One might have thought, as I thought myself, that his sisters and his cousins and his aunts would have been pleased to talk or to write about young Harry and his adventures abroad and in London, and of his encounters with Mr. Robert Browning, Mr. Longfellow, Mr. Ruskin, Mr. Whistler and so many other eminent gentlemen. But, no, not a bit of it. There was a baffling absence of any word, spoken or written about him by those who had reason to know him best. A portrait of a Cornish worthy, Dr. Charles Barham, painted by Dunn, hangs on the walls of the Council Chamber in the Town Hall at Truro. His fellow-townsmen clearly thought well enough of him.

One of his sisters, my great-aunt Frances, lived to be well over ninety, and as a boy I often stayed in her house in Edgecumbe Gardens, Newquay: when Harry's name was mentioned this exquisitely-mannered old lady would purse her lips, continue with her embroidery and gently, and very, very firmly, decline to breathe a word about her brother.

Another sister, Emily, my own grandmother, died before I was born. My father found his wife's uncle a fascinating character: he edited the *Recollections*, and persuaded Elkin Matthews to publish them as a small book.

This was in 1904, and since my father died when I was only five years old, we never had a chance to sort out the puzzle between us. My mother's information about her Uncle Harry amounted merely to what her elders were minded to tell her—and this was negligible. Although she was by nature the sunniest of women, I always had the feeling that my mother sympathised with the family's attitude towards Treffry Dunn. However adroitly I tried to introduce Harry's name into the conversation it was only to find that in a moment or two the subject had been changed, skilfully but with finality.

There was, then, precious little "family" evidence to help me. Harry's life, so far as we know, was blameless enough—apart from the familiar shortcomings shared by most of us who are given to the enjoyment of gay and congenial company. I suppose there are no two ways about it: whether he deserved it or not poor Harry came to be regarded as something of a black sheep. He was the only boy, and his mother spoilt him. He threw up his steady job in the bank. At the first opportunity he fled to London as though he had wings on his heels. For Harry, it was an artist's life or nothing and anyone who subscribed to the circulating library knew what that meant. Heaven knows what happened to young men who joined those godless, carefree circles in which young women were painted without their clothes, and everyone smoked tobacco and drank Scotch whisky.

His parents and sisters were glad when Harry was engaged by Mr. Rossetti: this at least gave an illusion of security. What is more, when tragedy scarred Edith's life and her fiancé died shortly before her wedding-day, could anyone have been kinder or more thoughtful than Mr. Rossetti? Indeed, Miss Dunn and her mother had found him so sympathetic that on her return to Truro Mrs. Dunn had set to work on some exquisite embroidery, the intricate pattern for which was inspired by his paintings. This has been known to the family ever since as the "Rossetti counter-pane", and it adorned his bed for years.

But as time slipped by, the family's attitude hardened. Harry's father died in 1870, and his son was disinclined or perhaps temperamentally unfitted to do what good sons are expected to do in such circumstances.

Both Edith and Harry would bring artistic friends down from London for sketching holidays and there may have been thoughtless gossip about the London way of life.

What the Cornish conscience could not, or would not, take was the story of how young Mrs. Rossetti's grave was opened years after her death so that the verses so romantically and tenderly buried with her could be rifled from her coffin, and printed—for personal satisfaction if not for profit. There were turbulent scenes in which poor Harry may have played merely the part of onlooker: although it must be said that if his nearest and dearest had seen the comings and goings at Number Sixteen, and heard the "language" and the stories, gazed on the golden-haired "stunners" and visited what Dunn himself called "the miniature South Kensington house and zoo combined", their darkest suspicions might have received a certain amount of confirmation.

There is one other circumstance which seems likely to have brought about the lasting disapproval of the family. Harry Dunn liked the company of his fellow-men and towards the end of his life any faint allegiance he may still have felt towards temperance (advocated so earnestly by his Cornish relations) reached vanishing-point. There is no evidence that Harry, in the years he spent at Cheyne Walk, drank more than the next man—although it can be surmised that the next man invariably possessed a strong head. Not until November 1884, two and a half years after Gabriel's death, did William Michael Rossetti learn from Watts-Dunton that "D. has taken to drinking of late, wh. is new to me and I am very sorry to hear it".

Writing to William in 1903, when, to quote my father's words, Harry "and his chief had long since solved the tremendous mysteries of life and death upon which they were wont to speculate together", his sister Edith wrote to Gabriel's brother about the publication of Dunn's *Recollections*. In her letter she says, "You once wrote to me the kindest of letters in connection with one of his *deplorable illnesses*, which I shall never forget."

It is hardly necessary for us to speculate on the nature of an illness which prompted such a strongly disapproving adjective. The following year there was a sojourn in St. Thomas's Hospital as a result of which

William Michael records that Harry was "discharged cured": although, he adds, with characteristic caution, "what use he will make of his comparative restoration to health remains to be seen: my expectations are not sanguine".

For once the kindly William did an old friend less than justice. Harry rented his own studio in Chelsea and, with his beard, wide-brimmed hat and flowing cloak, became a familiar and much-esteemed figure in Bohemian circles. Arm in arm with a boon-companion, great-uncle Harry would weave a majestic pilgrimage along the King's Road, stopping from time to time to share a glass—and his memories. This is the picture given me by the one friend I traced who knew H. T. Dunn at this period.

For ten years at least after that St. Thomas's Hospital "cure", he contrived to keep his head above water: for it was not until 1895 that his loneliness and lack of funds excited the compassion of a young actress, who was to become famous as Lena Ashwell.

I knew that Henry Treffry Dunn was born in Truro in 1838: that he died in St. George's Hospital, London, sixty-one years later. Much of what happened to him before he met Rossetti, and after Gabriel's death (when Dunn was forty-four), must be to some extent conjecture.

A year or so before Rossetti died there was a temporary rift in the friendship. Even art-assistants had financial responsibilities and Harry's salary was at one time so much in arrears that he departed to Truro in dudgeon to do some work on the new Cathedral. Gabriel begged him to return but he was too deeply committed to the Cathedral authorities: by the summer of 1881—Rossetti's last summer—he had been supplanted as companion, factotum and secretary by Hall Caine. One can understand a certain resentment on Dunn's part, and it is pleasant to know from William's diary that by January 1882, when Gabriel had but three months to live, the two men had "got on good terms again", and Harry was working on some pictures which had been promised to L. R. Valpy, one of Rossetti's patrons.

William Michael Rossetti decided that Gabriel's affairs could not be wound up efficiently without Dunn's help: and the Cornishman returned to Cheyne Walk. Here he did all he could to help William in the sad business of preparing for the sale of Gabriel's effects, working on replicas and completing unfinished work. This task over, he returned to Truro, but a year later he was in London, sharing a studio with another artist.

Eventually, desperately hard up and in poor health, he found a refuge with the good-natured Watts-Dunton and his wife.

In the shelter of The Pines at Putney he took possession of his own corner, painting away happily and with gentle humour, remembering to the delight of Clara Watts-Dunton what it was like to be the guardian angel of a genius. With Swinburne he would pace slowly up to the Heath and take a glass or two—no more—at the Green Man.

Before the old century ended, Harry was taken ill and he and his memories died together in the big hospital overlooking Hyde Park Corner. He was not entirely forgotten. His *Recollections* were published five years later, and when another five years had passed his portrait in oils of Rossetti was accepted by the Uffizi Gallery in Florence.

There is a striking pencil drawing by Rossetti of himself as a young man, made at about the time "The Blessed Damozel" was written. If there is a self-portrait in oils or water-colour I have not seen it. Certainly there is none showing the artist in maturity.

It seemed to me, then, that Henry Treffry Dunn deserved something of posterity even if the most important years in his career were spent in the shadow of an overwhelming personality. After all, the minds and the thoughts of great men, their frailties and their strengths, assume a clarity and charm when seen in terms of their relationship with others—and especially with others in whose presence they never had to be on their guard.

Dunn was for many years an indispensable human factor in Rossetti's life. The artist turned to him for help in a hundred different ways. The great man retreats, and the friend emerges when for example we read: "*My dear Dunn—your dress trousers are, I believe, in the drawer near the window in my bedroom. I saw two pairs lying there lately, and I believe I only possess one....*" And: "*My dear Dunn—many thanks for your beautiful sketch of Donatello's cherubs. I enclose a cheque for £50. having received this morning one for five hundred.*"

There is the urgent command about "locking all letters in the safe" and when the housemaid, Mary, is leaving, it is to Dunn that Gabriel writes, sounding a note of alarm, "*I should be glad if she were prevented from gossiping with the other people in the house, but made to take her things, and go promptly.*"

Who is to say that comments like these, trivial as they may be, do not add to our picture of the man who made them?

What a mistake it is to believe the more that is written about a great man the clearer his personality becomes. Millions of words may be read describing Rossetti's work, his character, his triumphs, his failures and his tragic end. The romantic Italian background, the youthful flowering of a rare double talent, his vitality, the sorrows of his private life—no wonder these attracted scholars and students of art and letters.

As a newcomer to this particular scene it seems to me that the true humanity of the man has escaped most of his biographers. They write of the Pre-Raphaelite Brotherhood not merely with erudition, but with awe. Where must we look for a full-blooded reconstruction of these lively, thrusting, ambitious young men?

It is true that by the time Harry Dunn came on the scene the friends of Rossetti's youth were successful, full of years and zeal, and—inevitably— respected. The photographs which illustrate their biographies show them stern of mien, handsome and forbidding. But for all their beards, for all their grave aspect, these were the men who, with Gabriel, had roistered and laughed, played and suffered schoolboy pranks, drank, talked—and loved—freely. They were ready to break a lance with all comers. They were clever and, in the main, attractive young men.

In Harry Dunn's day that early and blazing eagerness had been damped down: which is not to say that life at Cheyne Walk was uneventful. There were still parties when the talk and the wine flowed plentifully.

Handsome models—tall girls whose measurements matched the studio fashions of the day—knocked at the door of Number Sixteen. All were lovely to look at: all displayed a crowning glory in varying but most attractive gold and copper shades.

Is it hard to understand why I have felt compelled to make an affectionate attempt to endow with some substance the vague, shadowy but engaging person of my great-uncle, Harry? He was part of that strange, gifted and eccentric company which lived in or frequented the Rossetti home by the River Thames at Chelsea. He moves busily and anxiously across the domestic scene. With the honourable exception of Gabriel's kindly brother, William Michael, he was for years the only human being who constantly and at close quarters shared Gabriel's troubles, financial and spiritual. It was his nature to make life smoother for the man who turned to him for help.

Harry Dunn was Gabriel's "guardian angel": he was his "best of good fellows". But he was a painter, too; and a good one, whose work may be found in many famous galleries. It is no idle compliment to have a portrait in the Galleria degli Uffizi.

He was, I think, a gentle, self-effacing and discreet companion to a man of wayward but undeniable poetic genius and artistic talent, and this is an affectionate tribute to his genial shade.

AUTUMN LEAVES
(Verses for a picture)

Fast fall the leaves, blown by the Autumn blast,
   In swirling heaps on the green sward they lie,
   Sweet memories of the Springtime greenery
And the golden glories of Summer past.

The last red flushes of the sinking sun
   Shed over all a wondrous mystery,
   On toil-worn age nearing eternity,
And the young hearts whose lives are but begun.

And with departing light the conscience grieves
   O'er bygone days, and golden hours misspent
   In selfish deeds and empty merriment,
To find, where fruit should be, but withered leaves.

                —Henry Treffry Dunn, 27 February 1891.

2

Of all the shops in Lemon Street, Truro, the establishment of Henry Littlejohn Dunn had the nicest smell.

Mr. Dunn kept a tea and spice business and all his life Harry Dunn could recall at will the tantalising, heady aroma of coffee, cinnamon, nutmeg, cloves, pepper, caraway, curry powder and saffron which rose like a fragrant cloud to greet you as you pushed open the door.

"What a lovely aroma!" the ladies of Truro would say, as with crino-lines flaunting they swept into the dark and cosy shop, and even their sternly whiskered escorts would sniff appreciatively.

Mr. Dunn was also in a very fair way of business as a grocer and for special family treats, on birthdays and at Christmas—especially at Christmas—Harry and his sisters were the envy of their friends. There were crystallised fruits, sweetmeats from the Continent, ginger, sultanas and cakes which tasted very different from anything to be had from Mr. Trevithick, the baker, whose shop was two or three doors down the street, and had nothing mysterious about it at all.

Tea and spices were Mr. Dunn's main concern. They arrived in large boxes of fascinating aspect, bound with metal bands. It was not difficult to imagine them stacked in the dark, forbidding holds of the ocean-going cargo ships. One could almost hear the strange cries as the crates were loaded, and see the vivid splashes of colour, bright in the blazing sunshine.

Above all, the colour appealed to the children. They would inhale the perfumed air, and as though by magic the shop would be a vast cavern filled with contraband. Suddenly, the metal canisters were sea-chests filled with treasure, the porcelain jars on the shelves richly-painted vessels like those one read about in *The Arabian Nights*.

Mr. Dunn was an upright, God-fearing and sober citizen—above all, sober. He was a fervent member of the Baptist Church, and was frequently bewildered by the high spirits of his young family. It is true they did not always react to discipline as, by all the teaching of the Good Book, they should have done.

All the Dunn children were gay and mischievous: all were artistic. These were qualities they inherited from their mother, who worked the most delicate pictures in silks and who was always busy on some new and charming piece of needlework.

Henry Treffry Dunn was born in Truro in the spring of 1838. The family could not claim any connection with the County Treffrys, of Place House, Fowey. Harry was given his second name as a compliment to a Mr. Treffry, of Exeter, a friend who had encouraged Henry Dunn to set up in business in Truro. There were four girls. Emily who was a year older than Harry, Frances, Edith and Ellen. There was a second son, Leonard, born when Harry was seven: he died in infancy. Harry was his mother's favourite. Eighty years later, his sister Frances confided to her own daughters that their uncle was, in fact, outrageously spoiled. "He joined in all our pranks," she said, "but whenever we were punished he was always forgiven!"

This flair for avoiding trouble did not, as may be imagined, endear him to the rest of the family: and as they grew up, Edith was the only sister to whom Harry could turn with much optimism for sympathy.

Both shop and home were in Lemon Street: but the Dunns lived in a trim, narrow house on the opposite side of the road from their place of business and some distance further up. Religious discipline—especially in Cornwall—was an accepted part of domestic life in this early Victorian period. Mrs. Dunn clearly found nothing remarkable about it, and certainly declined to allow convention to interfere with her own conception of a happy home.

Frances Dunn was by any standards a poised and attractive woman. Her children remembered her as inventive and independent. She brought them up to appreciate the beauty of the world around them. None had any great understanding of the sterner ways of life, of commerce, of domestic arithmetic. One of the girls, Edith, was to become an accomplished artist. Of Emily's children two were musicians, one a sculptor whose work may be seen in half a dozen Cathedrals. Frances lived to be more than ninety— and the artistic strain was inherited by her own daughters.

Harry, more than the others, was fascinated by his mother's embroidery, her drawings and the dolls and figures she fashioned for their pleasure. Best of all he loved the miniature menagerie Mama made for them. The cages were fashioned from macaroni boxes, with knitting-needles as bars. The animals were first cut from cardboard. Then Mama covered the figures with finely-cut wool, so that the lions and tigers, the leopards and the bison looked exactly as though they had on their fur coats. The effect was extraordinarily realistic, and friends would come to the house specially to see the Dunn children's zoo.

The toy theatre, too, was one of Harry's keenest pleasures. Tiny coloured figures cut from cardboard, that was all: but light the candles, let the curtain roll upwards, and here was yet another enchanted world. Then there was the famous scrapbook on whose pages Mama drew and painted for each child its favourite animal. For Emily a dog; for Frances a cock, with scarlet wattle and comb; and for Edith a robin red-breast. Harry chose a horse, and they teased Ellen because she loved best her white pig— "it must be a little fat one".

Theirs was a happy home, apart from the storms which inevitably beset a group of high-spirited children, all a trifle more sensitive than most. The girls were, of course, furious when the single interloping boy was given special privileges. Why he was invariably permitted to do things for which they were punished was a continual and infuriating mystery. Mama insisted that Papa's passion for good behaviour should be respected, and on the whole the Dunn children were well-mannered and obedient. They romped, ran, and explored the loveliness of the Cornish countryside. They were encouraged to use their hands, to read, to draw, to write. Long years afterwards, when Gabriel showed him his sepia sketch of Lord Tennyson reading "Maud", Harry suddenly remembered his sister, Emily, at the age of seven, proudly reading her own "poem"—

> A faithful dog there was and good
> That found a purse within a wood
> He brought it to his master straight,
> And did not even make him wait!

Some of the Truro neighbours had reason to complain to Mr. Dunn about his children's conduct—but they were few. Miss Carlyon, who lived next door in Lemon Street at Number Eight, was one. She became known to almost the entire juvenile population as Miss "Eighty Carlyon", and was so annoyed that she moved to another house on the opposite side of the street.

Sometimes, there would be an unusual commotion, when even Mama's patience was tested. There was a scrubbing of hands, a rubbing of faces and a putting on of best clothes, freshly ironed. These proceedings meant one thing—a visit from Papa's eldest sister, Emily, who married John Rawlings, Clerk to the House of Commons. Mr. Dunn had two other sisters, Maria and Harriet—and these charming but ineffective ladies had their place in Harry's memories. They stubbornly remained maiden ladies, and with a faith which must have been sharpened by desperation, he set them up in a toy-shop in Union Place. It was an agreeably genteel occupation, but neither Maria nor Harriet had a gift for commerce, and they could never make the little business pay. In consequence Henry Dunn from time to time put his hand in his pocket and paid their bills. No doubt, looking at his family, he was often thankful to own a prosperous business —the business in which young Harry must one day take his place.

The aunts may have been a disappointment to their brother, but to have a toy-shop in the family—nothing could have been more satisfactory from the young people's point of view. They were always welcomed in the little shop in Union Place. You had to go down a little step to enter, which appealed to them as a quaint old-fashioned touch. For years a beautifully-made wicker toy pram hung in the window.

The roaring century sped by. But Cornwall, even in Harry's childhood and youth, was remote, in many ways cut off from the rest of England. West of Plymouth, people pictured the Duchy, as truly the land's end. These knew nothing of the mines, the thriving ports, the flourishing trade in the larger towns.

Although Harry's mother lived on into a new era—until December 1900, a year after her son's death—she had been born soon after Trafalgar. When the Dunn children were growing up, tinder-boxes were still being used as a matter of course: and what a slow and laborious affair it was to get a spark to ignite the charred linen.

It was quite clear that, spoiled or not, Harry had a more than ordinary talent. He possessed a natural gift for drawing, a feeling for colour, and an eye for a subject. No boredom was so acute, no domestic squabble so bitter that an hour with a sketch-book could not dispel it. His mother encouraged him to study and to experiment. With her own taste she could see that, properly directed, the boy might be a credit to her.

The boy would spend hours wandering about the old town—some of his sketches of old Truro are still admired by visitors to the Museum. At other times he would be off to Malpas, where you could hear the "curlies" cry, and it was fun to yell for the ferryman to row you across the river. The fishermen came to recognise his short, wiry figure as he clambered over the rocks, and stood looking out to sea, his long hair blowing about the eager face.

The boy passionately wanted to make a living with his brush. But for his son to become a professional artist in a small provincial town a hundred years ago—and that far away in a part of the country where prejudice and piety went hand-in-hand—was something no self-respecting male parent would entertain for long. There is nothing to suggest that Truro's leading Tea and Spice Merchant was not a kindly and affectionate man, but equally, he was affronted by the suggestion that his only son should join the ranks of a profession so notoriously unstable. He rejected the idea with all the force and conviction of his Nonconformist soul. It was bad enough that Harry had been favoured above his sisters and spoilt by a doting mother. One day Mr. Dunn informed his son that since neither the shop nor a place in his father's insurance agency appealed to Harry, he had obtained for him a place in a local Bank.

This was worse than anything the boy had expected. The prospect appalled him. But Harry was intelligent enough to know that to exchange a comfortable home for a dubious livelihood among the artistic set—so many of them by repute romantically poor—would show no profit. He swallowed his pride, clad himself in a black suit, bought a top-hat, had his hair barbered, and abandoned the poetic style which had made the belles of Truro turn their heads, some, it is true, to laugh, but many to smile with admiration. These were the girls who in some locked drawer or secret hiding-place kept a paper on which the young artist had sketched with lightness of touch an idealised portrait—the souvenir of a sentimental journey, a walk by starlight.

One Monday morning Harry Dunn presented himself before the Manager of the Cornish Bank in Boscawen Street. This was the beginning of a period on which Harry always looked back with distaste. He did his best, partly to please his mother, partly because it was his nature to make life as easy for himself as possible.

Later, he found comfort in the thought that Richard Carter (who later married his sister Ellen) had also started in a Bank—and yet Richard became a well-known and successful artist whose water-colours are to be found in galleries in many parts of the country.

Harry made a good pretence of settling at his desk in Boscawen Street, dressed with a certain natural elegance—there was always a touch of the dandy about him—and began, to his father's intense disgust, to smoke a pipe.

This was certainly not a lonely period, for Harry had a gift for making friends. He was what became known in another time as a born mixer. All his life he contrived to present to the world an attractive and quite imaginary helplessness. This invariably touched the hearts of generous friends, especially if they were women. It was the quality which persuaded Lena Ashwell to seek help for him. It was the quality which led Clara Watts-Dunton to hold out the hand of friendship without the slightest thought of recompense.

The truth is that a most engaging temperament hid a disinclination to fend for himself unless it was absolutely necessary. No-one can have been less suited to the routine of a provincial bank. It was poor consolation to know that the position offered a certain amount of prestige, that many young men with private means thought it a privilege to engage in such employment (even though private banks, Cornish ones included, were not immune from the occasional failure!). To arrive at the old building in Boscawen Street punctually, to hang one's high hat on the same peg each day, to bow ceremoniously to one's seniors, which meant almost every-one, to spend hours scratching away with a quill pen—this was to exist beneath an absolute pall of boredom.

3

The Cornwall of Harry Dunn's boyhood seemed to its more adventurously-minded inhabitants unbearably remote. The Tamar at Devonport divided the Duchy from the rest of England as finally as though it were a frontier between two foreign countries. East of the Cornish boundary lived a race of people who were deemed to be foreigners. Forty years or more would pass before the motor-car and the telephone came to be blessed and cursed by mankind. A number of artists, it is true, were drawn westwards by the picturesque coastline and the quaint fishing villages.

Harry Dunn knew most of the beauty spots in his native county. His early sketch-books were filled with studies of fishermen and farmers—rugged faces, full of character.

Distance made London even more desirable and he read eagerly every printed word he could about the world of art and treasured every reference to well-known painters and sculptors.

A name which made a profound impression was that of Dante Gabriel Rossetti. Harry Dunn and two of his friends subscribed to the *Illustrated London News*. One day, during the ten minutes' grace the clerks were allowed after their midday meal, Harry read one paragraph with special interest. It contained a quotation from a letter which had appeared in a recent issue of the *Athenaeum*: and it was to the effect that Mr. D. G. Rossetti had not given up oil for water-colour but that he still practised both. Apart from his burning interest in all that had to do with painting there was nothing outstanding in this statement, but as Harry wrote many years later:

"D. G. Rossetti?" I enquired of myself—"Why, I never heard of him. Who is he, and what kind of pictures does he paint?"

Thereupon I fell into a reverie over the announcement I had seen, and gradually and convincingly a strange presagement came to me that some day, not very far off, I should not only meet and know this man, but even be closely associated with him in his profession.

Summer that year seemed endless. Harry Dunn had arranged to take his annual fortnight's holiday in the middle of September. Planning his vacation for the autumn meant that he had longer to save. His idea was to see something of Holland and if time and funds ran to it, something of Germany, too.

The tyranny of the calendar was over. The day of departure was here, time at last for Harry to find a seat on the fast train to London. He was at Harwich by nightfall, in time to take the steam boat, and to quote his own words: "After a night's voyage, which was somewhat rough and tempestuous, I landed at an early hour in the morning in the Boompjes at Rotterdam."

In his diary Harry related with a certain engaging naïveté how he obtained a meal by a time-honoured method employed by generations of artists in many foreign countries:

> To get something to eat was my first consideration and after wandering vainly about the streets for some time in search of a place of refreshment, I at last espied a coffee-tavern. Forgetting that Dutch was the prevailing language of the greater part of the inhabitants of Rotterdam, I fancied there would be no difficulty in making known my wants with the few phrases of French and German that I had managed to pick up, but I was soon to be undeceived. Entering the house, I seated myself at the nearest table and rang for attendance. Presently, a slovenly, unkempt girl, broad of face, made her appearance, and in what German I could command I asked her to provide me with some breakfast.
>
> She nodded her head, stared in bewilderment, and said something in reply which was perfectly unintelligible: so, my German failing, I tried again in the few words of French I could remember. This seemed even more perplexing to her, and shaking her head once more, she went away with a grin on her expansive face. Anon, she returned with her mistress, who was even more fat and "Dutchier" looking than the maid, and both stood with their arms akimbo gazing at me with curiosity. Again I essayed to make myself understood, but only to find that in language the effort was fruitless.
>
> Suddenly, a happy thought struck me. Pulling out my sketch-book, I hastily drew a plate with a chop on it, a knife and fork, a couple of eggs, and a cup and saucer. To their delight, this gave them a clear idea that it was something to eat and drink that I wanted, and in a very short time I was furnished with a substantial and well-cooked meal.

Bathed in the late autumn sunshine the old city took on an even more mellow and gracious appearance. For Harry these were days of enchantment. For him, the streets glowed with a wealth of colour. By contrast, the quaint nooks and corners seemed cool, sombre and provocative. Each day seemed to bring its own atmosphere of leisurely grace.

"I think these must truly be the happiest days in all my life", he wrote to his sister Edith. There was a soothing quality in the air which made him feel at peace with the world and appealed to the indolent streak in his character. Could anything be more delightful than to wander along the quayside, as generations of visitors had done before him, to stroll through the newly-opened zoological gardens, to visit the old English church?

Only at the close of each golden day did nagging thoughts of the bank and the inevitable return cloud his pleasure. Such unbidden reminders he dismissed briskly. How perfect it would be to linger in Rotterdam, sketching, day-dreaming and answerable to no-one. This was the life for him—not that dull, daily grind in the counting-house with companions whose idea of adventure was a church outing and the pinnacle of ambition a few hundreds in the bank and a seat on the local council. Why pore over ledgers, adding interminable columns of figures, when there was so much in the world to gladden the eye and the senses? This was surely to make a mockery of the talent providence had given him.

Abruptly, he closed his sketch-book. It was pleasant to dream, but time and money were running out. He must make the most of every day, of every hour. Tomorrow he would go as far as Mayence and fulfil an ambition—to see the Rhine. That decision was to change the direction of his life.

"I've been watching you at work. May I see your sketches?"

The speaker was a tall, friendly man, with a pleasant voice. Harry had been struck by his air of authority and idly wondered what was his business and why he was travelling alone. His name, he said, was James Shepherd—his home, Blairgowrie. He was a young veteran of the Russo-Turkish war and (so Harry learnt later) had been decorated for bravery. Now he held an appointment in the War Office, in the Volunteer Department.

Shepherd talked knowledgeably about art. He had not asked to see Harry's work out of idle curiosity or merely as a gesture of politeness. His admiration was sincere, his criticisms well founded. Soon the younger man was talking eagerly about his dreams of becoming a professional artist.

"With your talent I don't see why you shouldn't," Shepherd said. "Look here, I'll give you my address. If ever you come to London, and somehow I think you will, look me up. I daresay I could give you an introduction or two. In any case, I'd be glad to see you again."

His holiday unsettled Harry. That brief taste of freedom made life in the Bank seem even more irksome. The desire to spread his wings became more urgent as the winter months dragged slowly towards spring.

It had been fun to show off the sketches he had made in Holland and on the memorable voyage along the Rhine. He did not need the fond pleasure they gave his mother to tell him they were good.

Even his sisters, who were all growing up into handsome young women, had to agree. Most of all, he valued Edith's praise for she, he admitted with affection, had the makings of an accomplished artist.

He recognised in her a strength of character he was never likely to match. For all her brisk manner and the air of mockery with which she received his confidences, there was a stronger bond between Harry and Edith than she cared to admit. Emily already showed promise as a writer. Ellen played the piano and sang with a dash and charm which astonished her family and her teachers. But while Emily sat curled up in the window-seat writing verses in her notebook, and Ellen worked away on some difficult piano study, Edith and Harry would be miles away on some sketching expedition, always searching for a promising landscape, or coaxing some old fisherman to pose for them. Sometimes their subject would be a farmer's wife selling eggs and butter in the market-place: next day, the piquant face of some solemn little girl carrying wild flowers in her folded apron.

Edith had a flair for finding the unusual subject and for catching the fleeting expression on a sitter's face. Running to earth some unusual subject became a game in which they both found delight.

At other times they would make their way to a lonely inlet, there to sketch the wheeling gulls, or a cormorant with wings outstretched. Then, idle but content, they would watch the sea-birds skimming the surface of the water and wait for the curlew, the redshank or the occasional puffin.

Many times they talked of Harry's meeting with Shepherd and his promise of helpful introductions.

"I mean to go," he said. "Can you imagine how Mr. Williams will look when I ask him if I can see him privately and then say: 'Mr. Williams, sir, I have the honour to give the Cornish Bank a month's notice!'"

Edith obligingly thought this would be the most amusing thing to do, but tempered her brother's enthusiasm by saying: "Yes—and can you imagine Papa's face when you tell him what you've done?"

The expression on Papa's face was something Harry could imagine only too well. The situation, when it came, arose without any special prompting on Harry's part. There had been talk in the town for some years that one day Truro would become a Cathedral city. If this were to happen, if was being said, a great new building would be erected, probably on the site of the Parish Church of St. Mary.

Harry thought this was the most imaginative and important step which had been taken in his home town for years. A modern Cathedral! What a challenge to the architect and to the designer and the artists who would be responsible for its making! What an opportunity to blend tradition with a bold and no less beautiful expression of the present. If only he could have a hand in such a mighty project . . .

There was an angry scene when Harry finally decided to leave the Cornish Bank. Mr. Dunn wanted to know, not without reason, what his ungrateful son proposed to live on. He pointed out that his Aunt Emily and her husband John Rawlings would be shocked and horrified by the whole idea. For once, Harry stuck to his guns. He bade farewell to the Bank, changed his frock-coat for a black velvet jacket, said goodbye to his mother and sisters and, considerably more triumphant than tearful, bought a single ticket to Paddington.

Between his old life and the new one now beginning Harry Dunn had deliberately set up an immovable barrier. There was to be no going back. His future, for good or ill, was to be found in this sprawling city, sulphurous fumes and all.

Carrying a carpet-bag in one hand and in the other a parcel containing his paints and brushes, his books and a selection of his best drawings, he took a cab to lodgings in Marylebone, recommended by an artist he had met in Cornwall.

In a very short time he had enrolled as a student at a well-known art school, Heatherley's, in Newman-street, a turning off Oxford-street. Harry himself has little to tell us about his experiences at Heatherley's, this "nursery for beginners", as he called it. But he did record, with some enthusiasm, "here quite a new life opened to me, and here I found quite a fresh and more congenial set of companions".

Harry Dunn's education was taking a step forward. In relation to the young visitor from Cornwall, "congenial" is an illuminating word. It has a ring of the boon-companion about it, and for all his diffidence, Harry enjoyed good company and was soon at ease with those whose company he found sympathetic.

In his Heatherley days he made many friends. One was William Gorman Wills, a writer whose plays were already being talked about. Wills was ten years older than the Cornishman, but they took an instant liking to each other: their friendship lasted until Wills died nearly thirty years later.

Harry Dunn was well established in his curious rôle as art-assistant and general factotum at Cheyne Walk by the time Wills wrote his most successful play. This was *Charles I*, which was staged at the Lyceum Theatre in London in September 1872, and promptly found a place in Henry Irving's repertoire. The piece clearly showed its author's flair for writing what Irving's public wanted and Wills became, as it were, resident dramatist of the Lyceum. My father, in a note to Treffry Dunn's *Recollections*, gives his opinion that *Charles I* was "inferior in form to its predecessor, *Medea in Corinth*, which contains Wills' best work". But he adds, "it sprang into high favour with the public and assisted Henry Irving to confirm the reputation he had previously achieved in *The Bells*. Several plays of uneven merit followed from Wills' pen in quick succession."

This somewhat acid comment underlines the fact that authors as a race do not greatly change their habits. Today more than ever, writers are tempted to work a successful vein until it is exhausted.

Harry became a great playgoer. His association with Wills brought him the friendship of many men and women in the theatre. Ellen Terry he admired, and met on many occasions—and it was Lena Ashwell, a protégé of Dame Ellen, who was moved to give practical help when Gabriel was dead and Harry was on the verge of destitution.

Congenial company is inclined to be expensive, and before he had been in London many months Harry's savings were "beginning to run low".

"I bethought me", he writes, "of my Rhine friend's promise of assistance. I resolved to call upon him and acquaint him with my position, which I did without further loss of time."

It seems rather odd that Harry should have waited so long before going to see his "Rhine friend", James Shepherd. But Shepherd "received me very cordially"—and in no time at all that friendly holiday footing was resumed.

The young soldier of the Russo-Turkish war found in Dunn a kindred spirit, and very nearly became his brother-in-law. Harry's sister, Edith—three years his junior—was enchanted by Harry's stories of London life and the new friends he was making at the Art School. She, too, made up her mind to leave Truro, and enrol at Heatherley's. One can only guess what scenes and arguments occurred, what tears were shed, but Edith got her own way. Harry found himself once more on Paddington Station, but this time in the rôle of a sophisticated elder brother who had become very much a man of the world.

Harry was glad to introduce his vivacious, gifted young sister to James Shepherd. The three of them spent a great deal of time together—in the art galleries, on the river, at the theatre. On fine summer days they would stroll in the gardens at Hampton Court and go for walks in Highgate and on to the Heath at Hampstead.

Edith and James, concluding they were made for each other, became engaged. A day for the marriage was settled, but two weeks before the ceremony, Shepherd died—on 26 July 1867. Edith, who was in Cornwall making plans for the wedding, was broken-hearted. By this time Harry was living at Cheyne Walk, and the sad event showed Gabriel in a solicitous and sympathetic light. He insisted that Edith and her mother should be his guests when they came to London for the funeral. It was a characteristically generous gesture.

At Heatherley's in Newman Street, Dunn was absorbed in his work and happy in his friends. These were of both sexes, for it is still Heatherley's proud claim to have been the first art school in London to admit women students on equal terms with men.

From the day he joined Harry found the atmosphere stimulating. The school had been in existence as a separate organisation for less than twenty years. Its founders—students of an independent turn of mind—had long been frustrated by orthodox methods of teaching. They were determined that there should be no nonsense about this school's approach to its work, and there was a refreshing absence of convention in the way it was run. Simply by paying his fees, for example, an artist could enter Heatherley's and paint from the nude: and for a great many years it was the only place of its kind in London where this could happen. No wonder Heatherley's flourished and drew within its friendly walls almost every artist of repute. The roll of students has on it the names of Sir Edward Burne-Jones and Michael Ayrton, of Sickert and Nicolas Bentley.

Heatherley men were never tired of telling their younger colleagues how J. R. Herbert, R.A., had led a band of happy rebels out of the Government School of Design in Somerset House—to set up a new and vigorous centre of their own. This was in 1845. The first step was to launch a separate class in premises in Maddox Street in the West End of London, then occupied by Dickenson's Drawing Gallery. Three years later the group had taken over Dickenson's and moved to Newman Street, where Harry Dunn and Edith sat at their easels and drawing-boards and absorbed the teaching of enterprising tutors. In Newman Street the first Principal was James Matthews Leigh, and according to custom the school took the name of its chief and was known as "Leigh's". He was succeeded by Thomas J. Heatherley, who directed the school for more than thirty years, and whose influence was so profound that his name was retained after his death. The school, now in Warwick Square, S.W.1., is still renowned in the world of art as Heatherley's.

Harry (and Edith Dunn in her turn) was enthralled by stories of "Dagger" Leigh, who had lived a good deal abroad and whose adherence to Continental methods had such tangible and satisfactory results. This nickname was an eloquent reminder of the barbed and sarcastic remarks with which he goaded his pupils: and at the same time put them on their mettle.

Thackeray, who had considered making painting his profession, was a student under Leigh, and readers of *The Newcomes* will recall how his hero was sent to Heatherley's. Leigh had the reputation of being a wit who could give and take on equal terms with Leigh Hunt and Douglas Jerrold. His supper parties to celebrate sending-in day at the Royal Academy were famous.

Harry was in his element. In his first days at Heatherley's he wrote enthusiastically to Truro, telling Edith how his work was improving and what the tutors had told him about it—and urging his sister to join him as soon as possible.

"Mr. Heatherley will not countenance carelessness of any kind", he wrote to his sister. "But at the same time he does not concentrate on technique. In fact, we are allowed—I should say encouraged—to develop our own style. This is a legacy from the days of Mr. Leigh. He spent a great deal of time in Paris, you know, and it was always his plan to allow his students to show originality. The result is that we feel we are individuals and that our work will not all bear the same stamp."

In some schools of art one particular style was enforced because a strong-minded principal left the imprint of his own personality on his pupils' work. But Leigh, and Heatherley after him, regarded the students as intelligent people with minds and talents of their own and, within reasonable limits, let them go their own way.

"It is hard work", Harry recorded. "We start at six o'clock in the morning, and one may work through for twelve hours. Then there are evening classes from seven o'clock until ten."

By modern standards the teachers in the mid-Victorian era were tough task-masters. True, Heatherley's was closed on Sunday, but apart from this concession, the only official holidays were Christmas Day and Good Friday. Soon after six o'clock each morning Mr. Heatherley's bearded countenance could be seen as he leaned out of a window, looking re-proachfully at the laggards as they rounded the street corner into New-man Street. He certainly did not spare himself, and his devotion to duty is the subject of a picture by Samuel Butler shown in the Tate Gallery. The title is "Mr. Heatherley's Holiday", and the old man is seen busily repairing the school skeleton on one of the few days when this indispens-able but grisly object was not in use. The benevolent old gentleman favoured a gown of black velvet which reached to his heels, and had a habit of humming gently to himself as he paced up and down the big rooms. His appearance must have been striking, for W. S. Spanton re-cords in his book *An Art Student and His Teachers in the Sixties* that Heatherley had been described as a "dissipated Jesus Christ".

Heatherley's successor was his nephew, John Crompton. The school had two more homes—one also in Newman Street, the other in George Street—before settling down in its present headquarters. After nearly one hundred and twenty years the famous academy, with its broad outlook and insistence on free style, flourishes and gives instruction to students from almost every country in the world.

Harry Dunn could not have had a better start—and he knew it.

It was a remarkable period: the influence of students who had paid their guineas in the twenty years or so before Harry's arrival was still powerful. Burne-Jones, Millais and Rossetti himself had worked at Heatherley's—and with them, many other artists who were in sympathy with what were then considered the most modern ideas. One contem-porary of Harry was Thomas Ballard who, some twenty years later, painted the scenery for *Ruddigore*.

It is intriguing to find in one proud list of "famous names" of artists who attended the school that of Mrs. Hume (Edith Dunn). She is one of four or five women (Miss K. Greenaway is another) who are in the company of Sir John Lavery, Sir Edward Poynter, Frank Salisbury, C. R. W. Nevinson, Walter Crane, Sir George Frampton and Sir William Russell Flint. Alas, H. T. Dunn does not appear: but it would have pleased him to see his young sister's name in such exalted company. Spanton recalls that "among the lady-students, Miss Dunn and Miss Mearns, who drew illustrations for *Once a Week*, lived in the house".

Edith was grieved beyond measure by the tragically sudden death of James Shepherd two weeks before their wedding-day. But she was a woman of courage and some independence of mind. It would have been easy for her to remain at home in prolonged mourning; to abandon her ambition to become a professional artist, content to help her mother in the sleepy, sedative atmosphere of a provincial town. Such a life was not for her. After a few months, Edith Dunn set her lips, resumed her career and earned a considerable reputation. She travelled much on the Continent, and in Holland especially her trim figure, clad in a long black dress and black straw hat, became familiar. Edith gallantly mended her life and painted a series of Dutch landscapes and many charming studies of family life. In the course of time she married another artist, Thomas Hume, and made her home at the foot of the South Downs.

Since both John Millais and Dante Gabriel Rossetti had been among the early students of the School in its Maddox Street days, their quality, both as men and as painters, was often discussed. One had only to say the words "Pre-Raphaelite Brotherhood" to provoke arguments which became progressively more heated as the hours ticked by and the room grew thick with tobacco-smoke.

The most startling fact to emerge—at least, so it must seem to all but the scholars—is that this group, or camp, or coterie, had such a brief existence. The Pre-Raphaelite Brotherhood is a phrase, a title, known throughout the world: the inexpert may be forgiven for believing it to be an influential movement sponsored by a number of mature, highly-respected men of art. In truth, the Brothers were young men, in their twenties, some quite unknown: and the Movement expired after four or five years.

Its life was over at least a dozen years before Harry Dunn met Rossetti. But some account of the "P.R.B.s", as they were called, is important—if only because the men concerned were important in relation to life at Cheyne Walk, and because their friendship affected Rossetti's life. One at least, Frederick George Stephens, remained loyal, and a year or two before he died Gabriel was writing of "dear, staunch Stephens—one of my oldest and best friends".

Creators of the Pre-Raphaelite Brotherhood were Holman Hunt, John Millais and Dante Gabriel Rossetti. Another four Brothers were enlisted —Thomas Woolner, a sculptor; James Collinson, a painter; Stephens, an Academy student of painting; and William Michael Rossetti, the indispensable William, who became secretary and editor of the P.R.B.s journal, *The Germ*. Woolner, a Suffolk man, became an R.A.; Stephens, an authority on the early schools of Italian art, made a reputation as an art-critic. Collinson "did not", says William, "rise to distinction in the pictorial art", and resigned after a comparatively short time. Even before he came of age, William Rossetti was writing ably in a weekly paper called *The Critic*: and he became art-critic of *The Spectator* soon after his twenty-first birthday.

The Brotherhood was a high-spirited affair with elements of profound sincerity, some vanity and (in its early stages) a certain amount of noisy exuberance. In writing to each other the Brothers would use the initials "P.R.B." instead of "Esquire". In his forties Rossetti rather testily told an inquisitive lady: "Madam, I am not an '-ite' of any kind. I am only a painter." But the secretary of the Brotherhood—who, of all people, was in a position to know—always held that Gabriel's belief in the principles he and his friends held in those youthful days did not waver. It was just that these good companions grew up. The "old fellows" grew older— and went their own ways.

What was the Pre-Raphaelite Brotherhood all about? Well, even the experts have tied themselves in knots trying to tell us. As each clue is followed up, as each shade of feeling is analysed, the more involved has become their exposition.

In the simplest terms, the Seven thought British art was in a rut and wanted to do something about it. Like young men in every generation they were in arms against the older men who were content with themselves and with what they believed. This seemed to the "P.R.B.s" to be precious like stagnation. They did not merely protest against the conventional in art. They had an answer.

New ideas: here was the key. To hit upon new ideas and breathe life into them, this was the way to send a fresh wind down the corridors of the Academy. To blazes with the fashionable belief that one should paint a certain way because it was the thing to do, and had been the thing to do for a very long time!

How, then, to express these new and genuine ideas? Our young reformers were convinced that the answer was to be found in studying Nature, and being faithful to her. This is where the authorities are inclined to bemuse us and themselves. It was really quite simple. Painting (the "P.R.B.s" thought) was hidebound by tradition. But Nature was true, there was nothing formal about her: and you could hardly go wrong if you took your lessons from her. In other words, they wanted to topple the self-satisfied leaders from their pedestals—and start afresh.

This did not mean the "P.R.B.s" all painted in the same way. They never did. Their styles differed from the very beginning. All they sought so fervently was "to produce thoroughly good pictures and statues".

In a sentence, they were in revolt against the dullness and smugness of mid-Victorian England.

The name Pre-Raphaelite merely meant that the members would never be the slaves of rules or traditions which had been observed by followers of the school of the great Raphael. To the disappointment of William and of Stephens, the first fine zest began to lose way and slowly but surely the spring unwound. It was inevitable. The "P.R.B.s" and what today might be called their "message" were given publicity in the Press and in the lecture-rooms. The public, having been amused, interested—and often misled by inaccurate reports as to the true ideals of the Brotherhood—were reluctant to abandon a picturesque talking-point. Having heartily condemned the stick-in-the-mud attitude of leading artists and critics—that inward-looking and protected world—the young crusaders were ready to turn their attention elsewhere, not least to their own affairs.

4

Shepherd had been as good as his word, and given Harry a letter of introduction to a Mr. Charles Augustus Howell. This gentleman, he remarked casually, was a friend of Dante Gabriel Rossetti. Dunn saw in this the hand of fate. He says:

"Upon hearing the name of Rossetti mentioned, I instantly recalled the announcement I had once seen in the *Illustrated London News,* and the premonition I had then received, and felt that what was then so strangely presaged was actually about to come to pass."

Howell's house was across the river in Brixton, and Harry found his way to it easily enough. Howell at this time was a good-looking young man in his twenties, dark, handsome, and of a distinctly foreign appearance. He invariably dressed with care, but with a touch of flamboyance. In his speech there was the hint of an accent.

Harry Dunn was young, he was impressionable. Although by leaving home he had taken one decisive step this was not truly in keeping with his easy-going disposition. Experienced and clear-headed men of the world liked Howell even against their better judgement. What chance did a young provincial have? It is not surprising that Harry Dunn went down before the notorious charm of Charles Augustus Howell.

He was meeting for the first time, of course, a man whose goodwill was likely to be of immense value to him at a critical moment in his life: but he was to see a great deal of Howell in the future. For much of that eventful period in which Harry Dunn "helped to keep things straight" in Cheyne Walk, Howell was to make his presence felt socially and in a series of business transactions. As agent for the sale of Rossetti's pictures he was remarkably successful. Long after their business relationship was ended, Rossetti made it quite clear that his finances had never been in better shape than when the sale of his work was Howell's responsibility. And, later, when others spoke slightingly of the man, Harry saw no reason to adjust his initial admiration to any great degree. Charles Augustus Howell was the man who brought Rossetti and his "guardian angel" together, and for this the Cornishman could have forgiven him much.

As time went by, Dunn was to learn with what distaste some in Rossetti's circle regarded this new friend. In her impeccable and restrained book *Dante Gabriel Rossetti: His Friends and Enemies*, Helen Angeli quotes from one unpublished letter to her uncle in which Burne-Jones called Howell "a base, treacherous, unscrupulous and malignant fellow". Howell was frequently the target for such adjectives, but Harry at that first encounter would have felt personally affronted had he heard Swinburne's vicious description "the pole-cat Howell: the vilest wretch I ever came across". He was frankly captivated by Howell's easy manner.

Madox Brown, it is true, called him "one of the biggest liars in existence" and "half mad", but the fact remains that where other members of Rossetti's circle could at times be pompous, boring, patronising and snobbish, Howell was unfailingly himself. His methods may have been suspect, but there was nothing petty about the man himself, even if that self were flamboyant, ruthless, egoistic and worldly.

Howell shared with Rossetti the quality of being larger than life. Only a man of such a strong personality could have aroused such antagonism among those with whom he lived and worked.

In later years, Harry was often to ask himself why Howell was so much disliked. Part of the trouble quite clearly stemmed from a widely-held belief that nobody could be sure when he was telling the truth. For one thing, his friends and acquaintances could only guess how much reliance could be placed on the account he chose to give them of his origins. Howell was a man of mystery, and the strange, macabre manner of his death in 1890 only served to heighten the sinister, cloak-and-dagger quality of the image he created of himself. He was found dying in a Chelsea gutter with his throat cut and a golden half-sovereign clenched between his teeth.

It was generally understood that Howell had been born in Portugal, that his father had taught drawing in Lisbon, and in this city had met and married a Portuguese girl. There was talk of his being mixed up in his youth with a plan to assassinate Napoleon III. He gave it out that he had been acquainted with the Italian patriot, Felice Orsini, who made the attempt. His tales of diving for gold among submerged hulks of Spanish galleons were taken by most of his listeners with a grain of salt. William Morris gave it as his opinion that Howell had "stolen" the imposing red sash he wore across his shirt-front and which, according to Howell, was a Portuguese order handed down in his family. The panache with which he wore his mantle of distinction amused and exasperated by turn those who respected him as a shrewd man of business.

Later, Harry Dunn came to believe that it was Howell's reputation for sharp practice in commerce which alienated his celebrated clients and friends—even when they themselves benefited by his lack of business scruples. The fact is, Howell was too clever for them by half. With all their eccentricities, fecklessness, talent and prejudice, Rossetti's friends were men of probity—and this glib, persuasive man, a born "fixer" if ever there was one, belonged to a type they could not understand.

He was notorious for his disregard of truth. Mrs. Angeli quotes this limerick written by Gabriel:

> There's a Portuguese person named Howell
> Who lays on his lies with a trowel;
> When I goggle my eyes
> And start with surprise
> It's at monstrous big lies told by Howell.

And Theodore Watts-Dunton paid him this somewhat backhanded compliment:

"If he had possessed a private income, and if that income had been carefully settled upon him, I believe he would have been one of the most honest of men; I know he would have been one of the most generous."

Howell was an immensely good-natured man, no-one denied him that. He was always ready to help anyone to whom he took a fancy—and from the start he was taken by this young Westcountryman with his clear complexion and bright eyes, and the Cornish burr singing in his voice. Howell made no special effort to impress his caller. He was merely dispensing the charm which came so easily to him. It is possible that since an eye to the main chance was equally a basic part of his make-up, Howell saw a potential ally in the pleasant stranger. Howell spoke affectionately both of Dante Gabriel and William Michael Rossetti. The brothers and he were the greatest of friends, he said, and had been for many years. He did not mention that he had first met the Rossettis through a mysterious military gentleman, whom Gabriel had befriended. Money lent had never been repaid, and this character, described by William in an unusual mood of censure as "a very disgraceful character", vanished from the

scene. Howell had taken some hand in the "unmasking" of this un-
desirable person and the brothers were grateful.

He spoke of Gabriel, of Ruskin, Whistler, Madox Brown, Burne-
Jones, as though they were intimate friends or neighbours. He talked
airily of dealings on the Stock Exchange and of that true connoisseur's
eye which could discern bargains in the antique shops, later to be disposed
of at a substantial profit.

In time, Harry learnt the advisability of treating such stories with more
than a modicum of reserve. None the less, part of the Howell charm
rested in the fact that while he could not help embroidering his tales
in a fashion all his own, he did know what he was talking about: only if
one made a personal study of the Howell technique was it possible to
guess the point at which truth and falsehood parted company.

When Harry Dunn eventually took up residence at Cheyne Walk and
Howell was everywhere recognised as a social and commercial asset in
Rossetti's life, Gabriel would talk for hours on end to his young art-
assistant about this intriguing character. Eventually, Dunn was in a
position to make his own assessment and to learn something of the facts
in Howell's life. For instance, that he had, for some years, been Ruskin's
secretary (Harry gathered that the introduction had been effected by
Gabriel). Howell's busy, supple mind was constantly bent on some new
project for making money: and before the rift in their friendship, Gabriel
would talk with affectionate amusement about these schemes. There were
companies to be formed which were going to make everyone's fortune,
although on the authority of William Michael, well founded, no doubt,
capital seemed always to be "not super-abundant".

There was a plan to go to Madrid "to bid for the picture of Queen
Christina". There was his claim to have been elected a Fellow of the
Royal Society on the strength of his distinction as a civil engineer. There
were his dreams of a political career and the conviction that if he stood
for Parliament he would most certainly be elected to the House of Commons. Harry learned that Howell's friends smiled at these ambitions and
boastings—that is, they smiled until the joke wore thin. For various
reasons many people were in the years to come to revise their first high
opinions of Howell—notably Ruskin himself, Burne-Jones, Gabriel and
others.

On that afternoon in Brixton there was nothing to suggest that Charles
Augustus Howell would ever be regarded as the "evil genius" who

2. Henry Treffry Dunn, as a young man: from a photograph taken when he worked in a Truro bank.

3. Henry Treffry Dunn, as he was when Rossetti relied on him to keep the business and domestic affairs of No. 16, Cheyne Walk, in order.

4. A characteristic painting by Edith Hume, Harry Dunn's sister, who studied with him at the Heatherley School of Art in London, and who became a well-known professional artist.

played a leading part in one of the most dramatic incidents ever to shed an eerie glow upon the history of an English poet—the recovery of the poems from Mrs. Rossetti's coffin. To judge from Howell's pleasant and informative conversation he was an intimate friend and confidant of a score of famous men: yet no-one could have been more friendly towards an unknown stranger from the West Country. He asked many questions about Harry's home, especially about the smuggling tales and the stories of Spanish treasure ships submerged around the coast.

After an hour or two Dunn had been smothered by a torrent of kind words and warmed by Howell's hospitality. He learned a great many personal details about his host's past life and his hopes for the future. He was, he told him, planning shortly to marry his cousin, a Miss Kate Howell. This hope, at least, was realised, for the wedding took place in the autumn of 1867—with William and Christina Rossetti present, together with the Morrises and the Burne-Joneses and the Madox Browns, whose daughter, Lucy, was a bridesmaid. Before Dunn left the house, his new friend promised an introduction to Rossetti but suggested that first Harry should copy two heads of Dante. They were both, he said, copies made by Rossetti himself.

"The first", he said, "is a copy of a fresco discovered by Baron Seymour Kirkup in an old chapel at Florence—in the Bargello. It had lain there for at least a couple of centuries, hidden under repeated coats of whitewash." This, Howell went on, had been drawn from the poet himself by his friend, Giotto. In his *Purgatorio* he had referred to Giotto as the coming rival of Cimabue.[1]

Kirkup was an English painter who settled in Florence in the 1820's, and was given the title of Barone of the Italian Kingdom. His discovery of the fresco in 1840 or thereabouts had brought him international renown.

In a letter Kirkup wrote to Rossetti he told him that Dante had actually drawn part of his own portrait and written his name under it to oblige him. Kirkup died, a very old man, in 1880.

The other head of Dante was copied from an old Italian oil painting of the same period. The style was similar, the artist unknown.

---

[1] The Longfellow Translation:
> In painting Cimabue thought that he
> Should hold the field, now Giotto has the cry,
> So that the other's fame is growing dim.
> So has our Guido from the other taken
> The glory of our tongue, and he perchance
> Is born, who from the nest shall chase them both.

D

Harry left Brixton, warmed by Howell's hospitality. With the precious pictures carefully packed and secure under his arm, he walked buoyantly back to his lodgings, his head in the clouds, and his mind full of a rosy future.

Each of the paintings had a characteristic style and some skill was required to reproduce them successfully. In the event, Rossetti was satisfied enough for an appointment to be arranged at Cheyne Walk.

5

My appointment [Harry tells us] took me for the first time since I had been in London, to Cheyne Walk, Chelsea, to one of the most picturesque houses in which Rossetti lived. Entering by the fine old gateway of seventeenth-century ironwork, before ascending the flight of stone steps leading to the street door, I paused for a moment to look at the house itself. A profusion of jasmine in full bloom spread over the lower part of its walls, and it gave me the impression that at one time it must have formed the central portion of a much larger and statelier mansion.

This, then, was the house in which as a young stranger from West Britain he was to find a home. It never became a haven, or a refuge where serenity reigned for more than a day or so at a time. But here, in this large and comely place, Harry was to work happily and to meet Swinburne, Longfellow ("who had absolutely no knowledge of painting"), the author of *Alice in Wonderland* (who "photographed the Rossettis on a little flight of steps that led to the back hall door"), George Augustus Sala, and a remarkable group of men and women who wandered amiably and often noisily in and out of Mr. Rossetti's home. Although, as art-assistant, he had his duties and was regarded politely enough, as an indispensable jack-of-all-trades, he did as the years went by become a member of the close circle of friends who loved Gabriel, and protected him at times when he was most in need of their care.

It was at 16, Cheyne Walk, that Harry's easy-going temperament became an insidious curse. Many promising young artists have found soon enough that talent not infrequently fails to keep pace with ambition. Harry Dunn's case was precisely the opposite. He had considerable gifts, but any driving force which might have become personal ambition soon spent itself.

In the years which were ahead he was content to dream away too many precious hours, to write verses when the mood took him, and to paint—for modest rewards. It was fun to live day after day in the company of a man he admired, to meet his master's brilliant friends, to savour their wit and listen to the endless stream of anecdotes (many of them irreverent) about men of distinction in letters and in art.

Then there were the many domestic distractions which came crowding in. As Gabriel came to rely on him more and more, there was the constant skirmishing with Fanny to fray the nerves and send him out to the Admiral Keppel on the Fulham Road rather more often than might otherwise have happened. Or to the White Horse; or to the handy Magpye and Stump, in Cheyne Walk, a little west of Oakley Street. It was here, so the tale went, that Colonel Despard plotted to kill the King and seize the Tower and the Bank of England—and had been beheaded for it.

With Gabriel turning to him for help, with plenty of work to be done in the house and plenty of good companionship to be had outside it, there was not a great deal of incentive to woo fame or, indeed, to think a great deal further ahead than tomorrow.

While on this day his visit to 16, Cheyne Walk, seemed to young Harry to open a limitless prospect, the truth is that it smothered and crushed ambition. For the best part of twenty years the house and those who lived beneath its roof fascinated him and made demands which left little time and less inclination to strike out confidently for himself.

It might have been better for Harry Dunn if he had married. It was in Cheyne Walk he thought himself in love with the delectable Alicia; Alicia Wilding (known also as Alexa or Alice), whose face looks out upon the world in "Veronica Veronese", "Monna Vanna" and "The Blessed Damozel".

Harry's trouble was that he was not a man who could take easily to discipline in any form. He liked to go his own way: and although hands were held, kisses exchanged, and verses written, and it is unlikely that Harry wasted the long journeys when he was ordered to "escort" Miss Wilding to Kelmscott and other Rossetti sanctuaries, Alice, all in all, was probably better off without her adoring Harry.

Now, he was about to meet a man whose work he admired, a man who already stood head and shoulders above the majority of contemporary artists. Howell, and the students at Heatherley's, had spoken of Rossetti as a man of genius and character: and the house in which such a man worked would have had a compelling interest even if this had been a single exciting visit.

He was eager to see the home in which the great man lived. It was the most natural thing in the world that before mounting the flight of stone steps which led to the massive street door, he should pause for a moment to look at the building itself.

The "mansion" had been variously known as Queen's House and Tudor House. Such titles have been known to give ground for beliefs with very little foundation. In fact, the London County Council states that the house was built in the year 1717 when Queen Anne had been dead for three years: and since in 1949 the Council went to the trouble of affixing a circular blue and white memorial plaque to the wall of 16, Cheyne Walk, there is no reason to question the accuracy of their research.

The plaque bears the inscription:

Dante
Gabriel
Rossetti
1828–1882
and
Algernon Charles
Swinburne
1837–1909
lived here

Hall Caine recalled a tradition that Queen Elizabeth lived in the Tudor House. It is true there was in the garden an imposing and fruitful mulberry tree which was known as "Queen Elizabeth's Mulberry Tree". The tale went that the place had been used as a "nursery" for the children of Henry VIII, but as William Rossetti most sensibly points out, if there were the slightest basis of truth in this, then the story must have applied to a mansion which once stood on the same site and not to the house itself. Plausibly enough, history links both Sir Thomas More and Katharine Parr with a Tudor residence which stood on the same spot: while Thackeray described the house as Rossetti and Dunn knew it, in *Esmond*.

Anyhow, Mr. Caine, who knew something about architecture, was inclined to think that Number Sixteen was the oldest house in The Walk. The wrought-iron gates and railings certainly lend some weight to his theory that the house once stood on its own—on land which was later occupied by neighbouring houses. The records show that it had been built for Richard Chapman, an apothecary of St. Clement Danes, and his initials "R.C." may be seen on the gates.

Caine did not think much of the bay windows. He called them "unsightly". But William Rossetti (who did not always see eye to eye with Hall Caine on matters of fact) differed, and tells us that Gabriel and he agreed that the windows made the house a pleasanter place to live in. By the time Hall Caine came on the scene—to give an impression of a courtyard overgrown by moss and weeds and much shabbiness indoors— Gabriel had been ill for years, and his picture of the house in which Rossetti entertained friends with grace and bonhomie is not a fair one. Harry Dunn, who had insisted that the rooms should be kept immaculately clean even if the tenant was not in residence, had left for Cornwall and Fanny was busy on plans for her own future. Obviously, if one looked for them, there were bound to be signs of decay and neglect by 1880.

But for most of Gabriel's tenancy the house was anything but gloomy. It was handsomely and expensively furnished—and if the domestic arrangements were casual and unconventional, the atmosphere was one of colour and vigour and good fellowship. As an establishment it would not, perhaps, have been very highly thought of in circles where the daily newspapers were stitched and ironed before being read by the master and mistress, and where the lady of the house would not touch silver money until it had been cleaned in boiling water. But it was very much a home, with a great deal of extremely comfortable furniture.

When Rossetti went to live in Cheyne Walk there was no Chelsea Embankment. The Thames was still a public highway, a preserve of the old longshoremen. Water-borne traffic moved up and down the River constantly. Sailing craft of all kinds looked at the same time picturesque and business-like. In front of the house, the water's edge was made squalid by the litter which, especially in the summer, had a penetrating smell of its own, compounded of ships and tar and many less attractive things.

When Harry Dunn first cast an appreciative eye on the waterfront, the atmosphere still bore an echo of the days "when gracious Anne became our Queen, the Church of England's glory. . . ."

Not so long before, wealthy residents used their own rowing-boats and barges, and the private landing-stages were as normal an adjunct to a home as the stable in the mews behind the mansions of Mayfair and Regent's Park. There were boat-sheds, tall shady trees, moorings, the projecting wooden balconies and the inns, the Adam and Eve, for example, and the little shop where Carlyle bought his tobacco—and the houses and the steps leading down to the water. City men still caught the steam boat.

Cremorne Gardens, a handy distance from Cheyne Walk, were still open. The more raffish pleasure-seekers turned their steps to Cremorne as a matter of course. With its music, dancing, fireworks and galas, it was an ideal place for a night out. You could find there adventure in its broadest sense, and gay young men who fancied their chances with the girls and had not too much money in their pockets were drawn there as naturally as a kitten is to milk. In their twenties, Rossetti and his friends went frequently to Cremorne. In the years which followed his first visit to Number Sixteen, Harry Dunn was often to saunter through those wrought-iron gates, turn westwards and make his way to the Gardens. After a day which called for precise and constant work on some mediaeval or mystical subject, it was a relief to come down to earth, to hasten one's steps as the twinkling coloured lights came into view, to smile at the plaster figures and lean against a tree smoking a pipe and watching the boisterous pageant. Then, in 1875—the year in which Gabriel was painting "Venus Astarte", at Aldwick Lodge, near Bognor, Cremorne, with its fireworks and balloon ascents, was voted by common consent a nuisance in a respectable and genteel neighbourhood, and was closed for ever.

Chelsea, even today, has more character than most districts in London, but changes, in the name of progress, there had to be. Two which greatly altered the prospect of anyone gazing from the high windows of Number Sixteen were the building of the present Embankment and the disappearance of the old Battersea Bridge. The wooden toll-bridge—gas-lit in Harry Dunn's day—was a tangible link with that remarkable age in which humanity breathed the same air but lived in two vastly different worlds. Already a century old when Rossetti paid his first quarter's rent, this highway across the river was a picturesque landmark regarded by those who lived at either end of it as their own special property. It is a way Londoners have. It was worth a halfpenny to stroll across the bridge and look up and down the Thames from the raised footpath or to gaze down from one of the bays—though the language used by the bargees and the steamship skippers as they made the tricky passage beneath was enough to make strong men turn pale. The view, of course, was superb, the bridge itself an object to delight the artist's eye—Whistler was not the only man to paint it. But its appearance of solidity was misleading and the old Battersea Bridge was to vanish from London river, three years after Gabriel's death.

There was much, then, in the appearance of Rossetti's house on the day Harry first saw it which cannot be recaptured today. The noise, the movement, the apple-woman, the cry of the shrimp-vendor and, in the distance, to borrow from Carlyle, "the green, beautiful knolls of Surrey, a most artificial, green-painted, yet lively, fresh, almost operatic-looking business".

Harry had lingered long enough. He braced himself, moved lightly up the steps to the front door and lifted a hand to a large, old-fashioned knocker shaped like a dragon.

> But I found [says Harry] it was not a very easy dragon to perform a respectable rat-tat upon, by reason of the awkwardness of its shape (I did not quite know whether to take it by its head or tail) and the stiffness in its joints which age had rendered.
>
> On gaining admission I was ushered into one of the prettiest, and one of the most curiously-furnished and old-fashioned sitting-rooms that it had ever been my lot to see. Mirrors of all shapes, sizes and designs, lined the walls, so that whichever way I gazed I saw myself looking at myself. What space remained was occupied by pictures, chiefly old, and all of an interesting character. The mantelpiece was a most original compound of Chinese black-lacquered panels, bearing designs of birds, animals, flowers and fruit in gold relief, which had a very good effect, and on either side of the grate a series of old blue Dutch tiles, mostly displaying Biblical subjects treated in the serio-comic fashion that existed at the period, were inlaid. The fire-grate itself was a beautifully-wrought example of eighteenth century design and workmanship in brass, and had fire-irons and fender to match. And in one corner of the room stood an old English china cupboard, inside of which was displayed a quantity of Spode ware. I sat down on a cosy little sofa, with landscapes and figures of the Cipriani period painted on the panels.

At Heatherley's Harry had learnt a good deal about Cipriani, the renowned Italian painter and designer who became a member of Britain's Royal Academy and who died, in Chelsea, in 1787. The house seemed to Harry an exciting and stimulating place—a storehouse full of surprising and beautiful things. Even the cellar, as he was to discover, was filled with broken furniture, seventeenth-century iron grates, fire-dogs and "lumber of every kind for which no use could be found upstairs".

William Rossetti was inclined to play down the picturesque atmo-sphere of the old house. He saw his brother's residence as comfortable, well furnished and stylish—but far from showy and predominantly a home.

Harry, in his youthful enthusiasm, was more likely to have agreed with Philip Hamerton, the art-critic, who called on Rossetti and wrote: "He lives in a magnificent house, furnished with very great taste, but in the most extraordinary manner. His dining-room is very large indeed, and most curious: the general effect is very good. His pictures . . . are splendid in colour, and very quaint and strange in sentiment."

Harry heard the click of the handle as it turned in the door behind him. He turned—and found himself face to face with Dante Gabriel Rossetti.

In later years, after what his sister Edith so primly described as "his deplorable illness", Harry's memory for dates was unreliable. He sets his meeting with Gabriel in 1863, but William Michael thinks it was much more likely that Dunn first went to Cheyne Walk some years later, though certainly before the end of 1867. Whether, as Harry writes, "it was in the month of June 1863", when Rossetti was thirty-five, or in 1867, when he was thirty-nine, his graphic artist's description has been accepted, gratefully enough, by a series of biographers. At all events, this is the impression Gabriel made on the man who was to be his faithful and harrassed companion for years.

His face conveyed to me the existence of underlying currents of strong passions impregnated with melancholy. His eyes were dark grey, and deeply set; the eyebrows dark, thick, and well arched; the forehead large and well rounded, and the strongly-formed brows produced a remarkable fulness at the ridge of the nose, such as I have often noticed in men possessed of great individuality. A thick, but not heavy moustache partly concealed a well-formed and somewhat sensuous mouth, and at this time he wore a trimmed beard of a deep chestnut brown, with the cheeks shaven; his hair was much darker in colour, curly, and inclined to thinness. He was about 5 feet $7\frac{1}{2}$ inches in height—his drawing-room door was a faithful recorder not only of his own stature but that of most of his intimate friends. Although there was a tendency to a rather too extensive form with him, this was not particularly noticeable, owing to his shapely figure and easy carriage. He possessed a voice which was peculiarly rich and musical in tone; and when, later, I had opportunities of hearing him read his poems, which he did from time to time to some of his intimate friends, it was delightful to listen to him. His hands were small and very white. Of jewellery he made no display; all that he wore was an old-fashioned gold chain attached to his watch. He was equally unassuming in dress. For studio use he generally wore a loose overcoat, with capacious pockets into which he could easily thrust a good-sized memorandum book, which was indispensable to him, as it was his custom to jot down his thoughts either for poetry or painting as they arose in his mind.

It is interesting to compare Dunn's description of Gabriel with that
of William who also said with characteristic candour that his brother's
appearance was more Italian than English. Some disagreed, and said they
would not ordinarily have suspected a foreign ancestry.

With a fraternally uncompromising regard for truth, William tells us
that Gabriel, "meagre in youth, was decidedly fat in mature age". And
he goes on:

> The complexion, clear and warm, was also dark, but not dusky or sombre.
> The hair was dark and somewhat silky; the brow grandly spacious and solid;
> the full-sized eyes blueish-grey; the nose shapely, decided, and rather pro-
> jecting, with an aquiline tendency, and large nostrils, and perhaps no detail
> in the face was more noticeable at a first glance than the very strong indenta-
> tion at the spring of the nose below the forehead; the mouth moderately well
> shaped, but with a rather thick and unmoulded underlip; the chin unremark-
> able; the line of the jaw, after youth was passed, full-rounded and sweeping;
> the ears well formed and rather small than large. His hips were wide, his
> hands and feet small; the hands very much those of the artist or author type,
> white, delicate, plump, and soft as a woman's. His gait was resolute and rapid,
> his general aspect compact and determined. . . . Some people regarded
> Rossetti as eminently handsome; few, I think, would have refused him the
> epithet of well-looking. . . . He wore moustaches from early youth, shaving
> his cheeks: from 1870, or thereabouts, he grew whiskers and beard, moder-
> ately full and auburn tinted, as well as moustaches. His voice was deep and
> harmonious; in the reading of poetry, remarkably rich, with rolling swell and
> musical cadence.

Rossetti put himself out to welcome Howell's protégé. He was amused
by the young Cornishman's ingenuousness—and modest enough to be
flattered by his frank admiration. Harry on his part understood everything
Howell had good-naturedly tried to tell him about Gabriel's special brand
of charm. It would have been astonishing in the circumstances if he had
not fallen under the spell. The man's friendliness was unforced, his
manner relaxed and paternal. Luckily, Harry Dunn came into Rossetti's
life at a happy and rewarding period, when skill matched inspiration.
Mercifully, the frightening compulsion of chloral was not yet making life
intolerable. In a few years' time, Harry would be doing his best to keep
those damnable bottles out of sight, talking hour after hour in an attempt
to help Gabriel fight the menace of depression which would yield only to
increasing draughts of the drug.

Rossetti had been overwhelmed with grief and dismay by the death
of his wife. But that tragic event had happened in the February of 1862,

and when Harry eventually turned up at Cheyne Walk with his paint-box, his palette and his carpet-bag, the cutting edge of tragedy had been blunted by time.

Many writers took it for granted that after Elizabeth's death Gabriel was a man forever tortured by remorse and regret. His brother pours cold water on this theory. What Rossetti felt when some pang of memory, some spoken word, some forgotten perfume, made his wife real to him again in one swift moment, who can say? We all know these unbidden flashes of pain and bitterness. But in William Michael's understanding, Gabriel "had too much energy of mind and character, too many ideas of his own, too earnest a desire to turn these into realised work, to be perpetually dwelling on the grievousness of the past, or moping over what once had been and could never be again".

In the company of wits and of men of brilliance, Rossetti shone with a natural gaiety, in spite of his personal tragedies. Haunted sometimes, perhaps: haunted forever—not so. Later, sleepless, crushed by illness and pain, his memories may, indeed, have been intolerable, but in the first few years Harry worked at Cheyne Walk Gabriel's manner was normal enough.

His sister, Christina, in a magazine article under the title, "The House of Dante Gabriel Rossetti", made the point with admirable firmness:

> Family or friendly parties used to assemble at Tudor House, there to meet with an unfailing affectionate welcome. Gloom and eccentricity, such as have been alleged, were at any rate not the sole characteristics of Dante Gabriel Rossetti. When he chose he became the sunshine of his circle, and he frequently chose so to be. His ready wit and fun amused us; his good-nature and kindness of heart endeared him to us.

It so happened that Gabriel's most successful and prosperous period began almost as soon as Harry Dunn came on the scene, and took an active part in the affairs of 16, Cheyne Walk. The Rossetti income increased, and there was about the house that pleasant and unmistakable atmosphere of prosperity. Of course, it would have been a great deal easier all round had Gabriel had a banking account. But this practical step was not taken until some years after Harry's unofficial election as keeper of the purse: and even when there was a banking account, the famous "money drawer" still remained the favoured financial system.

It is possible then that Harry allowed himself a little artist's licence when he spoke of those underlying currents of strong passions which "were impregnated with melancholy". He may have felt that this was something readers of his *Recollections* might, in the light of later events, expect him to say.

Harry's eyes were too busy absorbing the scene with all its rich detail to realise that in a way he was himself on trial, before an amiable judge. Although Rossetti did not follow the accepted practice and exhibit his pictures, he had for years been regarded as a successful and original artist. His poetry was admired—and (which meant so much more) discussed. These rare twin-talents helped to focus public attention on his work and attracted the buyers. He was kept busy enough to engage a professional assistant—Mr. W. J. Knewstub—to prepare "duplicates" of pictures and to make himself generally useful. Now, after a year or so, Knewstub had dropped a hint that he would like to branch out on his own. The commissions were still coming in with delightful regularity. Might not this trim, polite Cornishman make an excellent replacement?

In many ways Howell was the most unreliable fellow living, but he had spoken well of young Mr. Dunn and Gabriel was inclined to take a chance. The work he had seen (including some of the Cornish sketches) was not too bad by half—at least it had a certain firmness and originality and if Knewstub did indeed decide to take himself off here might lie the answer.

So, as he talked to Harry he weighed him up shrewdly enough, though he was affability itself. He enchanted his visitor by saying, with a glint of fun in his eye, "Tell me about your second name. It's most unusual, I think—though not perhaps in your own part of the world. Howell tells me you like us to pronounce Tre*ffry* with the stress on the second syllable."

Harry, a trifle embarrassed, remembered saying to Howell that he winced every time a new acquaintance called him "*Treff*-ry". It was clear that Howell had passed this on to Mr. Rossetti, that they had smiled at this Cornish idiosyncrasy. Gabriel, clapping him on the back, repeated his name correctly, saying: "Have I got it right? If you and I are going to be friends I must at least have the good manners to pronounce you properly!

"But we've other things to discuss, I think," he added. "You must let me show you my studio."

He took Harry's arm and led him into the large room in which the

Westcountryman was to spend so much of his working life. His first impression was of the excellent light: it could hardly have been better.

The studio, as Harry noted, "was liberally stocked with Chippendale chairs and lounges and various other inviting rests whereon one might sit at ease and enjoy a survey of his pictures, which stood about on easels. Several cabinets of Old English and Spanish design and work-manship filled up the odd nooks and corners that were left."

Later, Harry set down some of his thoughts about this first visit to Tudor House. In particular his memory of two pictures out of the many Gabriel showed him remained clear in every detail. They were "Lady Lilith" and "Beata Beatrix".

Gabriel had been strangely stirred by the legend of Lilith, whom Adam loved before Eve. His poem "Eden Bower" is proof of the effect the chill, disquieting tale had upon his imagination. But the painting which fascinated Harry Dunn as he stood in Gabriel's studio did not depict the Lilith of fable. The face and form of "Lady Lilith" were meant to proclaim one bold, uncompromising statement—the power and supremacy of physical beauty.

Rossetti himself made some water-colour replicas of the picture. In his sonnet, "Body's Beauty", the poet in him tried to explain the emotions which inspired the painter.

Of Adam's first wife, Lilith, it is told
   (The witch he loved before the gift of Eve)
   That, ere the snake's, her sweet tongue could deceive,
And her enchanted hair was the first gold.
And still she sits, young while the earth is old,
   And, subtly of herself contemplative,
   Draws men to watch the bright web she can weave,
Till heart and body and life are in its hold.

The rose and poppy are her flowers; for where
   Is he not found, O Lilith, whom shed scent
And soft-shed kisses and soft sleep shall snare?
   Lo! as that youth's eyes burned at thine, so went
   Thy spell through him, and left his straight neck bent
And round his heart one strangling golden hair.

Of the picture, Harry wrote:

It was the portrayal of a beautiful woman, sumptuously seated in some mediaeval kind of chair, combing out a cataract of golden hair that fell in masses over her shoulders. By her side was a mirror of curious form, in which was reflected the greenery of the forest glade, through which the glinting sunlight pierced here and there, lighting up the densely-leaved branches of the trees, and a large red double poppy in a goblet of old Venetian glass stood near her. The dreamy beauty of the woman, and the rich colour in which the whole picture was steeped excited my admiration. I desired to know its meaning, and in answer to my enquiry he told me it was suggested by Lilith.

"Who was she?" I asked.

Rossetti then told me the Talmudic legend concerning her, and then I understood the allusion to her in *Faust*, where Goethe introduces Lilith into the witch scene on the Hartzbrocken, and makes Faust ask the same question in almost the same words that I had used.[1]

"I am sorry to say", Harry wrote after Gabriel's death, "that Rossetti repainted the face some years later, for what reason I could never divine. To my thinking he by no means improved upon the original."

The first head was that of Fanny who in this instance was ruthlessly dethroned in favour of Alicia Wilding. There is no reason to suggest that Gabriel made this drastic change for any but artistic reasons of his own: but some may think the affair is probably the unkindest cut Fanny ever suffered at her master's hand. In all other matters, he was tolerance itself so far as his principal model was concerned: but he was determined that hers was not the head of Lilith posterity was to admire—and that was that.

Considering the trouble Fanny gave him Harry's was rather a generous opinion: especially as he found Alice so enchanting. One might have thought that in his eyes the lovely Miss Wilding would most certainly have "improved upon the original". But, Alice, after all, had also on occasion been difficult, and his memory of her may have been tarnished by her occasional periods of unreliability. As Gabriel wrote to "My Dear Dunn" from Kelmscott, the house he leased jointly with William Morris, "I have got a note from Alice W. saying she may not be well enough to come for two or three weeks! This may prove most inconvenient. Would you kindly look her up and see how she *really* is."

---

[1] FAUST: And who is that?
MEPHISTOPHELES: Do thou observe her well.
                        That's Lilith.
FAUST: Who?
MEPHISTOPHELES: Adam's first damosel.
Be on thy guard against her lovely hair,
   That tire of hers in which she peerless shines!
   When with its charm a youngster she entwines,
She will not soon release him. So beware!

At all events, on the subject of "Lady Lilith" Harry was to express the somewhat lofty view:

> Generally speaking, I hold it a dangerous experiment to alter a first conception; the charm, the quality of colour, and the inspiration are so apt to be lost.

William Michael agreed. He says, "Mrs. H . . . sat for the woman in 'Found', 'The Blue Bower' and 'The Loving Cup' and, in the first instance, for 'Lilith'; but another head—that of Miss Alexa Wilding—was after an interval of years, substituted in 'Lilith' and, to my thinking, very disadvantageously so."

The other picture which Harry found so touching and so disturbing was the "Beata Beatrix".

"I afterwards learnt from my friend Howell", he wrote to his sister Edith, "that the face of Beatrice was painted from Mrs. Rossetti." He might have added that the artist himself would say that no picture had ever cost him so much in mental effort and despair. At one time it was believed to represent "The Dying Beatrice" and was known by that title. Gabriel himself made it clear that the nobly conceived picture showed Beatrice "suddenly rapt from earth to Heaven". Life seems withdrawn from the pale upturned face in the golden light. Harry, as he looked, saw in Elizabeth Siddal's features an expression of fulfilment rather than mortality.

Howell told Dunn that he had found the picture, dusty and neglected, among a stack of other canvases in the studio. He had secretly taken it away, cleaned it and relined it, and then brought it back to Gabriel "in a most inviteable state to work upon". Gabriel had "taken fresh heart of grace and completed what is perhaps one of his most beautiful conceptions".

After Gabriel's death the "Beata Beatrix" was presented to the National Gallery by Lady Mount Temple, formerly Mrs. Cowper-Temple, and a personal friend of Rossetti and his brother.

> There was yet another of his works that incited my interest. He called it "The Loving Cup". Rossetti wanted a replica made in water-colours, and it was on this that he wished me to make my first essay.
> "Although I was in considerable doubt as to whether I could do it or not—his water-colour work was so different in method of execution to anything I had yet seen—I was delighted with the opportunity afforded me, and said that I would try, so arrangements were made there and then for me to come

and make a beginning. The beginning, I am happy to say, came to a good ending. Rossetti like my replica so well, that when it was completed he set me to work upon something else.

It proved to be a long and happy visit. Harry found himself after several hours still enthralled by Rossetti's conversation. This was not the brief, formal call he had foreseen, but a comradely, intimate meeting between two professionals. His host had no intention of letting his visitor depart until he had introduced him to William Michael who was expected to drop in at Number Sixteen. No doubt there had been a plan to bring the two men together. William naturally wished to see the young artist whose qualities had impressed Howell. It was, in its way, a momentous encounter for both. William Rossetti and Harry Dunn were to be friends and allies until a year or more after Gabriel's death. Allies in at least two struggles—one, the battle against what even William conceded were Gabriel's "unthrifty and negligent habits in household affairs"; and another, far more grim, the attempt to rescue Gabriel's health and, indeed, his reason, from the tyranny of chloral.

Harry Dunn gives us a pleasant and boyishly enthusiastic account of how he spent the remainder of what was, for him, such a memorable afternoon. The Chippendale bookcase was "well-stocked" and Gabriel and his new acquaintance were soon deep in discussion about William Blake. Both men revered and admired Blake's work.

> Rossetti went to the shelves and took down a little, unpretentious volume that looked just like a schoolboy's exercise book. Such it was originally intended to be, but the use to which it had been put made it very precious in my sight, for on turning over the leaves I saw it was filled with Blake's first thoughts for his *Songs of Innocence*, interspersed with pen-and-ink and slightly-coloured pencil designs for the same. Rossetti told me he had bought the book many years previously from one of the attendants in the British Museum, who had let him have it for half-a-sovereign.

After he had read Harry's *Recollections* more than thirty years later, William Michael made the point that the contents of this little book did not refer only to the *Songs of Innocence*. There were many "miscellaneous designs" and a great deal of verse and prose. It was a collector's treasure, and the individual who paid rather more than a hundred guineas for it at the sale of Rossetti's effects in 1882 had a bargain. Gabriel was among the most generous of men, and it is on record that when Alexander Gilchrist died with his *Life of Blake* unfinished, he willingly helped the widow to

5. A childhood study by Henry Treffry Dunn: the subject,
a daughter of his sister Frances.

6. The three children of the Cornish artist, Richard Carter, with the city of Truro in the background. Painted by their uncle, Henry Treffry Dunn, this picture is now in the County Museum and Art Gallery in Truro. The elder boy, Reginald Carter, became Headmaster of Bedford School.

edit and prepare the final manuscript. As Harry was to discover in the next dozen years or so, Rossetti was always ready to help a fellow-artist down on his luck. He was, to use the jargon of a later day, an "easy touch". And many times Gabriel's "guardian angel" had to scale down some contribution when the money drawer had been opened rather too often.

When the Blake manuscript was well conned and discussed, another curiosity took its place, in the form of *Hypnerotomachia Poliphili*, of great interest to book collectors, because the numerous woodcuts illustrating the text are said to have been designed by Botticelli. [Harry was probably off course here. Bellini seems a more probable name than Botticelli: and the experts are reluctant to be definite.]

Rossetti's copy was faulty, as it lacked the original title-page and binding; but this did not interfere with my enjoyment of the designs. Many other books there were in that Chippendale case of a similar kind, such as the *Nuremberg Chronicle*, with its quaint and interesting illustrations.

As the afternoon wore on, William Michael Rossetti, the painter's brother, came in. He generally spent three evenings a week at Cheyne Walk. I had heard and seen his name pretty frequently in connection with critical papers upon Art which had from time to time caught my eye in some of the periodicals that came in my way. William Michael Rossetti I soon got to like, and as he was a smoker it gave me an opportunity of producing my pipe and blowing a cloud with him. A special tobacco box, always on the mantelpiece, was reserved for William Michael Rossetti, who invariably brought a two-ounce packet of some choice brand of tobacco which generally disappeared by the time his next visit came about. A good many of the visitors to Cheyne Walk were smokers, and if their own stock ran short, William Michael Rossetti's was usually drawn upon. The box itself was a bit of eighteenth century pewter work, four-square shaped, designed in high relief with sporting and rural scenes. I always intended to make a cast of it for my own use, and as a memento of the house, but never did so.

Rossetti's fancy for collecting old blue Nankin and other china was just at this time in full swing. James McNeill Whistler had set the example with his "Long Elizas", and was closely followed by Rossetti and Howell.

These were specimens of china porcelain on which figures of slim Chinese ladies are painted. The term "Long Elizas" was a characteristic bit of Whistler nonsense. The correct phrase was "Lange Leises"—that is, long, tall or slim damsels, this being the name given by the Dutch to porcelain of the kind.

Each tried to outvie the other in picking up the choicest pieces of "Blue" to be met with. A pair of splendid blue hawthorn ginger pots stood on a table in the studio. These were not the first ginger pots I had seen; I recollect

E

that when a boy they were common enough—of course, not such magnificent specimens as these were, but very good ones—although they were then thought very little of, and many a one such as would fetch ten or fifteen shillings now were given away to anybody who chose to ask for them. The two hawthorn pots in question were certainly beautiful, and exquisite in their blue and design, nevertheless when Rossetti informed me he had paid sixty pounds each for them, I confess I was astounded. The investment, however, proved a good one, as some time later, when money was needed, the pair was disposed of for six hundred pounds.[1]

Whilst the hawthorn pots were being admired and discussed, Rossetti was hastily pulling out drawer after drawer from an old cabinet that stood in one of the recesses of the room. He was searching for something suitable to paint round the neck of the girl in his picture "The Loving Cup", and before him lay a rare store of necklaces, featherwork, Japanese crystals, and knick-knacks of all kinds, sufficient to stock a small window. At length his choice was made of a necklace, and when this was satisfactorily settled, his costumes, which were kept in a large wardrobe at the back of the studio, were over-hauled for one that was needed for another painting which he had in progress.

In going towards this wardrobe, I noticed upon one of the walls of the studio a gilt frame containing about half a dozen drawings and sketches, chiefly by members of the Pre-Raphaelite Brotherhood, with the names of John Everett Millais, William Holman Hunt, Thomas Woolner, William Bell Scott, Ford Madox Brown, and James McNeill Whistler attached.

Wherever I went, I noticed musical instruments of some kind or another; all were old and mostly stringed—mandolines, lutes, dulcimers, and bar-barous-looking things of Chinese fashioning, which I imagine it would have been a great trial to the nerves to hear played upon—and yet in all the after years that I lived in the house I never heard a note of music. It had no home there. Our neighbours in the next house, however, were abounding in it, and often in the summer evenings, when the windows would be thrown wide open, the fine baritone of Theo Marzials, the poet and musician, who was frequently there, would come floating into our front rooms. Rossetti had a great admiration for Marzials as a poet, and often spoke of the high quality of his poems and songs, which were then becoming very popular and much discussed. But for music itself he did not care a whit, and was very much of the opinion of Dr. Johnson, who, when once he was asked if he liked music, replied that perhaps of all noises it was the most bearable!

In relation to this indifference to music shewn by Rossetti, I recollect in the course of one of our conversations whilst working together, something led to his giving me an idea of what he thought of Handel's *Messiah*, which was at the time being performed at one of the Crystal Palace festivals. Once, he said, he had been induced by a friend to listen to it, and it seemed to him

---

[1] William, more cautious where money is mentioned, thinks two hundred pounds a more likely figure.

that everybody got up and shouted at him as loudly as possible! Another time, Mr. Frederick Leyland took him to the Royal Opera House to hear *Fidelio*. The next morning I was curious to know what he had to say in regard to such a masterpiece, but he could not give me a clear idea of what it was all about. The only notion he had of it was that of a man who was taken out of prison, where he had been for a couple of days without food, and who, when a loaf of bread was given to him, instead of eating it like any starving man would do, burst out into a long solo over it lasting for ten minutes— which he thought was obviously absurd!

But the musical instruments were only a few of the many odds and ends of all sorts that were stacked away wherever a place could be found for them. Anything Rossetti saw in his rambles that might be of possible use to him for a picture he would buy. He delighted to take an evening's walk through Leicester Square, visiting the various curosity shops in that neighbourhood, or through Hammersmith, a district where many a Chippendale chair or table could be met with and bought for next to nothing, such things not being then in the repute that they have become since the taste for Queen Anne houses and fittings sprang up.

When Howell joined us unexpectedly in the studio, the flow of talk became lively. Howell had a lot to say, and it consisted of the most astounding experiences and adventures he had gone through. He had just left Whistler, and was full of a "Long Eliza" he had picked up somewhere, of his etching of old Battersea Bridge, of which he had been shown a proof, and of his latest witticism. The main object, however, of Howell's visit was to get from Rossetti a drawing he had made of a lady. I infer some bargaining had been going on between them, and that the drawing formed part of the bargain, but as Rossetti prized it highly, to gain possession of it was not a very easy matter and required much diplomacy.

I now had an opportunity of looking over and admiring a series of Rossetti's first ideas and sketches for many of his pictures, and studies of heads, which were contained in a large, thick book, lying on a little cabinet in a distant corner. It was a great and unexpected treat to see this collection, a most varied one, amongst which were many carefully finished likenesses, some in red chalk, and others in pencil and in pen and ink, including pencil sketches of John Ruskin (not bearded then), Robert Browning, Algernon Charles Swinburne, William Morris, and other well-known men.

At last we came to the page at which the drawing Howell had come to secure was affixed. It was a beautiful face, delicately drawn, and shaded in pencil, with a background of pale gold. Howell, with an adroitness which was remarkable, shifted it from the book into his own pocket, and neither I nor Rossetti ever saw it again.

As we turned over the contents of this volume, a small, hasty, but exceedingly realistic pen and ink sketch, that had nearly got passed over, arrested my attention. It was of Tennyson, seated and reading out his poem "Maud". This reading took place in Browning's London residence, in the presence of Browning, Mrs. Browning, Rossetti, and his brother. Whoever possesses the little sketch ought to prize it very highly.

The pages of the book were still being turned over, slowly, by reason of the accompanying flow of lively recollections and stories of this or that individual whose face formed the subject of a sketch. The book was a rich record of past days and memories. And many a tender little sketch of his late wife was to be found there, with the same sad, beautiful weary expression that had struck me so much in his "Beata Beatrix".

When it was time for farewells Harry was elated and sanguine. It had been quite the most remarkable day in his life. Three important and successful men had talked to him on equal terms. Gabriel himself had drawn the young stranger into the circle with the greatest courtesy and friendliness. He had been given the promise of work and an invitation to come again.

Above all—although the significance of the incident no doubt escaped him at the time—he had, on his first visit to Cheyne Walk, been given an example of the notorious Howell technique. With enormous effrontery, and in full view, Charles Augustus, the likeable scamp, the "Portugee", the arch-fixer, had calmly walked off with a friend's property. He wanted something: he took it.

The Frederick Leyland mentioned in the extract from the *Recollections* quoted above was a hard-headed Liverpool shipowner, whose London headquarters was a mansion in Princes Gate. He was one of Rossetti's greatest admirers, and bought many of Gabriel's pictures for his splendid art collection. It was for Leyland that Whistler painted his famous "Peacock Room", but a quarrel ended their association. How these art-lovers enjoyed a good row! Leyland was more than a purchaser of Gabriel's pictures: he was a good friend, and Harry was to meet him frequently in the next ten years.

He was a welcome and reliable source of income. Gabriel was writing to Madox Brown in 1874: "Leyland and Graham have both turned up trumps as to tin, so, instead of demanding, I can offer, if needed, without the least inconvenience."

Whistler was a neighbour of Rossetti. With Howell, too, in full cry, the two artists searched the antique shops of London for Nankin. They were years ahead of fashion and between them collected a unique assortment of rare china pieces. This is not the place to examine Whistler's gift for verbal clowning, but as Harry Dunn suggested, he and Howell had a flair for planting the barbs of repartee, and enjoyed baiting each other. Of the artist's newly-built house in Tite Street, with its simplicity of style and light yellow interior decoration, Howell said: "To be in Whistler's house is like standing inside an egg." It was here that Whistler, shortly to be declared bankrupt, climbed a ladder to write above the door: "Except the Lord build the house, they labour in vain that build it. E. W. Godwin, F.S.A., built this one."

6

Harry had made an excellent impression. As an artist he was something more than capable. He had an eye for detail and his brushwork was meticulous to a degree. The first modest commissions led to others, and by the time six months had passed, Harry found himself a regular and welcome visitor to Cheyne Walk.

One day Gabriel, smiling, put an arm round his shoulder and said, "My dear fellow, I have a matter to discuss with you. Think well before you answer—but what would you think of joining me here, making your home under this roof? Knewstub's leaving me, and I've every confidence that you are the only man who can take his place."

Harry had met Walter John Knewstub and liked him. This talented and agreeable man was Gabriel's first "art-assistant", having been engaged several years before Harry's introduction by Howell. He has also been described as Rossetti's "only articled pupil". By 1862 Rossetti had plenty of work, and should, indeed, have been fairly prosperous. His wife's death had shaken him badly, but to outward appearance at least he settled down to a comparatively disciplined programme of work. A number of commissions were coming his way, and other paintings found buyers quickly and without difficulty.

Gabriel was rarely short of inspiration but attention to detail and routine could be a bore. When a new idea came to him he would develop it with an imaginative zest—to the exclusion of everything else. It was a recognised practice for busy artists who found the work getting on top of them to engage studio-assistants to help them. By 1862 Rossetti's work was so much in demand that he felt secure enough to employ Knewstub, a man of wit and intelligence, and a welcome addition to the circle. The association between the two men was a happy one, never to be regretted by either.

Knewstub had a gift for comic drawing and much of his work then and later reflected a pleasant and penetrating sense of humour. His professional value to Rossetti was, of course, in his skill as a painter, chiefly in water-colours. He and his employer enjoyed each other's company, talking endlessly on many topics and going for long walks together. It was on one of these walks that Rossetti's roving eye lit on an extremely attractive young woman—a "stunner", no less. It was not Gabriel's habit to allow such chance encounters to go to waste and one can imagine the affectionate amusement with which Knewstub imparted to Gabriel the information that the lady in question was a friend of his. In fact, she became his wife.

Knewstub was not the kind of man content to live and work under the wing of a celebrity and it was only a matter of time before he decided to make his own way in the world. Gabriel, the first to recognise talent in others and the last to prevent them from using it to the full, understood Knewstub's feelings. He encouraged him to become independent—and then found himself casting about for someone to replace his pupil.

Knewstub went on to make a reputation in the art world of the time. He married, and one of his beautiful daughters became the wife of William Rothenstein, father of Sir John Rothenstein, who retired in 1964 after so brilliantly directing the fortunes of the Tate Gallery.

Harry had a naturally sunny disposition and from the beginning he fitted snugly enough into the easy-going atmosphere of Number Sixteen. He was quick and willing and had a ready grasp of the work he was expected to do. Gabriel, the most companionable of beings, and a man of boisterous good nature, found the young Cornishman's quiet manner and shy smile appealing. He liked the ready smile and Harry's boyish desire to please.

There was nothing of the recluse about Gabriel. He liked his fellow-men, enjoyed hearing their voices raised in argument and laughter. He had been on easy terms with his previous art-assistant, and it never occurred to him to countenance any master-and-servant nonsense about Walter Knewstub's successor. The result was that in a remarkably short time, Harry felt as though he had lived in Cheyne Walk for years. For a man of his tastes it was a delight to exchange a modest lodging for a civilised and gracious home filled with rare and expensive possessions.

By day, Harry would spend hours in the big studio mixing the paints, watching Gabriel at his easel, and taking instructions from him.

From time to time his employer would stand by Harry's side as he worked, throwing in now a word of advice, of praise, perhaps now underlining a point with some memory or jest. The rich laughter rang round the room as a point struck home. He was entertained by Harry's story of how he first heard the name—on reading of Mr. Rossetti's decision to abandon water-colour.

"True enough," he said, "but a man must live—and that's the only reason I stuck to such 'sloshy' work for as long as I did."

Everything pointed to the fact that the arrangement would be a permanent one. Harry lost some of his nervousness and after a month or two of daily meetings his timidity fell away and he was able to see Gabriel as a man rather than as an employer. As they shared the same table for the mid-day meal or took a drink together at the end of a day's work, Harry felt a natural curiosity about Gabriel's background. He made it his business to study the way Gabriel liked things done, to anticipate his instructions: to run an errand before the order was given. It took him very little time to learn that this dark, rather portly, striking-looking man was, professionally, a perfectionist. In appearance, the two men made a complete contrast. The Westcountryman, with his high complexion, thin intelligent face and spare figure: the other, London-born, but at times having a distinctly foreign air about him. From various sources Harry soon came to know something of Rossetti's parentage and ancestry.

Gabriel was one-quarter English, was born in Charlotte Street and had never been to Italy in his life. Harry learnt that Gabriel was born in the year 1828—the date, May 12th. His name in full was Gabriel Charles Dante Rossetti. The form Dante Gabriel Rossetti was his own choice. Few names, once heard, were harder to forget.

His father, Gabriele Pasquale Rossetti, was wholly Italian. The son of a blacksmith, he had been born in 1783 on the Adriatic coast at Vasto in Abruzzi, at that time in the Kingdom of Naples. Force of character and a true, natural talent, carried Gabriele from an unspectacular beginning to a position of importance in the literary world of his adopted country. His mother could neither read nor write, but a local landowner, the Marchese del Vasto, was so impressed by the boy that he undertook to see him properly educated. As a young man he was employed in the Museo Borbonico in Naples, his special interest the custody of ancient bronzes.

Gabriele's poetic and fiery temperament landed him in trouble and in exile. Politics were the breath of life to the liberal-minded young patriots of the day. An idealistic outlook made him violently critical of the King of Naples—Ferdinand the First—and when the King betrayed the Constitution, broke his word and made a mockery of his promises, Gabriele not only wrote inflammatory poems, but talked and worked with equal ardour for the cause.

As a result he was condemned to death, and the venom of the King was such that Rossetti was one of two patriots who were excluded from an amnesty.

In common with many other distinguished men before him, Gabriele preferred exile to a disagreeable and premature death. He arrived in England in 1821, and became Professor of Italian at King's College in London. He wrote a number of scholarly books and is remembered as one of the great authorities on Dante. Gabriele Rossetti thought and wrote profoundly about Dante's Hell, Purgatory and Heaven, and his love for Beatrice, and it is not difficult to understand the fascination Dante was to have for Gabriele's brilliant son.

The young political exile married Frances Mary Lavinia Polidori, who was English-born and whose mother, Anna Maria, belonged to an English family called Pierce: it was through her that Dante Gabriel Rossetti was "a quarter English".

Gaetano Polidori was also an exile from Italy, though not for political reasons. He was a Tuscan, and Helen Angeli makes the point that two men, one from Tuscany, the other from Abruzzi, may well have been as un-alike as a Cornishman and a Scotsman.

Polidori was at one time Secretary to the well-known dramatist and poet, Count Vittorio Alfieri: indeed, he was with Alfieri in Paris when the Revolution was under way. Shocked by the rioting and the excesses of mob law—to say nothing of his own patron's somewhat hysterical atti- tude to the whole gory business—Gaetano left Paris and sailed for Dover. Like Rossetti, he made his home in London and taught his native language. Polidori also worked on an English/Italian dictionary, wrote plays and poetry, and translated Milton into Italian. His wife had a small income of her own and was an educated and elegant woman. It seems from most accounts of Dante Gabriele's forbears that they all enjoyed good looks in some measure; handsome, striking and pleasing are the adjectives most freely used.

John, brother of Frances Polidori, has his own curious niche in the history of English letters. This "gifted and very handsome young man" became Byron's friend and physician, was inspired to write *The Vampyre*, and did away with himself at the age of twenty-six.

Gabriele Rossetti, the much-loved Professor, and his wife Frances

Polidori (one of her brothers anglicised his name to Polydore), had four children. These were: Maria Francesca (1827–76), author of *A Shadow of Dante*; Dante Gabriel (1828–82); William Michael, the poet and critic (1829–1919); and Christina Georgina (1830–94), the author of *Goblin Market*, *The Princess's Progress* and a poet whose work was acclaimed throughout the world.

From the many details Gabriel himself later let slip in conversation, Harry eventually had a clear picture of his friend's youth, his ambitions and his adventures—romantic and otherwise.

Maria and Gabriel were full of spirit and mischief: William and Christina quieter and less demonstrative. A Punch and Judy show; daily walks in Regent's Park; a camera obscura; and the smoke from the still magical railway-trains puffing away near the Park—these were some of Gabriel's cherished memories.

The boys' interest in animals (one day to bring notoriety to 16, Cheyne Walk) stemmed from frequent childhood excursions to London's comparatively newly-opened Zoological Gardens. William recalls how they would "run shrieking through the tunnel to arouse the echo". Generations of children played that same game. By today's standards, the specimens were few in number and not specially exciting; but there were plenty of parrots, some lions and tigers, elephants, bears—and a "singing antelope", which could never be persuaded to live up to its name. The first "collection" of animals assembled by Gabriel consisted of a dormouse which enjoyed its winter sleep in a drawer; and a hedgehog of unpredictable behaviour.

There was never, so it appears, any doubt that Gabriel, or Dante, as he was called in childhood, would be a painter. He had taken a pencil from his father's desk and was soon rapt in a world of his own. Wondering, the milkman said, "I saw a baby making a picture." Their mother taught the children with affection and much thought for their future. Dante enjoyed Shakespeare, the tales of Walter Scott, and the rich, resounding lines of "Marmion" and "The Lady of the Lake". After a spell at a day-school in Foley Street, off Portland Place, W.1, he and William went on to King's College School, where the elder boy stayed for five years. He was no more than thirteen when serious training as an artist began—first at a drawing academy in Bloomsbury, run by F. S. Cary (a friend of Gabriele's), and known as "Sass's". Here, before passing on to the Antique School of the Royal Academy, he had the name for drawing "chivalric and satiric subjects": the dark mysteries and romances of the Middle Ages appealed to him even then.

Except when deeply engaged in creative work, Gabriel was not the most patient of men—although his loyalty to Fanny, of course, was marked by patience of an almost saintly quality. Even at nineteen he was beginning to be thoroughly discontented with his progress at the Academy. There seemed to him only one sensible course—to study under a man who had already proved himself. Schools, to his way of thinking, were too impersonal. Gabriel wanted to work closely with someone else, to hear voices—one of them his own—raised in argument, to learn how to bring out the best of himself in competition, as it were, with a friendly rival.

Very well then—first to choose the artist. A name which came to mind without any prompting at all was that of Ford Madox Brown. Here was someone whose work he admired, someone who had sipped the sweet savour of success, and who was an older man—twenty-six is maturity when you are yourself only nineteen! So, impetuously, Gabriel posted a letter. "The hope suggests itself", he wrote to Mr. Madox Brown, "that you may possibly admit pupils to profit by your invaluable assistance." If this were the case what would be Mr. Madox Brown's terms for six months' instruction?

Still in his twenties, Brown had hardly outgrown his own boyish enthusiasms. No-one knew more about the practical jokes beloved by art-students, and the somewhat fulsomely-worded request aroused his darkest suspicions. The story goes that Brown strode off wrathfully to confront the writer at his address in Charlotte Street, and teach him a lesson—if necessary, with force.

"Is your name Rossetti?"

"Yes."

"Is this your writing?"

"It is."

"What do you mean by it?"

Madox Brown's anger melted in the warmth of the Rossetti charm. Very well: Mr. Rossetti could come and work with him—in his own studio—but he was certainly not in the habit of charging for such a service. After a reasonable time, Mr. Rossetti could show something of his quality as an artist, and if the results were satisfactory, Mr. Madox Brown would be glad to advise him.

So began a life-long friendship between the two men. Madox Brown set Gabriel to work. He was to copy a picture and make some still-life studies. "Bottles and pickle jars, if you can believe it", Gabriel told Harry years later. This had not been exactly the advice the young Rossetti expected: and it did not specially commend itself to him. More to the point was Brown's hint that he should attend evening classes at an Academy in Maddox Street, where models accustomed to posing in the nude were employed. Rossetti promptly agreed. The fee was half a guinea a month: the school was Heatherley's.

It was at this time Rossetti met Holman Hunt, Millais and Woolner and in no time at all the Pre-Raphaelite Brotherhood linked arms and swung jauntily into their own appointed place on the fringe of immortality.

7

It did not take Harry long to appreciate the self-effacing but vital part William played in his brother's life. When Harry took over from Walter Knewstub, William was still a bachelor: he did not marry Ford Madox Brown's daughter, Lucy, until he was well over forty. From the start, he and the new man were on good terms and William was clearly relieved to recognise in the Cornishman someone who was both reliable and anxious to please.

Harry liked Gabriel's younger brother, and welcomed the courtesy and friendliness William was ready to show a shy newcomer. Without reading more into William's own expressed opinion of Harry than he intended to convey, it is true to say there was, for the best part of twenty years, a bond between the two men, a bond based on their affection for the charming, wilful master of Tudor House. Harry soon realised how attached the brothers were to each other and how much Gabriel was dependent on the good sense and generosity of William.

Gabriel in life and after death was the Rossetti the world talked about and knew best. It was on Gabriel the spotlight was trained and of whom all the colourful, dramatic and tragic stories were told. By the nature of things, William was bound to play a secondary rôle, but Harry quickly came to understand that this was not because William himself, as some writers have hinted, was in any sense a neutral personality. He belonged to that company of realistic, clever men of letters who, from the time of Chaucer, have found it sensible and convenient to obtain a steady job in the Civil Service and stick to it. He had a brilliant brother, but he was far from being a negligible quantity. Helen Angeli says of her father: "He was quite willing to take second place but he played his own fiddle." Certainly, he was out of sympathy with Gabriel's haphazard way of life. He did not approve of casual love affairs or his brother's theory that to have his own way was the most normal thing in the world. But he understood the origins of Gabriel's faults and stood by him throughout his life.

In a word, William was always there when he was wanted: and wanted he often was. He advised Gabriel shrewdly, he lent him money, he looked after him when he was ill and he left one of the most remarkable, penetrating and well-balanced books ever written about a great man. It was William who (with the help of Harry Dunn among others) did everything in a layman's power to halt Gabriel's decline and diminish his reliance upon chloral. Dame Edith Sitwell was near the truth when she called William "that saintly and sweet character whose whole life was given to his family". His contemporaries thought highly of him as a critic and editor and of his flair for discovering talent in many young men who later made international reputations.

Like Gabriel, William was devoted to his mother and to the sisters. The family shared a lively sense of humour and typical of the friendly family joke was Gabriel's description of his elder sister, Maria Francesca, when she joined an Anglican Sisterhood. "Dear Maggie has turned herself into a penwiper", he said, and again, "One of those old things you see going about in a sort of coal-scuttle-and-umbrella costume." But there was a strong affection between Gabriel and Maria, and in a letter to his mother he wrote that Maria was "much the healthiest in mind and cheeriest of us all, except yourself. William comes next and Christina and I nowhere."

William passed on as much as he thought Harry should know about his brother's earlier life and the reasons why he had come to live in the house in Cheyne Walk. Chatham Place, where Lizzie died, held nothing but unhappy memories and it was clearly desirable to find another home for him. The Tudor House had been seriously considered some time before Rossetti finally signed the lease and paid his two-hundred-and-twenty-five pounds premium. The original plan was for the entire Rossetti clan, including their mother and sisters and even their maiden aunt, to take possession of the house with Gabriel nominally in charge. Happily for all concerned, this remarkable plan was never put to the test. What happened was that the house was taken over by Rossetti, William Michael, Algernon Charles Swinburne and George Meredith. The idea was for these four friends to live (in the words of A. C. Benson) "a kind of collegiate life". The rent was one hundred pounds a year, modest even by the standards of a century ago, and the "special tenants" each contributed towards this liability. It was arranged that the four men should dine together, while Swinburne and Meredith had sitting-rooms where they could entertain their own guests.

Rossetti felt he needed some lively companionship and this Swinburne could undoubtedly provide. Meredith's was a somewhat more sober approach to life and it is not surprising that he failed to stay the course. Swinburne stayed on and long after Dunn's arrival the poet still treated Cheyne Walk as his home, coming and going as he pleased. Swinburne's behaviour was, to say the least, exceedingly odd. It is a matter of record that he was unstable and when he had had too much to drink was exasperating to a degree. More kindly biographers have taken with reserve the accounts of how he would slide shrieking down the bannisters and of his tendency to appear from time to time as barely clad as a Heatherley model, but nothing like so pretty.

Harry soon found that there was one topic on which Gabriel was silent —his wife. The story of Gabriel and Lizzie has been told many times— sometimes with sympathy, more often by authors who have gone out of their way to make the most of its tragic aspect, who have, in fact, been heavy-handed about the whole matter.

It was—who can deny it?—a tragic tale, dramatic enough, inevitable enough to take on in certain hands the red glow of melodrama. More detached observers see it as a sad story beginning with genuine love but moving, through illness and misunderstanding, to early death. Lizzie's was a situation in which many other women had found themselves: but the affair was magnified for the very simple reason that Rossetti was in the public eye. His personality and his work came under the scrutiny of men and women whose approach was not only academic but journalistic, and these were only too ready to seize on the more sensational elements.

Lizzie and Gabriel were unlucky. They were profoundly and emotionally drawn together. But this was not enough, as countless couples have since discovered. Lizzie stirred in Gabriel a true romantic feeling, which is reflected in the best of his verse, and in the pictures for which "the Sid" was his model. They were by temperament unsuited to set up house together, or to live in constant harmony beneath the same roof.

Too many things went wrong. Their marriage did not take place until after too long a period of home-sharing. There was a child who did not live. Lizzie was delicate, Gabriel robust and often craving more than she could give him. She died as the result of an overdose of laudanum. And long after Mrs. Rossetti had been laid to rest in Highgate Cemetery, there was the macabre incident of her exhumation when poems buried in her coffin were removed—and printed.

All this could not fail to add up to high drama and the less scrupulous chroniclers had their way with it. Harry, meeting Rossetti only a few years after Lizzie's death, saw nothing exceptional in the story of Rossetti's marriage except that it had been broken by death in melancholy circumstances. Later, he was to be on hand when plans were made in secret to recover the poems: and was to observe with sympathy the effect the affair had on Rossetti's mind—on his nerves, as we should say today.

Gabriel first set eyes on Elizabeth Siddal in 1850. Ten years went by before they married. As man and wife they were together for less than two years, from May 1860, to the time of Lizzie's death in February 1862.

The future Mrs. Dante Gabriel Rossetti had been "discovered" by one of Gabriel's friends, the artist, Walter Howell Deverell. Lizzie worked in a milliner's shop in Cranbourne Alley, Leicester Square (one prefers William Michael's charming Victorian term "bonnet shop"). He felt that throb of excitement familiar to most normal young men when their roving eye is caught by a girl with striking good looks and, what is more, with lovely red hair. Even in those days artists had a head start when it came to obtaining an introduction to such a "stunner". Deverell very properly persuaded his mother to ask if the goddess of Cranbourne Alley would sit for him. The answer was yes, and from that moment the life of the milliner's assistant changed its course irrevocably. The name Elizabeth Siddal, which might otherwise have remained obscure, was to have its permanent place in the history of British art; her face and figure were to be painted by artists of renown, and admired by millions. She is the Viola in Deverell's "Twelfth Night" (in which Gabriel sat for the Jester) and she was painted by Millais—and by Holman Hunt.

Gabriel met Lizzie soon after she had begun to sit for Deverell. She had everything which appealed to his ardent nature. He liked girls with red hair—and hers was a splendid coppery gold. He saw in the dignity of her bearing, in her heavy-lidded rather brooding eyes of greenish hue, in her graceful neck, in her tall finely formed figure, some ideal he had long despaired of finding in a model. Miss Siddal had a brilliant complexion. She had simplicity and a natural reserve which rightly or wrongly gave her a reputation for being enigmatic. William admired her, but was baffled. He found her difficult to understand. "I hardly think I ever heard her say a single thing indicative of her own character, or of her serious underlying thought."

7. Dante Gabriel Rossetti with Ruskin.
The negative of this photograph was found in Harry Dunn's effects

8. A copy by H. Treffry Dunn of Rossetti's "The Loving Cup". It was this picture which, at their first meeting in Cheyne Walk, Rossetti asked Dunn to copy as a test of skill.

The long and short of it was that Gabriel could not resist her. He quite ruthlessly brushed aside all Lizzie's other admirers in his circle and made it clear that he wanted Lizzie for himself. No-one else was to have her, and to this extent she may have played, unknowingly, some part in the dissolution of the P.R.B.s. Ruskin appreciated her. Madox Brown liked her. Swinburne adored her. With these friends Gabriel correctly knew that his treasure was safe. By 1852 there was an "understanding" and his family and friends accepted the fact that Gabriel was engaged to Lizzie. But it was an engagement that dragged on, and both Madox Brown and Ruskin were among those who found it hard to understand why there was no talk of a wedding.

By the time they did marry it was too late to hope that Lizzie would ever be anything but a sick woman. In the course of that lengthy "engagement" the future Mrs. Rossetti learnt to paint and to write verse. If all his friends failed to share Gabriel's faith in the quality of her work, there can be no doubt that she was a woman of intelligence and of some talent. "A noble, glorious creature"—these were the words in which she was described by Ruskin (who at one time suggested that he should pay her a hundred and fifty pounds a year in return for all the work she did up to the value of that sum). To say that she and Gabriel were on affectionate terms is to put it mildly. Gabriel drew and painted her again and again. Madox Brown wrote that he "showed him a drawer full of 'Guggums' (his lover's name for her). God knows how many." She had her own term of endearment for Gabriel, "Gug", which may have been, as William says, "sort of short for Gabriel". It was, in whatever light one may judge it, an extraordinary relationship. Helen Angeli says it was accepted as a fact that their relations were platonic—"in that Puritan mid-Victorian age and England, there was never any suggestion that their relations were other than platonic—never a breath of scandal".

At last the hour arrived when the pawnbrokers could carry on business without his patronage, and Gabriel felt secure enough to settle down as a married man. The wedding took place at St. Clement's Church, Hastings, on 23rd May 1860, and they sailed away on a wedding-trip to Paris. The Burne-Joneses had planned a joint honeymoon with them, but Edward caught cold and couldn't go. The young Rossettis appeared to be happy in spite of Lizzie's "very alarming" state of health. But once again it is impossible to feel that the pair had not themselves to blame for the aura of foreboding and gloom with which the biographers have found it so easy

F

to surround them. It was chance, maybe, but how grim a chance, that Gabriel's principal work in Paris was that haunting picture with the doppelganger theme, "How They Met Themselves". A newly-married couple meet in a forest two ghostly doubles. Lizzie was the model for the bride ("and very like her", says William Michael) and she is depicted as swooning or perhaps dying as she beholds the apparition in her own likeness. This was hardly a cheerful honeymoon subject, for the legend goes that death follows such an encounter. Lizzie herself produced a curious picture of her own kind at this time, its subject hardly less forbidding. It was called "The Woeful Victory", and shows a woman shielding her face as she is claimed by the winning suitor in a duel to the death. But there it is. We are thinking of Dante Gabriel Rossetti and his wife Elizabeth, and such an odd method of expressing the bliss of a new marriage must not surprise us too much. After all, one doubts if they were more solemn or held hands with less pleasure or affection than if the subject of their pictures had been lovers on the beach at Margate. Indeed, Gabriel did find time to work on his study of Dr. Johnson and the Methodistical Young Ladies at the Mitre Tavern.

They returned to live in London at 14, Chatham Place, which could hardly have held, for Lizzie, the novelty of a new home, although a wall was knocked down and the flat made more roomy and comfortable. Any possible happiness the married state brought them was brief. Gabriel was busier than at any other period in his career. Lizzie, on her part, was easily tired and slowly weakened by consumption. She suffered a great deal from that most wearing of complaints, neuralgia, and to ease this laudanum had been prescribed. She took it frequently.

Lizzie died at seven o'clock on the morning of 11 February 1862, having taken an overdose of the drug. The coroner's verdict was "accidental death". The intention was clear enough: although because she was already under the influence of the drug Lizzie could not in any event be deemed responsible. It is inevitable that some writers should seize on the tragic manner of young Mrs. Rossetti's death as an excuse for highly-coloured accounts of what they imagine must have happened. When Gabriel's own clouded and melancholy life ended, the drama was heightened still further. Had Dante Gabriel Rossetti in any sense been responsible for his wife's death? It has been suggested that Lizzie was hurt bitterly by his waywardness, that she was jealous, that there had been arguments, recriminations, quarrels.

This was almost all guesswork. The handful of loyal friends who may have suspected the truth are long dead. Lizzie did take her own life. There is no doubt of this. Whether there was some final crisis which tipped the balance of a mind made feeble by pain (and by repeated doses of medicine which alone could dull that pain) will never now be known. It could have been that at twenty-eight she knew she was doomed. It is unlikely she would have lived for more than a few years. Life at the moment she chose to destroy it may truly have seemed insupportable. She had grieved cruelly for her dead baby: there is the heart-breaking story of how the Burne-Joneses called on her and found Lizzie rocking an empty cradle which had been bought by Gabriel with such love and hope.

Not for many years was it revealed that Gabriel had in fact found a few scribbled words with the plea "Take care of Harry" pinned to her night-gown, this Harry being a brother for whose well-being Lizzie had always been concerned. On being shown the note, Madox Brown, strong-minded and far-sighted, had burnt it. Gabriel's brother, too, must have been aware of what happened, though he never spoke of it. Madox Brown himself told his daughter what, for the best of motives, he had done, and Lucy before her death confided it to her own daughter Olivia. Years later (when those who would have found the revelation so painful had themselves died) Hall Caine wrote how when Gabriel had himself only a short time to live he had confirmed the finding of the note. According to Caine he added that the dying message "had left such a scar on his heart that would never be healed". Caine says he had the impression that Gabriel had never thought of his wife's death without reproaching himself, as though it "had been due in some degree to failure of duty on his part, or perhaps to something still graver".

Lizzie, then, wished to die: her own verses tell us so.

> I wish I were dead, my foe,
> My friend, I wish I were dead,
> With a stone at my tired feet
> And a stone at my tired head.

On another day she had written:

> How is it in the unknown land?
> Do the dead wander hand in hand?
> Do we clasp dead hands and quiver
> With an endless joy for ever?

To sum up—there is no proof that Gabriel's conduct led to Lizzie's "accidental death".

Most of Dunn's life in London had been spent in the company of artists. His friends were almost all painters and sculptors—with the exception of a number of men and women of the theatre (Forbes-Robertson among them) whom he had met with his friend William Gorman Wills, the playwright. Many times he had heard acquaintances, some of them ill-informed, discussing the mournful circumstances of Mrs. Rossetti's death. On his part, Harry felt that it was not his affair—and until their friendship ripened, and Gabriel took him more and more into his confidence, the younger man never seriously considered that in Lizzie's early death and Gabriel's later moods of depression there might be cause and effect.

On the other hand, he had learned in some detail the remarkable story of the Poems; as we know, when the grim denouement came he was in on the secret. Most of the people who called at Cheyne Walk had their own versions of how Lizzie died and some of them talked about Gabriel's dramatic gesture of homage quite openly. Swinburne, with whom Harry struck up an almost immediate friendship, was not the man to be reticent on the subject of Lizzie, about whom he talked and wrote with extravagant admiration, while on the lips of Howell the tale certainly lost nothing in the telling.

Gabriel had been shocked and hurt by Lizzie's death—for reasons he could not share even with the dearest members of his family. His brother records how at one moment Gabriel stood by the coffin and cried: "Oh Lizzie, Lizzie, come back to me!" The anguish seems to sear the very page, breaking through the guard of William's formal prose. On the day she was buried at Highgate in Grave 5779, Gabriel felt the need to give the woman he had loved for twelve years some supreme token of his grief. What, he must have asked himself, would she prize more than anything else? She had loved his poems—had, indeed, tried to model her own verse on his style, as she had made her painting a reflection of his. The poems he had read aloud to her in his powerful but caressing voice had been copied into a book. He fetched it from his desk and placed the manuscript volume between her cheek and the red-gold hair which had been his delight from the day he had first seen her in Deverell's studio. Madox Brown, instinctively distrusting such a gesture, felt—though he did not express his disapproval in words—that this was a quixotic thing to do. Gabriel said: "I have often been working at these Poems when she was ill and suffering, and I might have been tending to her, and now they shall go!" All Brown could find the heart to say roughly was "Let him do it, it does him honour." Gabriel's distress was as bitter and as genuine as that of any man who was losing forever a woman he had loved tenderly and with all his heart. Seven years later, some of his closest friends, Harry Dunn among them, were to wonder if in a single night that grief had not been tarnished.

8

As the weeks sped, and then the months, Harry began to feel that he had been accepted in Cheyne Walk. William, kind and considerate, seemed to take Harry's presence for granted.

At first, when visitors called, Harry would politely make himself scarce, but before long—unless some intimate matter were being discussed—Gabriel would tell him to remain. Then, if a few friends stayed late, it came to be understood that the young assistant would be there to see that the fire was kept alive and the glasses filled.

These nights, with a single lamp glowing, and the coals sending their shadows across the lofty ceiling, held a magic Harry never forgot. Often the meetings would go on until the early hours of the following day, and Harry acquired the habit—it was one he never lost—of working, reading or, when the mood took him, of walking by the river until far into the night. His chief seemed tireless, and Harry had been living at Cheyne Walk for some time before Gabriel began to show signs of the sleeplessness which was to become insupportable without the help of chloral.

Harry's relationship with Rossetti changed more quickly than he realised. Before he had been a year at Number Sixteen the two men had slipped into an agreeable intimacy—though neither forgot the basic situation: Dunn had certain duties for which he was paid a salary. These duties were never clearly defined. There was, indeed, a characteristic but charming vagueness about the arrangement. If Harry had been asked why Rossetti had engaged him he would have said simply that he was paid for preparing replicas when these were needed, keeping the studio tidy, buying materials, attending to all the necessary detail involved in the life of a man who earned his living as a painter. It would have surprised him to learn that in a remarkably short space of time he would be acting as secretary, engaging models, keeping the accounts, lecturing the maids, occasionally sending them about their business with the inevitable week's wages, keeping unwanted callers at bay, acting as a voluntary assistant zoo-keeper, and maintaining the peace whenever domestic warfare broke out below stairs.

For many months the prospect was without a cloud. Harry was in luck—so he told himself as each fascinating day came to an end. To sit at the feet of Dante Gabriel Rossetti, to share his studio, to watch him at work, not once in a while but every day—what would some of his friends at Heatherley's give for a privilege like this!

Rossetti's mastery of colour, as he soon realised, was superb; and no-one, except the departed Knewstub, had been able to study his methods at such close quarters. Staying behind to clear up the confusion of each day's artistic battlefield, Harry would observe the progress of the canvas clamped to the easel at which Gabriel had been working. He learnt to recognise the signs of inspiration, impatience or satisfaction.

As an artist himself, Harry was absorbed by Rossetti's skill in painting the subtle effects of light, and spent many hours studying, for example, some telling impression of sunshine stealing through the leaves of a forest. Rossetti's handling of artificial light—the glow from lamp or lantern—was remarkable. In his visits to art galleries in Britain or on the Continent, Harry had never seen the atmosphere of twilight more cunningly achieved.

He was quick to understand and appreciate the two Rossettis. One, a robust, thrusting talker, human and humorous. The other, a meticulous professional to whom the perfection of a chosen word, or of an artistic effect, meant everything. As Gabriel's assistant, Harry learnt how carefully the palette had to be mixed at the start of each day—it was a task which took the best part of an hour—and how scrupulously it must be cleaned at the end of it.

He would follow every movement of Gabriel's hand as, the design for a picture complete and clear in his mind, he would draw it on the canvas in thick red chalk.

In the words of A. C. Benson:

"Then the whole was covered with thick white paint mixed with copal varnish, so that the outline glimmered dimly through. The flesh was laid in a monochrome of ultramarine, which produced a peculiar grey shadow. Then, when the stiff white paint had dried, he carefully painted in from the life."

For hours at a time when the mood was right, Rossetti painted in silence and with intense concentration. At such times Harry worked quietly in a corner, taking care to make his presence as unobtrusive as possible. He was instinctively tactful and now and again Gabriel would flash a friendly smile of thanks. At other times he would talk softly about the importance of style and his own appreciation of colour. A clear light green was one of his favourite colours, he would say, while he loved a deep gold, certain tints of grey, steel-blue, brown with a crimson tinge, and scarlet.

As time went by Harry, from his own perception as an artist, was to see the gradual development of the Rossetti mannerisms. These were expressed in Gabriel's habit of painting the full lips and the long neck which gradually became more marked. Working at Rossetti's side Harry Dunn had an unrivalled opportunity of studying the older man's methods. It is worth quoting his own description of Rossetti at work.

> When a design germinated in his brain, it was all thought out and shaped into a pen-and-ink or pencil reality before the subject was transferred to canvas. When the sketch was to his liking, then came the question, What model was best fitted for the subject? And exercising the same fastidiousness as when composing poetry, several drawings of the model's face would be made ere he was satisfied. This accounts for such a number of carefully-finished chalk heads continually cropping up. They are all valuable, because they tend to show the progress and development of his most notable pictures. When all these careful preliminaries had been gone through, the painting would be commenced. But never in a hurry: no attempt was made to partially cover his canvas at once; his invariable rule being to do so much in the time that the model was present as could be well done, and required no alteration the next day. Alterations, he maintained, meant muddling, and were the death of colour.

In the light of his mature experience Harry even permitted himself some mild criticism of the master.

> All Rossetti's best works glow with rich tones and qualities. In the matter of drawing, however, I am obliged to confess he was not so strong. His curious habit of giving oft-times an unduly long neck to a figure threw him into difficulties in regard to the due proportions of the human body. For his models, he did not rely upon those who were strictly professional. He preferred finding a face for himself, and often a work would be delayed in the execution because the desired face could not be immediately found.

William Michael tells us that Rossetti's income in 1865 was rather more than two thousand pounds. It was somewhat less in the following year but by 1867 (by which time there can be no doubt that Harry Dunn was firmly installed in Cheyne Walk) "it will be seen that he had made £3,725 in the preceding twelvemonth, and that he regarded as about his then average".

Although from the personal point of view Gabriel's finances were involved and unstable, his annual income, for the rest of his life, reached a handsome total. He had the casual, day-by-day approach to money which often goes with the artistic temperament. As Harry was to discover very early in their association, Gabriel was constantly short of "the ready". He lent money, and gave a great deal away. He certainly had no banking-account when Harry optimistically drew on his own unlamented counting-house experience and attempted to keep some sort of household accounts.

The curious thing was that Gabriel had quite a formidable talent when it came to dealing with money on a grander scale. He had a remarkably shrewd sense of business when it came to bargaining for the sale of a picture. He would fix a price—and that was the end of it. This unexpected streak of commercial ability exasperated some, but amused authorities of the calibre, for example, of F. R. Leyland, whose close friend he became. In fact, the only debts of any consequence which Gabriel left were moneys due to Mr. L. R. Valpy and to Mr. W. Graham in connection with pictures he had been unable to finish for them. By the time his effects and unsold pictures were disposed of there was quite a reasonable sum to be divided between his mother and his brother.

In *Recollections of Dante Gabriel Rossetti and his Circle* by Henry Treffry Dunn there are printed at the end of the book more than a hundred "Notes" on a variety of subjects. These were written by the editor, with the help of William Michael Rossetti. This was an accepted practice at the time the *Recollections* were published, and it worked well enough in the case of a short book. The "Notes" were mainly concerned with fact, and when quoting from Harry Dunn's memoirs I have, when necessary, embodied the information in the text.

In Chapter Four, for example, Harry takes up the story of his initiation into the "Circle":

Rossetti was now, at this period, in the prime and fullness of his mental powers. He was in that happy state when all that he painted was eagerly sought after. The abundance of his work in the years previous to my meeting him shewed ample proof, both in pen and pencil, that those years had been busy ones. And although as yet his poems were only known to a few of his friends, he had written enough to justify him in publishing a volume which, but for a strange romance in his life, would have appeared long ere it did.

It was now that the association started by William Morris, having its home in Queen Square, Bloomsbury, and for its object, it is said, the education of the upper classes in the knowledge and right discernment of the really beautiful in Art, began to bring forth fruit. Its work-contributing members were Morris, Rossetti, Ford Madox Brown, Edward Burne-Jones, and one or two others, with Morris as manager and controller.

The "association" was Morris, Marshall, Faulkner & Co., its business the designing of wall-papers, fabrics, furniture, windows, mural decorations and so forth. The new headquarters in Queen Square were known as "the Shop", and when the Morrises returned to London from Upton in 1865 they lived above it. Once more Gabriel was to be near the woman whose beauty, according to Watts-Dunton, was "incredible". Lizzie, Fanny, Janey: theirs were the faces and forms Rossetti loved most to paint, and whatever the first two meant to him emotionally it was with Janey ("the silentest woman I have ever met" said Bernard Shaw) he felt most relaxed and at peace.

To return to Harry and Morris's work in "the Shop".

For this firm Rossetti made numerous designs for their stained glass department, and what always struck me in these conceptions of his was, that they worked up as finely into pictures as stained glass which, as far as my observation goes, is rarely the case in the majority of glass designers' inventions. For instance, his series of six illustrations for the story of St. George and the Dragon rendered it unnecessary to make any alterations in them when some years later they were turned into important pictures. The designs of the "Parable" were executed for the church of S. Martin-on-the-Hill, Scarborough. The series begins with the Labourers of the Vineyard, and ends with the procession of the rebellious vineyard workers to punishment.

Some of the St. George and the Dragon series, perhaps all, were turned into water-colour pictures (and bought by the late Mr. Geo. Rae, of Birkenhead).

In his series of designs—for St. George and the Dragon and the Parable of the Vineyard—Rossetti made great use of his friends, and introduced their heads freely into his conceptions.

Into his first exhibited painting, hereafter noted, Rossetti introduced the portraits of his mother and his sister, Christina. In the first of his "Three Designs from Tennyson's Poems"—"Mariana in the South"—the face of his wife is seen; again, with that of his sister, in the second—"King Arthur 'watched by weeping Queens' in the vale of Avalon"; and again in the third— "S. Cecilia". "Queen Guinevere" is the first, or very nearly the first, head that Rossetti drew from Mrs. Morris.

In one of the compartments of the "Parable" he has William Morris, who is generally the strong, wicked man of the lot, concealed by a door, in the act of dropping a big stone on the head of the Lord of the Vineyard's collector, who has called for the vintage dues.[1] In the last of the set the rest of the bad husbandmen include Algernon Charles Swinburne and Ernest Gambart, the then great picture-dealer, all woebegone and roped together, on their way to receive condign punishment. Edward Burne-Jones, by reason of his gentle disposition and refined face, was the "good boy" of Rossetti's designs. Howell figures twice in the "Saint George and the Dragon" story—first, as St. George himself in the act of slaying the monster, and next in the final scene, where he enters triumphantly into the city with the Princess, as her deliverer, the dragon's head being borne in front of the procession as a trophy of his prowess. The cartoons of this romance were framed and used to hang from the staircase wall, but three of them having been removed and turned into water-colours—"The Casting Lots for the Victim", "The Slaying of the Dragon", and the "Triumphant Entry"—the rest were taken down and given away or lost.

Sketches for the wings of the altar piece of Llandaff Cathedral were also noticeable works. The subjects were David as shepherd for the one, and David as Psalmist and King, for the other. Rossetti always spoke very slightingly of this triptych to me, and considered it as a work that he would rather not discuss. But it surprised me by its originality and breadth of treatment when it made its appearance after his death in the exhibition of his collected works held at Burlington House. In execution it was by no means so weak as he had always led me to believe.

One day, passing through a dark part of a back hall, my foot caught the corner of a picture stacked with others against the wall. I picked it up and found it to be a photograph. Seeing me looking at this, Rossetti told me it was taken from the first picture he had ever painted in oils, which was exhibited in the Hyde Park Gallery when he was about twenty years of age. The subject was "Mary the Virgin", who is represented seated, and embroidering a white lily upon a piece of dark-coloured cloth or silk, under the guidance of S. Elizabeth. In the foreground is a lily, growing from a vase, which she is evidently copying, whilst a child angel is employed in watering it. The full title of this picture is the "Girlhood of Mary Virgin". It was painted late in 1848 and in the Spring of 1849, and shewn in the latter year.

The first completed oil picture of Rossetti's is a head of Christina Rossetti (June 1848); then began the "Girlhood of Mary Virgin", and then, before this was finished, came the head of Gabriele Rossetti (October 1848). The tutor of the Blessed Virgin (it is the Annunciation lily, of course, which she is embroidering) in the picture under notice, is not S. Elizabeth, but S. Anna, the mother of Mary; in the background occurs her father, S. Joachim. The

---

[1] William Michael is quoted in the Notes as differing from this judgement: "The person who drops the stone is of quite different physique from Morris . . . The head of Morris occurs, however, in the same design; he is putting his head out through a wicket, wearing a smile of hypocritical civility, whilst the other man, his accomplice, casts down the stone."

head of the Blessed Virgin is that of Rossetti's sister Christina; that of S. Anna was done from his mother.

In this picture the mystic adoration and faith of mediaevalism is wonderfully and finely realised. I learnt from Rossetti, that it was to a great extent painted under the instruction of Ford Madox Brown, from whom he had gained much of his knowledge in the practice of oil painting, and who had contributed to the same exhibition a work of his own, the subject being taken from *King Lear*. Rossetti sat for the head of the fool.

Howell, who had joined us, wanted to show me a bit of old oak carving in Rossetti's bedroom, which I thought a most unhealthy place to sleep in. Thick curtains, heavy with crewel work in 17th century designs of fruit and flowers (which he had bought out of an old furnishing shop somewhere in the slums of Lambeth), hung closely drawn round an antiquated four-post bedstead. It had belonged to his father and mother, and he had been born in it. A massive panelled oak mantelpiece reached from the floor to the ceiling, fitted up with numerous shelves and cupboard-like recesses, all filled with a medley of brass repoussé dishes, blue china vases filled with peacock feathers, oddly-fashioned early English and foreign candlesticks, Chinese monstrosities in bronze, and various other curiosities, the whole surmounted by an ebony and ivory crucifix. The only modern thing I could see anywhere in the room was a Bryant and May's match box! On the other side of the bed was an old Italian inlaid chest of drawers, which supported a large Venetian mirror in a deeply-carved oak frame. Two or three very uninviting chairs, that were said to have belonged to Chang the Giant—and their dimensions seemed to warrant that statement, as they took up a considerable amount of space—and an old-fashioned sofa, with three little panels let into the back, whereon Rossetti had painted the figures of Amor, Amans, and Amata, completed the furniture of the room. With its rich, dark green velvet seats and luxurious pillows, this sofa looked very pretty and formed the only comfortable piece of furniture visible.

The deeply-recessed windows, that ought to have been thrown open as much as possible to the fresh air and cheerful garden outlook, were shrouded with curtains of heavy and sumptuously-patterned Genoese velvet. On this fine summer's day, light was almost excluded from the room. The gloom of the place made one feel quite depressed and sad. Even the little avenue of lime-trees outside the windows helped to reduce the light, and threw a sickly green over everything in the apartment. It was no wonder poor Rossetti suffered so much from insomnia!

A few pictures, not of a very cheerful description, hung on the walls where there was space. One, I remember, was particularly gruesome. It represented a woman all forlorn in an oar-and-rudderless boat, with its sail flapping in the wind about her, alone on a wide expanse of water. In the distance was a city in flames over which the artist had inscribed "The City of Destruction". In the sky were numerous winged dragons and demons, whilst swarming around were horrible sea monsters, all intent upon upsetting the boat. It was not a bad picture as far as finish and colour went, but the subject was too dreadful.

On returning to the studio we found Rossetti engaged over some letters. Four little magazines called *The Germ* were lying on the table, and these I looked over with much interest. *The Germ* was a collection of prose and poetry published monthly, with an etching in each number contributed by one of the members of the Brotherhood. Only four numbers made their appearance, the receipts arising from their sale not being sufficient to cover the cost of production.

Rossetti contributed the poems the "Blessed Damozel", and "My Sister's Sleep", and a romance entitled "Hand and Soul". These were the first verses and the first prose published by Rossetti. "My Sister's Sleep" and "Blessed Damozel" were afterwards included in his volume of *Poems* that came out some time after. The etchings were by Holman Hunt, Ford Madox Brown, James Collinson, and Walter Howell Deverell.

9

There was, when Harry went to Cheyne Walk, no suggestion that the garden and its curious collection of boarders would cause more trouble than an occasional irate cry of rage from neighbours. Yet the future of the garden itself was to upset and harrass Gabriel in the last two or three years of his life.

It was made known to him that if the lease of Number Sixteen were to be renewed he would have to part with a large part of the garden—to make room, in fact, for a new block of flats. At a time when his nerves were near the point of collapse he could have dispensed with arguments about what he called "the bloody question as to the wall".

Even so, the old sense of humour bubbled up when a Mrs. Watts, who lived at Number Nineteen, bewailed the loss of some of the trees in the garden. "A most frantic note", he records, "from my old and most senti-mental friend Mrs. Howitt Watts at Number Nineteen as to the unspeak-able horrors of these trees in question coming down." A little later comes one of the last recorded flashes of fun when he wrote: "Several of the elm trees fell today and Mrs. Watts is doubtless a weeping willow."

For an artist to be a collector of old blue Nankin and other china was the most natural thing in the world.

The same can hardly be said of Rossetti's passion for collecting animals. It was a strange and disturbing hobby: at least Gabriel's neighbours found it so. It must have been an alarming experience suddenly to be confronted by an armadillo on the prowl. Yet more than one householder in Cheyne Walk reported that with a rending of privet these armour-plated animals would plough through the hedge and scurry across their lawns at terrify-ing speed.

Incident followed incident, and the armadillos were the spearhead of many attacks on long-suffering residents who lived within burrowing distance of Number Sixteen. One which vanished for several weeks was an expert sapper. He grimly and efficiently scooped out a tunnel and to the horror of a cook suddenly appeared through the floor of a basement kitchen. When hysteria subsided, the cook was heard to exclaim: "If it isn't the Devil, there's no knowing what it is!" One can understand her feelings.

No wonder the local residents felt themselves justified in forming an unofficial protection society. When the night air was liable to be rent with the shrieks of a mate-hungry peacock, the screechings of an assortment of owls, the cries of a laughing jackass, it was time to form a united front. Even Harry Dunn, accustomed to walking by night through lonely Cornish lanes, would start up from sleep, trembling, with a medley of animal sounds ringing in his ears.

A truly remarkable menagerie of "beasts" dwelt in the spacious back garden. William Michael, who was certainly not given to exaggeration, lists among his brother's pets "a Pomeranian puppy named Punch, a grand Irish deerhound named Wolf, a barn-owl named Jessie, another owl named Bobby (described by Christina as 'a little owl with a very large face and a beak of a sort of egg-shell green'), rabbits, dormice, hedgehogs, two successive wombats, a Canadian marmot or woodchuck, an ordinary marmot, armadillos, kangaroos, wallabies, a deer, a white mouse with her brood, a racoon, squirrels, a mole, peacocks, wood-owls, Virginian owls, Chinese horned owls, a jackdaw, laughing jackasses (Australian king-fishers), undulated grass-parakeets, a talking grey parrot, a raven, chameleons, green lizards, and Japanese salamanders."

There was also a small Brahmin bull, or zebu. The wombat, a small Australian marsupial mammal, the size of a badger, was the favourite. Rossetti obtained the creatures from various sources. He was a valued customer of Jamrach of Liverpool.

There is no doubt that the chief offenders were the peacocks. Their raucous and unlovely noise—"shrill trumpetings" was Harry's own description—was intolerable to all who lived near. Representations were made to Lord Cadogan, the ground landlord, and the complaints were so numerous that the birds had to be got rid of, and a clause was introduced into the leases of Lord Cadogan's property that "no peacocks should be kept in the gardens of his tenants".

Gabriel's neighbours were not alone in their dislike of these handsome but infuriating birds. There was at least one effective protest from the animal population. In his *Recollections* Dunn tells us:

"Before these complaints were made, a fallow deer was added to the collection—a graceful, beautiful creature, which, from its first introduction to the garden, evinced the greatest curiosity in regard to the peacock. Perhaps it was the feeling of surprise experienced by the animal at the peacock continually displaying its gorgeous tail, which induced it to follow the bird up and down the garden, and eventually to stamp out every feather the tail of the poor thing possessed."

It was difficult to determine just how Gabriel felt about this extraordinary family of assorted and sometimes tiresome dumb friends. William Michael says Gabriel was "fond of beasts", but adds "he had no particular liking for an animal on the mere ground of it being 'pretty', his taste being far more for what is quaint, odd or semi-grotesque".

Dunn says quite bluntly: "Experience of Rossetti and close intercourse with him, led me to the conclusion that the Poet-painter had not any great love for animals, nor knew much about their habits."

This, I take it, was the restrained comment of one who, at times, must have suffered more than most the inconvenience of these creatures. No doubt Harry helped from time to time to feed and care for them, to supervise the burial of those which died or were "disposed of". Anyhow, Harry wrote that in his opinion "it was simply a passion he had for collecting (just as he had for books, pictures and china), which impelled him to convert his house into a sort of miniature South Kensington Museum and Zoo combined".

It was not until the concerted and drastic attack by his neighbours that Gabriel bowed before the storm and "disposed of" the peacocks. If they had not acted with such determination he would, no doubt, have continued blandly to add to the aviary. In August 1865 he was giving his mother the news that "the pea-hen has hatched out two of her four eggs and now stalks about with two little whining queernesses at her heels— no bigger or brighter than ordinary chicks, but perhaps a little steadier on their pins".

At all events, there is a slightly acid touch in Harry Dunn's own stories of "Rossetti's pets, or his animals, rather, as it would be wrong to describe them as pets". He says:

His collection of queer, outlandish creatures was mostly kept in a series of wire-woven, outhouse compartments, located in one portion of the garden. In one of them I noticed a large packing-case covered over by a heavy slab of Sicilian marble. My curiosity led me to enquire of Rossetti what it contained, when he told me there was a racoon inside. On hearing that I had never seen such a creature, he asked me to help him remove the stone, and then, to my astonishment, he put his hand in quickly, seized the "coon" by the scruff of its neck, hauled it out, and held it up, in a plunging, kicking, teeth-showing state for me to look at, remarking—"Does it not look like a devil?" to which I agreed. It seemed to me a most dangerous creature to tackle, and I would not have held it as he did upon any consideration.

This beast gave a world of trouble and annoyance by constantly escaping. At one time it suddenly disappeared, and no one knew what had become of it until there came a letter from a lady, who lived some doors away, containing a bill for eggs destroyed by the "coon", which had made its way regularly down a chimney into her henroost! With some difficulty it was captured, and once more put back into what appeared safe keeping, but ere a few weeks had elapsed it was out again on the warpath.

This time no trace could be found of it, until the necessity arose of looking up a lot of Rossetti's manuscript poetry, lying in the bottom drawer of the massive Elizabethan wardrobe, when, to my surprise, I found the manuscript gnawed into little bits! The "coon" had been hiding there all the while, prowling about the house at night in search of food. This accounted for certain mysterious noises which had occurred in the dark hours of the night— sounds, as it were, of a faint, flat footfall up and down the stairs, which to the housekeeper, who had just lost her husband and was in a chronically hysterical state, seemed to be that of his ghost! Eventually the troublesome creature had to be sent back to Jamrach, the great animal importer of Liverpool, from whom it was purchased originally.

There were two other curiosities—a pair of armadillos which, under the idea that they were harmless, had the run of the garden. They, too, seemed to have caught the contagion for mischief. Now and then our neighbour's garden would be found to have large heaps of earth thrown up, and some of his choicest plants lying waste over the beds. This was the work of the armadillos.

As in the racoon escapades, letters of complaint were received, and so baits were laid for the pests in the form of bits of beef saturated with prussic acid. The beef disappeared, and so, it was hoped, had the armadillos; but no—after about three months they re-appeared in a sadly mangy and out-at-elbows state; they had evidently shed their scales during their absence, and new ones were forming. I suppose that after taking the dose of poison, feeling the worse for it, they must have betaken themselves to a hospital, and were just discharged as convalescent. Very soon after their return, I am sorry to say they slid back into their old mischievous habits, and at last had to be made over to the Zoological Gardens, where no doubt they were better guarded.

Amongst this curious collection of odd animals were a couple of kangaroos—mother and son. As far as my observation went, I do not think they lived on very good terms with each other. At any rate, the mother was found dead one morning, murdered by her bloodthirsty son. There must have been an unusually fierce quarrel over family matters in the night, with this as a consequence. Nemesis, however, overtook the wicked son, for he also was found dead in his cage some few days after, but whether he committed suicide through remorse, or whether the racoon, who was strongly suspected, polished him off, was an open verdict.

Amongst the indoor pets was a singularly wicked and morose parrot. Its sole delight seemed to be to get visitors to stroke its head, and then, without any warning, suddenly to fasten upon their fingers and finish up with a sly, low chuckle. Now and then the parrot would utter quite apropos sentences in the most unexpected manner. One Sunday morning, I recollect, Rossetti was sitting in his lounge chair, and warming his feet. The bells from the neighbouring church of S. Luke were in full swing. For some time the parrot had been unusually silent, when all of a sudden it broke the silence with the exclamation, "You ought to be in church now!" It is possible the servants had taught it this speech, but, at any rate, it gave Rossetti great amusement, and he was never tired of relating the story to his friends.

I told this story in a BBC talk, and a day or two later had a friendly letter written from East Yorkshire by Mrs. Margaret Middlebrook. She wrote:

My grandparents (George and Mary West) lived in the first house in Manor Street, Chelsea. Their family consisted of five sons and six daughters, my mother (one of the latter) often spoke of the "goings on" at the Rossetti household. Their bedroom windows overlooked the garden and studio of Cheyne Walk from which they could watch Rossetti painting. I remember an account of a ferocious bird (possibly the parrot you mentioned) which attacked the Wests' parrot—an aged bird whose star turn was to imitate the tapping of a stick and say "There goes old Carlyle." Thomas C. was a customer of my grandfather (a tailor by trade). He made the Doggett coat and badge and would possibly be patronised by the Pre-Raphaelite Brotherhood.

For the wombat Gabriel did display some affection: and there is a rather charming story concerning a Mrs. Tebbs (she was the wife of a solicitor, Mr. Virtue Tebbs) who sat for him. When the sitting was over, she was unable to find her new hat. There was consternation, and it was only too obvious that the wombat had eaten it, and with relish, since only a few pieces of straw were left. The only consolation Gabriel had to give his indignant visitor was: "Oh, poor wombat! It is so indigestible!"

William Rossetti was surprisingly indulgent about the animal population of Number Sixteen. His brother relied on him to supervise the purchase of various "beasts", and in his magnificently documented account of Gabriel's life William writes about them with genuine amusement. He gives an entertaining picture of the wombat and the woodchuck.

"No more engagingly lumpish quadruped than the wombat could be

found, and none more obese and comfortable than the woodchuck."
Both were agreeably tame, and their owner would play with them for
hours at a time, nursing them in his lap and gently scratching their heads
and cheeks. These two companions both died without warning. Gabriel
was not exactly overcome by grief, but, as William says, "his heart was
sair".

He was staying at Penkill Castle when the wombat was taken on the
strength at Cheyne Walk, and he wrote these lines before ever seeing the
creature:

> Oh, how the family affections combat
> Within this heart, and each hour flings a bomb at
> My burning soil! Neither from owl nor from bat
> Can peace be gained until I clasp my wombat.

Apart from the peacocks, the most colourful and anti-social of all
Gabriel's acquisitions was the zebu, or "small Brahmin bull". One can
almost hear the echo of Ellen Terry's mischievous, feminine chuckle as
she expressed her opinion that Gabriel bought the animal "because it had
eyes like Janey Morris".

Gabriel's friends (especially Whistler, "who is just the man for a few
humorous embellishments") were soon having great fun in passing
round the story that the bull—so ungallantly likened to Mrs. Morris—
chased him out of his own garden. It really seemed as though Gabriel, the
arch-joker, had for once overstepped the mark.

William, characteristically cautious, declines to confirm this story
because he was not "present on this occasion", but he does not dismiss the
episode as improbable. What did happen for certain is that Gabriel and
his brother were strolling in Cremorne Gardens in 1864 and were boyishly
delighted to find a "beast show" on view. The entrance-money was well
spent, for Gabriel was captivated by the zebu—"a beautiful animal not
larger than a pony of small size".

"I want it," he told William, but the price was steep and they had not
enough "tin" between them to take the bull with them, which Gabriel
would have done without hesitation or embarrassment. Back he went
next day to negotiate a price with the owner.

"Five pounds payable by next Monday, and the balance of fifteen
pounds within a fortnight" were the terms. "I shall have plenty by then,"
he wrote to William, "but just now have none." Could William raise the
five pounds instalment? If so, Gabriel would send his man Pope around

to Somerset House for the "needful". If not, he would find some other way of raising the money. Whether or not it was that look in the zebu's eye, Gabriel was determined to possess it. "I co-operated", writes William, with his usual choice of the *mot juste*.

Gabriel took pains over the entire transaction. Was the beast tame? Pope went into the zebu's pen and reported that its manners left nothing to be desired. How much for its keep? Oh, about half a crown a week, according to the owner. Nothing to worry about at all. The bull would need some sort of shelter for the cold weather, but winter was far away. This was April and a shed would not be needed for many months.

As a postscript to his request to William, Gabriel added with eloquent brevity: "I have let the peacocks out in the garden." Perhaps he was thinking that with an old enemy in full cry, the neighbours might not take too much notice of a prospective new one.

The story, according to Whistler and Val Prinsep—and passed on by Joseph Knight, a friend and biographer of Rossetti—had some more vigorous touches.

William would not commit to his diary any fact for which he could not vouch personally; but his account says that when the zebu was delivered to Number Sixteen "it charged at a fine pace through the passage into the garden", where the estimable Pope tied it to a tree.

Having secured the prize, the animal's new owner promptly gave his attention to more pressing matters: and a day or two passed before he had an opportunity of making the zebu's closer acquaintance. As all animal-lovers know there is an etiquette to be observed in these matters. It is more than likely that small Brahmin bulls have their own ideas as to how humans should approach them.

This particular beast may well have disapproved heartily of his new quarters. Whatever the cause, the zebu threw a fit of tantrums and was more than prepared to bite the hand that fed him. Wisely, Gabriel retreated in haste. The more colourful accounts present a picture of the enraged zebu tearing up by the roots the tree to which Pope had tied it, and then giving chase, with Gabriel tearing across the garden in alarm.

Gabriel's animals could make all the noise they wished so far as he was concerned, but he did like them to be friendly. The zebu's eyes may have been melting and beautiful, but at this moment they had a nasty glint in them—and Gabriel decided (as he had decided about other members of his establishment) that it would have to go. It was sold: but its short sojourn in the garden at Cheyne Walk was something his friends would not allow Rossetti (always boyishly amused by the discomfiture of others) to live down.

With most of his specimens Rossetti was on the best of terms. In letters to his family there are affectionate references to the chameleons, the rabbits and, of course, to the wombat which "follows people all over the house!"

Sometimes the animals and birds displayed a remarked reluctance to show off their paces, or to be as amusing or decorative as their master hoped. When was the parrot going to talk? When would the peacocks display their plumage in all its glory? He told his mother that one peacock "may be expected with confidence to start a tail next year, as he will then be three years old, which is the proper age", and added, with chagrin, "he shows no sign as yet".

He was intrigued by the way the female rabbit, expecting a brood, pulled off some of her own fur to make a soft bed. "This indeed I witnessed in one of my own rabbits."

10

A favourite story recounted by Dunn and quoted by most of Rossetti's biographers is concerned with his passion for collecting. At dinner in a friend's house one course was served to him on a plate he had seen in a shop—or thought he had seen—and meant to buy. To make sure, he turned the plate upside down to examine it, and promptly upset the meal on the table-cloth. Whether the tale is true or not, it is something which might easily have happened—and is in keeping with what has been called his "mania" for getting his hands on a bargain.

It was the fashion in the "circle" to collect things. That Gabriel went to extremes and collected living creatures was a personal eccentricity, with more than a hint of mischief in it.

In Harry Dunn's day, 16, Cheyne Walk was the repository of a fantastic number of picturesque and sometimes expensive objects. At the same time, there was some method in this. Few artists can resist buying odds-and-ends for which one day a use may be found. Many of the Cheyne Walk "treasures"—articles of furniture, imitation jewellery, silver, robes, lengths of brocade, are seen in Rossetti's pictures.

Whatever Gabriel did he did thoroughly and with vigour. This certainly applies to his single-hearted quest for examples of blue china. Harry Dunn's memories of excursions and forays into various territories annexed by the second-hand dealers have been borrowed by many authors who have in turn given their own versions of the Rossetti story. In Harry's words:

> Between Rossetti and Howell there existed a friendly rivalry as to who could display the finest show of old Nankin. Howell, perhaps, possessed the greater facility of the two for picking up china bric-à-brac—or anything that was worth buying—from the fact that his time was generally spent in ferreting out all the old shops in the most likely neighbourhoods, as well as in the various sale rooms which he was always frequenting. He had, moreover, a keen eye for what was good, together with an unrivalled amount of assurance, that assisted him wonderfully in all his bargains with dealers, who were wont to get the advantage of customers less acute.

On one occasion, Howell's rambles took him to some out-of-the-way and unfrequented part of Hammersmith, which at that time abounded in small furniture-dealers' shops. Often, some very valuable thing might have been purchased there for a few shillings, that at present could not be procured for pounds. In one of these old furniture shops, Howell, with hawk-like eye, espied the corner of a blue dish peeping out from a pile of miscellaneous odds and ends in the window.

It was not so much the shape of this visible portion of crockery but the colour, that attracted him; it was the blue, the sweet, rich blue, only to be found in the choicest Nankin. He entered the shop, and began prying about asking the price of first this thing and then that in the window until at length, as though by an accident, the whole of the dish that had lain almost hidden was exposed to view. O heavens! What a thrill of delight passed through his soul when it was pulled out for inspection. It was a veritable piece of Imperial ware, and a fine specimen, too!

His mind was made up. Have it he must; but, not to appear too anxious to get possession of it, he commenced by buying one or two things he did not want rather above their value, and then, by artful cozening, got the dish thrown in as a final make-weight to his other purchases for next to nothing. His afternoon's work was done; he had secured a prize which would fill Dante Gabriel's soul with envy when he saw it. A cab was called, and away he drove home, chuckling with delight to himself over his acquisition.

That evening was spent in arranging the menu of a choice little dinner, which was to be given in order to display his treasure, and in selecting the names of those of his friends who should be chosen to see the dish. Invitations were written and duly sent. Dear Gabriel's name, of course, was first on the list; then that of Whistler—better known amongst his friends as "Jimmy"—as he was one of the triumvirate of Chinese worshippers; then came the Ionides Brothers, Leonard R. Valpy, George Howard, George Price Boyce, Burne-Jones, Morris, old George Cruikshank, John William Inchbond, and several others who were habitués of the house.

As it had got about that Howell had something to show that would knock them all into fits, there were no absentees. The table was set, and the guests had all arrived, brought thither not only by the prospect of spending a pleasant evening, but also by curiosity to see what Howell had to exhibit. When the substantial part of the feast came to a full end, Howell felt his guests were in a sufficiently appreciative state of mind, and so the dish, for the advent of which each one of the party had been on the tip-toe of expectation, was at length produced, Howell himself bringing it in, carefully wiping it with a silk handkerchief.

There was a concentrated "Oh!" from all assembled at the table, which, having been partially cleared, had space enough to allow the dish to be placed in its centre, that all could view and admire it. And it bore the closest inspection, for it was certainly as good a piece of Nankin as could be found in the best of a lucky day's hunt. Rossetti waxed enthusiastic over it; he turned it round, and examined it from every point of view, and not a flaw could he find, nor the ghost of a crack, or a suspicion of an inequality of colour in it.

Everyone congratulated Howell on his being the possessor of such a beautiful specimen of "Blue". After it had been admired and breathed upon, coveted and delighted in, fondled and gushed over, hustled and almost fought for—in short, after having created as much squabbling and controversy as, once upon a time, the partition of Poland did among the Powers, the dish was tenderly removed by its owner, and carefully deposited in its shrine on a cabinet in an adjoining room.

As there were ladies present, a little music was indulged in, but as a rule Howell's parties were chiefly composed of people who were not very musically inclined. As in Rossetti's house, the place abounded in musical instruments, but never a one that could be played upon; all were of antiquated construction, only to be looked at, and talked about in a hushed whisper of admiration for their workmanship and adornments.

It was now getting well on towards midnight, and most of the party began to think of getting home—Howell's Fulham villa was not a very easy place to get at, and after twelve o'clock it was only by chance a cab could be found. Whilst the ladies of the party were upstairs wrapping themselves up for their journey, and the men were downstairs occupied with their hats and overcoats, Rossetti was hanging about the hall in a thoughtful kind of way.

He had on the Inverness cape which he generally wore at night, and I saw him go into the room where the dish was deposited, to have, as I thought, a last look at the treasure, but—shall I tell it?—he hastily dislodged that dish by stealth, concealed it beneath the cape of his cloak and carefully wrapped its ample folds around it, that none could perceive what he carried under his arm. Having so done, he took leave of Howell and his wife in the most charmingly innocent manner possible.

We walked towards Cheyne Walk together, but on the road Rossetti hailed a cab that happened to be in view, and the rest of the distance was soon got over. On our arrival at his door, having dismissed the cabman, he let himself in, and pulling out the dish from under his cape had a good look at it by the gaslight in the hall, chuckling the while with glee, for in his mind's eye he saw the long face Howell would pull on discovering his loss. He cautioned me not to let him know anything which would give him a clue as to the disappearance of the dish, or its place of concealment. Then, finding his way to the back hall, he proceeded to carefully hide it in the recesses of the massive oak wardrobe that stood there, and the more effectually to conceal it, swathed it round and round with model's dresses and other artistic draperies for the custody of which the wardrobe was employed. Having done all this to his satisfaction, Rossetti took his candle and went to bed.

Next morning, when he made his appearance at the breakfast table, we had our usual chat respecting the day's work, and whatever else required to be discussed. In the course of our conversation, Rossetti said, suddenly,

"Dunn, I shall give a return party to that of Howell's last night. This is

Tuesday: I'll ask him for Friday, and tell him he must come as I have picked up a piece of 'Blue' that I think will rival his."

Accordingly, he wrote him a note to that effect, and also dispatched invitations to most of those who were present at Howell's party, and to a good many more, making altogether enough to fill the dining table, which was able to accommodate at least twenty.

On the afternoon of the day of the dinner, Howell called in a cab, bringing his factotum with him, a useful fellow by whom he was generally accompanied in his expeditions. He left his man waiting in the cab, and on gaining admission to the house, and hearing that Rossetti was in the studio, he went in and found us both there.

After an inordinately long confabulation over everything that could be talked about, but without a word concerning the dish, Howell, by and by, went from the room upon some pretext or other and left Rossetti busily painting away. As I afterwards learnt, Howell guessed pretty shrewdly who had his dish, and where it was to be found. Instinct took him to the old wardrobe; softly opening its massive doors, he peeped in, then searching about with his hands, felt his precious dish underneath the pile of draperies that Rossetti had heaped over it.

To remove these and disentangle his property was the work of a few seconds; recovering his prize, he softly stole away along the back hall, round to the front door, which he opened, and went out to his man who was waiting his instructions. To him he handed the dish through the window, receiving in return another of the same size and shape. Howell went back, and after putting this dish into the wardrobe in the place of the other, re-entered the studio, and with the accompaniment of Irish cold and the indispensable cigarette, resumed the conversation for another hour or so.

When he could find nothing more to talk about, he took his leave in order to dress for the dinner. Rossetti was strangely unsuspicious of Howell's movements; I suppose he thought the hiding place he had fixed upon was so secure, that it never occurred to him to go and see what Howell had been up to and whether the dish was still there.

At the appointed hour, our guests came flocking in until the whole of them had arrived. When they were assembled in the dining-room, and had taken their seats around the table they formed a goodly company. The dinner was well served, a professional cook having been engaged to prepare it, and a distinct success; the wine was excellent and the conversation sparkling. At last, Howell managed to divert the talk to the subject of Blue china, and the dish of his that had excited so much admiration on the night of his party, whereupon Rossetti declared he had something just as fine.

Howell challenged him to produce it, so off went Rossetti to the wardrobe most confidently: he fished out the dish and brought it away swathed in drapery, just as he supposed he had left it. In a few minutes he returned to the dining-room with the package, and began to carefully remove the wrappings. As the dish became uncovered, a curious, puzzled expression came over his face, and when it was entirely exposed to view, he stood still in blank astonishment. For a few moments he was silent; then his pent-up feelings burst out in a wild cry.

"Confound it! See what the spirits have done!"

Everyone rose to look at the dish. A dish it was, certainly, but what a dish! Instead of the beautiful piece of Nankin that was expected, there was only an old Delft thing, cracked, chipped, and discoloured through the numerous bakings it had undergone. The whole party, with the exception of Howell, who looked as grave as a judge, burst into a roar of laughter. Rossetti soon recovered himself and laughed as heartily as any of his guests at Howell's ingenious revenge.[1]

The fact that Rossetti so spontaneously attributed this matter to "the spirits" is a reminder that he was always intensely superstitious in grain. According to his brother, any writing about devils, spectres, or the supernatural generally, whether in poetry or prose, had a fascination for him; at one time—say 1844—his supreme delight was the blood-curdling romance of Maturin, *Melmoth the Wanderer*.

There follows a delightful glimpse of social life in the old house by the river.

Rossetti's greatest pleasure was to gather around him those whom he liked, and his little social dinners, when they took place, were events to be remembered. When the party was an exceptional one—I mean as regards the number of friends invited—the table was laid in the so-called drawing-room, an apartment comprising the entire width of the house and boasting of five windows which afforded an extensive and interesting view of Chelsea Reach and its picturesque old wooden bridge.

It was a beautiful room by day, when the sun streamed in and lit up the curious collection of Indian cabinets, couches, old Nankin, and the miscellaneous odds and ends with which it was crowded almost to the point of superfluity; and at night, when the heavy Utrecht velvet curtains were drawn and the dining table was extended to its utmost limits, when the huge Flemish brasswrought candelabra with its two dozen wax lights, that hung suspended from the ceiling midway over the table, was lit up, and the central, old-fashioned epergne was filled with flowers, the room was filled with a pleasant warmth and glow anticipatory of the company expected.

On such occasions, Rossetti would relinquish his poetry or painting, and devote half an hour or so to allotting to his guests the several places that they were to occupy.

"Dunn," he would say to me, "we'll have Howell here; so-and-so is slow and he shall sit next to him; he'll be sure to be amused and wake up when that droll fellow begins pouring out his Niagara of lies. And here", he would add, "Sandys (a distinguished painter and designer) shall have his place, just

---

[1] William Gaunt, in his informative book *Chelsea* points out that "a comic legend grew round Howell's legerdemain. Oscar Wilde, for example, told a tale of how one night the ghost of Howell appeared to Ellen Terry. The spectre vanished—and so, as she discovered, had a diamond necklace!"

opposite, so that whatever Howell relates, Fred shall have a chance of capping his romances with some more racy." And thus with each guest; all were placed as he considered would be most conducive to the harmony of the evening. And so happily did Rossetti arrange matters, that his dinners never failed to be indeed festivals of exuberant hilarity. Christopher North's "Noctes Ambrosianae" might have equalled, but certainly did not surpass them, for wit and humour danced rampant up and down the table. At such times, would be present Burne-Jones, George Augustus Sala, Westland Marston (poet and dramatist), Ford Madox Brown, Morris, and other well-known men.

But it was not really until the feast was over, and an adjournment to the studio came about, that the night's enjoyment commenced. If the conversation took a turn to suit Rossetti's humour, he was pretty sure to be first and foremost in the fun. Howell was the greatest romancer of all the Rossetti circle, and he had always some monstrous story to tell about anybody who happened to be enjoying notoriety at the time, with whom he would claim to have a perfect intimacy. Rossetti had a keen relish for these yarns, and would roll back in his chair with delight at Howell's latest adventures, the relation of which used to proceed in the most plausible and convincing manner possible. Fred Sandys was also a splendid raconteur, and these two men between them would keep us all listening and set us all laughing until long past midnight.

Smoking was indulged in by most of Rossetti's friends, although he, to his frequent regret, could never venture to touch either pipe, cigar, or cigarette. William Michael Rossetti, however, made up for his brother's inability on this score. Swinburne was also a non-smoker. I do not think I ever saw him attempt even a cigarette. Howell was never without one; from morn till night he smoked, and the amount of cigarette ends he threw away in a day might well have made a good ounce weight of tobacco.

During the period in which these convivialities were rife, the Tichborne trial formed the all-absorbing topic of the day, and though Rossetti as a rule carefully avoided reading the newspapers, he nevertheless took a keen interest in the claimant, and followed the record of the case closely from day to day; that the claimant was an impostor, I believe was his conviction at an early stage of the proceedings. It was upon one of these evenings, when the conversation respecting the great case had set in, and the opinions of those present as to the rights and wrongs of it fizzed about as confusedly as squibs on a Guy Fawkes night, that Rossetti propounded a highly original solution of the question.

"Let", he said, very gravely, "the carcass of an ox be taken into the court, and let the claimant be brought forward and told that he must cut that ox up in the presence of the judge and jury. It would be seen at a glance," he maintained, "whether that man had ever been a butcher; unconsciously he would hold the knife in a way no tyro could, and unconsciously he would set to the task of cutting up the carcass and betray himself at every slash he made."

Such was Rossetti's idea. It was an ingenious one, but whether reliable or not was a matter of opinion, and led to a protracted discussion in which nobody was convinced.

With his questing, poet's imagination Rossetti was always fascinated by the great question mark: what lies beyond death?

> Ye who have passed Death's haggard hills; and ye
>   Whom trees that knew your sires shall cease to know
>   And still stand silent:—is it all a show,—
> A wisp that laughs upon the wall?—decree
> Of some inexorable supremacy
>   Which ever, as man strains his blind surmise
>   From depth to ominous depth, looks past his eyes,
> Sphinx-faced with unabashed augury?

Harry Dunn knew more than most of Gabriel's approach to the matter.

It was about the first year or so of my intimacy with Rossetti that table-turning, spirit-rapping, planchettes, and spiritualism under its many phases had taken hold of society, and provided the trifles of the day. Whether Rossetti had any real belief in spiritualism, or whether he wanted to persuade himself that he had, I can hardly say. He was of a highly imaginative nature, and everything that appertained to the mystic had a strange fascination for him. In spiritualism he took an interest for some time; he went to all the private seances to which he happened to be invited, and now and again would give me an account of some of them, when such well-known mediums as Mrs. Guppy, Mrs. Fawcett, and Daniel Home, and others were present.

The result of witnessing the performances of these professionals was that Rossetti thought that he, too, would have little seances at home, and from time to time Whistler, Bell Scott, and a few other friends would meet together at Cheyne Walk to have their own experiences of the matter. On these occasions the spirit-rapping and gyrations of tables would be carried on until the uncanny hour of midnight. As each of the experimenters was suspicious of his neighbour's honesty when the table became rampant, the results were mostly unsatisfactory. At one or two of these meetings, I remember, some remarkable messages were received from the spirits, which could not be accounted for.

Mesmerism Rossetti had a reasonable faith in. He was in a great measure led to this belief from having met one night, at a friend's house, a Mr. Bergheim, an American, of early middle-age who spoke English quite well, who possessed extraordinary powers in this direction. So impressed was he with what he had seen on this occasion that he asked him to come one evening to Cheyne Walk to give a proof of his mesmeric powers to a few friends he intended to invite to meet him, and who would be interested in Bergheim's experiments. Amongst the party were Morris, the Master of Lindsay (Sir Coutts Lindsay, founder of the Grosvenor Gallery), Leyland and Sala.

The entertainment in question was held in a lordly pleasure-marquee, which Rossetti had caused to be erected in the spacious garden at the rear of the house. This tent was furnished in a very luxurious manner; couches, comfortable chairs, many-countried cabinets, Persian rugs, and such flowers as were in bloom were dispersed profusely within, and gave it a delightful Eastern appearance.

When all the party were assembled, conversation upon the occult became general. After a while, the Master of Lindsay related a wondrous story: that some time previously he was with Home the spiritualist—whose name was then on everybody's tongue—and saw him, whilst in a mesmerised state, rise from the floor and ascend to the ceiling of the apartment he was in, which was a very lofty one, sufficiently lofty, indeed, to enable the narrator to catch hold of Home's foot as he rose above his head, and to find that in spite of all endeavour to keep him down he still ascended, leaving his shoe in his hand. And also that, on another occasion, he had seen him float out of one of the windows of the room they occupied into the open air, and re-appear a few minutes afterwards floating through the next. This was related by the Master of Lindsay in such perfect belief and simplicity, that we could but listen and, wondering, accept his assertions accordingly.

Of course, Howell had something equally wonderful to tell and, as far as I recollect, it was in connection with Richard Burton, the traveller and orientalist, with whom he professed to have gone through supernatural experiences of a most astounding nature. Then arose and spoke Sala. He had just come from the Broadmoor criminal lunatic asylum, and he gave us a most interesting account of some of the inmates confined there for murder. He had seen Constance Kent. (Of the "Road Murder". She was the daughter of a man reported to be a natural son of the Duke of Kent, and therefore a half-niece of Queen Victoria. At the age of fifteen or so she murdered, out of spite, a brother—or half-brother—of hers, aged perhaps three. She was not known to be the murderess, but after some four or five years she confessed it, having come under religious influences. She pleaded guilty and was sentenced to death, but the sentence was commuted.)

Usually she was very quiet and reserved, but she had recurrent fits of madness that came on with the full moon. Then her depravity would break out and find vent in the most violent actions and Billingsgate language, so that it was only with the greatest difficulty she could be managed. It was on one of these occasions he had seen her.

Edward Oxford, who shot at the Queen some years ago, he also mentioned as having seen. There was nothing remarkable about him in any way. He was very quiet, and employed in doing portions of the rough painting-work that was required in the establishment. Another and much more interesting criminal was the artist, Richard Dadd, who was detained there for murdering his father on Blackheath Common many years ago. A terrible idea had weaved itself into his disordered brain—that it was his mission to kill the devil! And that notion, worming itself deeper and deeper into all his thoughts, caused him to wake up one morning with the conviction that his father was the devil. He took him for a walk and slew him. The Broadmoor authorities were allowed to furnish him with paints and brushes, and other necessaries for painting, and much of his time was occupied in making designs of the wildest and most ghastly character.

Sala found him at work upon a picture of Job suffering from the plague of boils. The boils were depicted in every stage, and in the most microscopic manner, and he seemed to take a delight in painting them, licking his brush over an extra ulcerous one. There were a good many of his designs, so Sala said, about the cell he occupied, all painted with extreme finish and photographic minuteness. One especially noticeable was of Richard III, after having slain his two nephews. He was depicted as holding up his sword high aloft, and catching in his mouth the blood drops as they fell.

Then, in parentheses, Sala told us how Dadd, having killed his father, escaped from the scene of his crime, and took his guilty flight to Dover, and from thence crossed the Channel with the intention of going to Paris. On his way thither, he still found himself in doubt as to whether, after all, he had accomplished his mission or not. In the compartment of the railway carriage that he had taken a place in, was a fellow-traveller. They entered into a conversation which lasted well-nigh the whole journey. Dadd, still in doubt, began to fancy his companion was the devil incarnate, whom it was his mission to kill. Through the window of the carriage he gazed at the heavens and looked for a sign from it. The sun was setting and the sky full of threatening rain-clouds. It seemed borne in upon him that if the sun sank in serene and unclouded splendour, his fellow-traveller's life must be spared, but if otherwise, he saw his duty and was resolved to do it. The sun sank below the horizon cloudlessly, and his companion little knew of the fate he had escaped.

These various relations were interrupted by the arrival of the two young women whom Bergheim had arranged should be his mediums for the evening. Hearing that they were on their way to the tent, he mesmerised them before they appeared, so that they both entered in a clairvoyant state. Rossetti's surprise at this was great. Not long after, Bergheim asked him to act in an improvised little drama that he had thought of.

Rossetti was to be a sailor, and act with the medium selected as though he were going to join his ship, which was about to sail on a long-service cruise. So, taking his cue, he told her a prettily-concocted tale of his being ordered away that night on Her Majesty's service, which the girl listened to with the greatest emotion. Another of the party then came forward, and represented himself as a naval officer sent by the captain to take him aboard; the anchor having been weighed, the captain was anxious to set sail.

When this was told her, and she found her sailor must leave her, she got into a terribly excited state, and threatened to stab the man who would separate them. At last, however, she allowed Rossetti to be taken away, and as soon as he had disappeared through the tent awning and could no more be seen, she fell to the ground in a fit of hysterical weeping.

Another of the party, a somewhat heavy man, was then asked to lie down on the ground, which he did. The mesmerist directed the medium's attention to him, scolding her as if she were a careless nursemaid in charge of a small child, and telling her that there was a carriage and a pair of runaway horses galloping down a supposed lane, and that unless she could rescue the child in time it would inevitably be run over and killed. In a terrible fright, she ran to the suppositious child, picked him up and carried him away to a safe place with all the ease that a grown-up young woman would a child of three or four years of age.

There were many other scenes of a similar kind enacted, until Bergheim thought his mediums were exhausted. When he restored them to their usual condition, by a few passes and a smart tap on the shoulder, I asked one of them if she knew what she had been doing, but she seemed quite unconscious of what had taken place, save that she thought sleep had overcome her, in which she dreamt something too indistinct to remember.

I witnessed all these things, and to me they appeared quite unaccountable. If the two girls brought hither by Bergheim were in collusion with him, why they must have been equal to the best actresses that ever trod the stage. Even granting that they were acting their parts, I cannot make out how the medium who lifted up one of us off the ground could have got her strength, for it was done without any undue exertion, and she was but an ordinary type of a little London milliner.

In recalling the foregoing scenes, I have many times asked myself why I should relate them, and whether such things were not too trivial to set down in writing? And my answer to myself was always, that the interest displayed by Rossetti towards everything bearing on the occult gave an insight to his nature, and however inconsequential these incidents may appear, they show how largely both his poetry and his painting were influenced by the best of his mind in that direction, and his yearning for the unseen. He would often talk about spiritualism for hours, and many were the curious experiences of ours which we revealed to each other. And, as in a disconnected dream, the conversation would sometimes wander into paths not thought of before, and hence these relations occasionally had their uses.

I recollect on one occasion I had just come from visiting a neighbour— a lady who possessed the original dreaming stone of Dr. Dee which she allowed me to look at. It was a small, unpretentious bit of crystal, but having such a reputation as it had, I felt as though I too must have a look into it. Full half an hour I spent in gazing into it, but I saw nothing. Perhaps the time was not long enough, or perhaps I was not in tune; during the afternoon, however, I learnt that my hostess had seen much and written much more from the pages of antiquated lore that it had unfolded to her—Hebrew, Sanscrit, and heaven only knows what else had been opened up to her enlightened vision.

Full of all this mysterious discourse, I went back to Rossetti and told him all. He listened to my narration with the greatest interest. I spoke of the dreaming stone as the magic "Beryl".

"What did you call it?" he asked.

I repeated its name—the "Beryl".

"Good," he responded, "that is the very word I want for the title of my poem; it never occurred to me before. I shall now use it; it is better than crystal in every way; it is more rhythmical, and has a greater seeming of mysticism in its sound. Moreover, it is one of the mystic stones named in *Revelations*."

So from that time he substituted the word "Beryl" for "crystal" and built up a wondrous poem.

Swinburne was a frequent visitor at Cheyne Walk, and I remember well his calling one evening when Rossetti was absent on some china-collecting expedition. It had been a very sultry day, and with the advancing twilight, heavy thunder-clouds were rolling up. The door opened and Swinburne entered. He appeared in an abstracted state, and for a few minutes sat silent.

Soon, something I had said anent his last poem set his thoughts loose. Like the storm that had just broken, so he began in low tones to utter lines of poetry. As the storm increased, he got more and more excited and carried away by the impulse of his thoughts, bursting into a torrent of splendid verse that seemed like some grand air with the distant peals of thunder as an intermittent accompaniment. And still the storm waxed more violent, and the vivid flashes of lightning became more frequent. But Swinburne seemed unconscious of it all, and whilst he paced up and down the room, pouring out bursts of passionate declamation, faint electric sparks played round the wavy masses of his luxuriant hair.

I lay on the sofa in a corner of the studio and listened in wonder and with a curious awe, for it appeared to me as though the very figures in the pictures that were on the easels standing about the room were conscious of and sympathised with the poet and his outpourings. The "Proserpine" gazed out more mournfully than I had been wont to see her gaze; her longing to return to earth seemed to have Swinburne as an additional reason for it.

On the other side looked out through her frame the "Blessed Damozel", and "from the gold bar of heaven", "Cassandra", away in the farthermost part of the studio, peered through the gloom, as though joining with the others in watching the poet as he impetuously strode up and down the room, each flash of lightning revealing him as one inspired, his wealth of hair giving forth a scintillation of tiny electric sparks which formed, as it were, a faint halo round his head. Amidst the rattle of the thunder he still continued to pour out his thoughts, his voice now sinking low and sad, now waxing louder as the storm listed.

How long his ecstasy would have lasted I know not. I was wondering, when the sounds of a latchkey and the closing of the hall door were heard. In another minute Rossetti entered the studio, boisterously shaking off the raindrops from his Inverness cape, and with a "Hullo! old fellow!" welcomed

Swinburne. Divesting himself of his cape, he lit the gas, sat down with his friend, and the night began anew. Their conversation, upon many things, went on hour after hour, until the dawn began to appear, and I arose as one in a dream, and betook myself to bed.

John Trivett Nettleship, the painter, would sometimes bring his sketches of wondrous, yet hardly worked-out ideas. Those of the Blake-like kind amazed and delighted Rossetti with their audacity of treatment. Nettleship's intense admiration of Browning's poetry and his almost idolatrous worship of the fantastic endeared him to Rossetti: in fact, had he known him a few years earlier, he would surely have found in him a valuable collaborator in the book exhibiting the poetic genius of Blake that he, in conjunction with Gilchrist, brought out. He regarded him as a genius and the various anecdotes which I told him from time to time concerning Nettleship and his peculiarities vastly amused him and excited his curiosity.

Ted Hughes (Edward Hughes, the artist, nephew of another well-known painter, Arthur Hughes) once showed a little picture to Rossetti—or he saw it at Hughes' house—entitled "Hushed Music", which delighted him very much. He spoke to me afterwards about it on several occasions, remarking that such a work gave fine promise of greater, and that Hughes would surely make a name for himself.

Lewis Carroll (The Rev. Charles Lutwidge Dodgson) the author of *Alice in Wonderland*, was another frequent visitor at Cheyne Walk in the early days of Rossetti's occupancy of the house there. Being an adept in the art of photography, he took several very good studies there. One of Rossetti, his mother, and his sister, Christina, seated on a little flight of steps that led to the back hall-door, was especially happy in the likeness and arrangement of the family group.

One day Longfellow, who had not long arrived in London from a tour in Italy, called on Rossetti. He was a grand-looking man, although somewhat short, with a fine silver-white beard, and still a goodly amount of snow-white hair on his head. He had absolutely no knowledge of painting, and his remarks concerning pictures were not only childish, but indicated an utter indifference to them. Although having just completed his translation of the 'Paradiso' portion of Dante's trilogy, he seemed quite at a loss to know what Rossetti's pictures represented.

From the midnight gatherings and conversations that I have mentioned, it will be seen that Rossetti's hours were very late ones. As a matter of course, he was not an early riser, and it was not his wont to commence work much before eleven o'clock in the morning. But when he did, he began right earnestly.

12

Harry would have been more than human if, during his first year at Cheyne Walk, he had not felt some curiosity about Rossetti the man as opposed to Rossetti the writer of verses and painter of pictures.

Imperceptibly almost, the formal relationship between them thawed. Daily contact smoothed the sharp edge of distinction between employer and employed. Harry came to realise quickly enough that beneath the appearance of a man who worked successfully with words and paint was a character complex and fascinating, a prey to changing and conflicting emotions.

There came the moment when Rossetti introduced his new assistant to Mrs. Hughes. It was an encounter Harry Dunn must have faced with a certain misgiving leavened, no doubt, with anticipation. He had probably already made his own assessment of Gabriel's relationship with his "Dear Elephant". Bearing in mind what he had learned about Lizzie, it called for no great perception on Harry's part to see that Gabriel had taken the qualities of two women in his life and saw in the blend of both his ideal partner. More bluntly, this is to say that what he needed he found in a fusion of both.

We know that Gabriel's affections could be easily engaged by what one might call the everyday commerce of physical attraction. But both to Lizzie and to Fanny he was faithful after his fashion. For his wife—and especially during their long-drawn-out engagement—he had a romantic and tender regard. With her tragic beauty, her remote expression, she appealed to all the imagination on which he had balanced the artistic part of his life. How many times had the sight or the touch of her given him that preliminary shock, that heart-quickening throb which meant that the poet in him had to find expression.

On the other side of the medal was the likeness of Fanny, no less lovely in her youth than Lizzie and, without doubt, more urgently desirable. As scholarly biographers have said—and in very much the same words—the two between them shared in satisfying Gabriel's frankly selfish emotions.

There was nothing passive or pensive about Fanny. She did not sit like some medieval maiden sighing for an absent lover. Fanny was fair and amiable and when in the fullness of time she acquired the inevitable discomforts of middle-age, they were solid, everyday complaints—colds, toothache, and rheumatism.

Could Gabriel live without Elizabeth Siddal?

He could: he had to. He never had to live without Fanny—except when the shadows were closing around him. She lived on into a sad and mind-clouded old age. But while Rossetti lived his affection for her—based on a matter-of-fact partnership of the flesh between a passionate man and an easy-going woman—endured almost until the end. Harry Dunn's understanding of Mrs. Rossetti had to be put together from words dropped casually by those who had known her. But of Gabriel's loyalty to Fanny he was to have all the embarrassment of proof. When scarcely a shred of true romance could have lingered in their relationship Gabriel still treated the Elephant with courtesy and good humour. In one of his last lucid intervals he whispered a name, and asked a tender and solicitous question. The name was Fanny's.

There were several accounts of how she and Gabriel first met. According to one, Rossetti was walking along the Strand when he saw a girl cracking nuts with her strong teeth and throwing the shells away. She had striking good looks and Rossetti, never a man to hide his pleasure at the sight of a pretty girl, stood and stared at her with frank admiration. Cheekily, she threw some of the shells at him, there was a lively exchange, and before Fanny knew what had happened she was in his studio and he was painting her portrait.

According to another, Fanny went to some noisy celebration some time in the summer of 1856 in one of the public parks: there were fireworks and a good deal of rowdy and robust conduct. There she met Gabriel in company with some of his boon companions—possibly Ford Madox Brown and Burne-Jones. They seemed to be taken with her beauty and one of them touched her hair so that it came undone and fell to her waist. There were apologies, a great deal of laughter, some compliments—and an appointment made for her to visit Mr. Rossetti's studio next day.

Later, as Harry heard these and other stories of how Gabriel met his famous models, he came to realise that however the detail varied the denouement was always the same. They all ended in Mr. Rossetti's studio.

In any case, there is not much doubt that Fanny had met Gabriel and Burne-Jones in 1856 and that she had sat for both of them from that time on. According to her own account the first painting for which she posed was what she called the "calf picture". This was the celebrated painting "Found". Gabriel painted her as the country girl who had taken to an evil way of life in the city. She is recognised in the street by her lover, a young farmer, in whose cart is a calf confined by a net. Thereafter she sat for Rossetti for "Fazio's Mistress", "Bocca Baciata" and, of course, "Fair Rosamund" and the "Lady Lilith".

Fanny, it seems, was born in Steyning, in Sussex. The year was 1824 and her real name was Sarah Cox. Professionally, she became known as Fanny Cornforth—the Cornforth being borrowed from one of her maternal grandmothers. Her husband, the shadowy Hughes, was credited with having been an engineer or mechanic and with having had some kind of business connection with the art-students at the Academy, but his most memorable characteristic was his addiction to the bottle.

This then was the redoubtable woman to whom Rossetti introduced the young Cornishman. The encounter itself was no doubt uneventful enough. Harry would have been eager to please, while Fanny was expansive and good-natured enough in the normal course of events.

But what emotions were to spring from this encounter—what a clash of wills, what arguments, what calling of names . . . what outraged dignity. Fanny, proud of Gabriel's trust, saw herself as the privileged manager of his household. The lean young provincial, with his quick gestures, was soon to be seen in the rôle of spy and interloper, poking that long nose into her business, a meddlesome nuisance. Dunn's efforts to keep the affairs of the erratic household on an even keel were to be the cause of endless and wounding quarrels, to Gabriel's amusement and alarm. In a curious way, he was flattered to observe two people so devoted to him at odds on matters affecting his welfare.

The blunt truth is that Fanny and Harry Dunn never hit it off. Could there have been two more ill-assorted characters? Their single point of contact was their determination to make life easier for Gabriel. Fanny was convinced that she and she alone should rule the house: the possibility that she might be carrying out her duties in a casual, not to say slapdash manner never entered her handsome head.

On the other hand, Harry saw his responsibilities clearly. His task was to protect a man for whom he felt great admiration. Fanny was possessive.

She had queened it too long to take kindly to the intervention of a young stranger. Knewstub had been different, a great man for a joke and in no sense a rival.

No wonder that after a year or two the Fanny–Dunn association developed into a running battle of wits—Dunn darting into the attack with the speed of a frigate, withdrawing as soon as he was out-gunned. When the majestic man o' war which was Fanny bore down on him and fired her broadsides, he scuttled back to harbour—a trip to Cornwall, a visit to friends in Croydon.

After one of these engagements Dunn would vanish for days at a time and bearing in mind the venom of Fanny's tongue, it is hard to blame him.

There is no need to speculate as to one reason why Fanny took a dislike to this young stranger from some outlandish place at the other end of nowhere. In his banking days Harry had had enough experience of Cornish thrift to realise that the Cheyne Walk budget was hopelessly organised. Under Fanny's rule expenses would always outrun income.

Thanks to Mrs. Troxell, who owns the complete and uncut version of the *Recollections*, we know from Harry's own words what steps he felt called upon to take.

For some inexplicable reason, the following account was deleted in the published volume.

> Being so continually in the house I had ample opportunities of seeing to a great extent the management or rather mismanagement of the very considerable income that Rossetti was now making by his profession. I found him often in a depressed state over the house expenses and I became aware that in spite of what he was earning there was much too frequently a request from one tradesman or the other that their several accounts should be reduced or that a three months' acceptance be given or renewed. This state of affairs perplexed me not a little and for the life of me I could not see why with his ample income there should not be always a good balance in his hands to meet every requirement. Pondering over this matter for some time I came to the conclusion that there must be great waste and improvidence in the housekeeping, and therefore when I felt I might do so I broached the subject to him one day and besought him to let me look into his accounts, as I felt confident that with proper supervision over household expenses there ought not to be this continual request from his tradesmen for more money on account of supplies.

One can imagine the quizzical look with which Gabriel received these suggestions, but according to Harry he "gladly acquiesced", no doubt with the lift of an eyebrow and a half-smile. The young art assistant's anxiety to help was the cause of the first major clash with Fanny. "Greatly to the opposition and annoyance of the servants," he says, "I looked thoroughly into the expenditure and found as I expected the greatest waste and improvidence by them."

His first step was to visit the local tradesmen and insist that their accounts should be rendered weekly. Once this arrangement had been made satisfactorily, Harry ordered that the accounts should be brought to him regularly by the servants for his inspection.

"By these means I was able to check the extravagance that was going on below stairs," he writes, "and it was not long ere Rossetti had a considerable amount of cash in hand: too much to keep in the house, so a banker's account was opened and for the first time, I believe, since he had taken up his residence in Cheyne Walk he found himself with a bank book and a handsome sum at his disposal to draw upon."

It is difficult to understand quite why this little piece of unrecorded history was not passed for publication. In his Foreword to Harry's little book William spoke generously enough of "Mr. Dunn's efforts" to keep Gabriel's finances in order. It may be that he could not go all the way with Harry's suggestion that having found himself not only solvent but a man of some substance, Rossetti was "enabled to give up pot-boilers and devote himself to designs into which he could throw all his genius and to give them the proper time for the development so essential to all serious work".

Perhaps William, in passing the *Recollections* for print, found this just a trifle too complacent.

Harry was young enough and fit enough to take the erratic Cheyne Walk timetable in his stride. It was nothing new for him while a pupil at Heatherley's to stay up smoking and enjoying the cut-and-thrust of friendly debate. For some time he did not give a thought to the late hours kept by Rossetti. Even when there were no visitors an occasional cough or the sound of footsteps on the ground floor would be evidence that the master of the house had not gone to bed.

It was a year or so before Harry realised that Gabriel did not stay up until all hours as a matter of choice. He was indeed one of those unfortunate people who found it hard to get to sleep. Insomnia is one of the abominable curses of mankind: and it was the grim prospect of sleepless nights which finally caused Rossetti to turn to the new drug, chloral.

This had been discovered in the eighteen-thirties but many years went by before it came to be prescribed for nervous conditions. When Gabriel first started taking chloral for its soothing powers the seriousness of the long-term effects was not appreciated. It brought refreshing sleep and gave the patient a feeling of restfulness and serenity: but taken in quantity it led to depression and a state in which the sufferer came to rely more and more on the drug—and this meant taking the stuff in larger quantities. The only cure was to break the habit completely.

Long before he saw the drug tighten its grip, Harry had plenty of evidence that Gabriel's health was vulnerable and that he was frequently given to exaggerating the symptoms. The following extract from the *Recollections* (to which I am indebted to Mrs. Troxell) was deleted from the original manuscript. Dunn wrote:

It was not long in these early days of our intimacy ere I became aware that Rossetti suffered from illusionary fears with regard to his health. In fact his nervousness over trifling symptoms turned him at times into a veritable "malade imaginaire". This impression was more fully strengthened when on one morning after giving me his usual visit of instruction for the day's work as was his wont, I noticed that he was in a perturbed and distressed state of mind; and on my expressing concern at seeing him thus he confided to me his conviction that he was suffering from incipient cancer on the tongue. I got him to give me some reason why he fancied such a dismal calamity should befall him, but the symptoms he described did not seem to me like those connected with cancer; so I comforted him as well as I could by suggesting indigestion as the probable cause, and how marvellously it simulated every known disease under the sun that a nervous mind could conjure up to itself; and that more exercise and fresh air would banish all such morbid apprehensions.

Harry devised his own method of restoring Gabriel's confidence in his health. Knowing the fascination that "curious bits of furniture" and bric-à-brac had for Gabriel, he would mention various interesting pieces he had seen in secondhand shops in Chelsea and elsewhere, and would persuade Gabriel to go on foraging expeditions in different parts of London. Now that he was living in Cheyne Walk Harry had bought a number of books concerned with the district, among them Faulkner's *History of Chelsea and Fulham* and Croker's *Londoners' Walk from Charing Cross to Fulham*. And, partly with the idea of taking Gabriel's mind off his symptoms, imaginary and otherwise, and partly to give him a pleasant physical fatigue, he worked out a number of these mild conducted tours. The two men went to see the house in which Richardson wrote *Clarissa*.

Another day their destination was a house in which Pitt had lived, and if Harry's well-intentioned expeditions did not always have the desired effect they at least added to his own and Gabriel's knowledge of the city.

Harry's rôle was becoming more and more that of comforter and friend. Letters from Gabriel to Dunn, and a few rare despatches from Dunn to William Michael Rossetti prove that this is not putting the case too strongly.

When Harry was still a visitor only, and before he had made his home at Cheyne Walk, Gabriel had been in despair on another count. He was threatened, so he believed, by the greatest blow which can afflict an artist —loss of sight. He felt pain in his eyes. Sunshine as well as powerful artificial light made him feel sick and giddy. Even street lamps bothered him. In search of company, he sought out the Irish poet and excise officer, William Allingham, an old friend of the "P.R.B." days, and spent a holiday with him at Lymington. The visit was not a success, and a proposed visit to Tennyson one wet and windy day was abandoned for fear of sea-sickness.

Allingham, who has been credited with being the first of Rossetti's friends to see the incomparable Miss Siddal (it was he who told Deverell about her), returned the visit a couple of months later. Oswald Doughty describes an odd dinner-party, when Gabriel, Madox Brown, Howell and Fanny sat down with Allingham. The guest of honour later complained that Howell's stories were distasteful, and he took an exceedingly poor view of Fanny's "pretence of decorum".

Harry Dunn joined the party and at one period he and Howell went to the kitchen in search of food. Allingham saw no reason to change his never flattering opinion of Fanny when Howell, returning with some food, announced that while below-stairs he had seen "a mouse eating a haddock". The friends talked until three in the morning, when the ever-willing Harry went off to find a cab for Madox Brown.

No amount of good company could make Rossetti forget the fear of blindness. He recalled the failing sight of his father, and began to worry about his ability to fulfil commissions. He saw not one doctor but a number—including Sir William Bowman, a leading specialist, who prescribed cold water baths and rest. As the doctors knew very well, there was nothing fundamentally wrong with his sight. The trouble was caused by overwork, nervous strain, insomnia. Spectacles helped—but not enough. He worried his friends by talk of suicide.

In restless mood Gabriel left London, returned, and was off again. With Harry as companion he explored Warwickshire. Then came the invitation to stay with Miss Alice Boyd (a friend of Bell Scott) at her home in Ayrshire—Penkill Castle.

Under pressure, and still unable to see distant objects except as though in a haze, he forced himself to work. The bills had to be paid. There was one redeeming circumstance in this sad and extremely trying period. His brother and his friends urged him to remember that he was poet as well as painter; and his interest in poetry stirred again.

13

It often happens that those who are closest to a sequence of dramatic events are the least conscious of what is happening. Only when one can look back through the spy-glass of time is it possible to see events in perspective.

Harry Dunn was one of Rossetti's closest companions at a time when the extraordinary pattern of Rossetti's life reached a sombre and decisive moment. In 1869, seven years after Lizzie's death, Rossetti was given permission by the Home Office to recover the book of poems he had placed in his wife's coffin. In October, a party of workmen made their way to Mrs. Rossetti's grave in Highgate Cemetery and, watched by Howell, Mr. H. V. Tebbs the solicitor, and a doctor, uncovered the coffin and hoisted it to the surface. The starkness of the scene silenced even Howell, who never told a tale without embroidering it with fancies of his own.

There was never any real need for the more sensationally-minded writers to romance about this grim episode. Indeed, the tragic elements in Rossetti's life were so marked that invention is superfluous. Of course, there was light as well as shade, but it was a life touched with sorrow at so many points that it seemed to be moving slowly towards a predictable end. A marriage overshadowed by ill-health and the loss of a child; Lizzie's early death by her own hand; failing sight and sleepless nights; depression and a sense of persecution; the exhumation and its effect on a mind already a prey to melancholy; recourse to alcohol and insidious chloral; illness, pain, and death at fifty-four. These things happened to a man who even in youth was pre-occupied with the mysteries of life and death.

When Rossetti despaired of his sight he turned again to poetry and found solace in it. He wrote with more insight, more passion and more skill than ever before. Circumstances (fate or destiny, say the romantically-minded biographers) had thrown Gabriel and Janey Morris together again. Whatever their relationship, Mrs. Morris was clearly the inspiration for his finest verse.

His friends, who had persuaded him to start writing again, were delighted by the success of their treatment. Some of his poetry had been printed privately. For it to reach a wider public seemed a wise and sensible thing. To do this it was desirable to include Rossetti's early poems—those which in that instant of grief he had placed between his dead wife's cheek and the lovely hair he had so often painted and caressed. Some of the lines, of course, he still carried in his memory. Friends, Swinburne among them, helped him to recall others. But the manuscript poems, bound in rough grey calf, were needed in their entirety, especially for the long and beautiful poem "Jenny".

It could not have been an easy decision to make. The grand gesture was spoiled—and no amount of glossing over could make it otherwise. The affair left a scar. Remorse is too easy a word to employ but it is hard to believe that the incident did not distress Rossetti for the rest of his life.

Once he had made up his mind Gabriel wanted the business to be over and done with as soon as possible. These matters cannot be hurried (unless there is some question of criminal investigation). There were papers to be signed, negotiations, formalities. Howell, the "fixer", was obviously the man to direct the affair. Gabriel wrote to William that he knew no-one else "who could well have been entrusted with such a trying task". It was not to be expected that he would keep such a secret, and the circle of those who knew about the exhumation widened.

Dunn by this time was fully in Rossetti's confidence, but he was too fond of his chief and of William to breathe a word. Madox Brown, who had thought his friend's sacrifice to be quixotic at the time, was aware of every move. William, Swinburne, Bell Scott and Fanny must have shared the secret, and their loyalty was beyond question. On the other hand, a number of officials at the Home Office, the cemetery authorities and employees dealt with the matter at one level or another, and there was inevitably a certain amount of gossip.

The exhumation itself was carried out smoothly and discreetly. It took place at night by lantern-light and the flames of a fire which had been kindled by the side of the grave. A Dr. Williamson, of Camberwell, removed the poems, saw to it that the pages of the book were adequately disinfected and dried.

Many imaginations have been fired by the drama of this remarkable and eerie scene.

"The body is described as perfect upon coming to light", reports Hall Caine. It is possible, as was suggested, that the drug she had taken in such quantities and which destroyed her did indeed delay the normal process of decay. It seems strangely fitting that the girl whose frail beauty had so spiritual a quality in life, should defy the cruel disfigurements of death.

Later, when the story was being passed from mouth to mouth, it was said that Lizzie's lovely hair had not only retained its famed colour, but had continued to grow after death. This item shows the characteristic Howell touch so clearly that there could surely be only one source for it.

The *Poems* were published in 1870 by Ellis of New Bond Street, and made secure Dante Gabriel's reputation as a "poet among poets". The critics and the public were stirred by lines which are still among the most-quoted in the language:

> The blessed damozel leaned out
> From the gold bar of Heaven;
> Her eyes were deeper than the depth
> Of waters stilled at even;
> She had three lilies in her hand,
> And the stars in her hair were seven.

In "Jenny" the poet draws with pathos and pity a picture of a girl whose way of life has not yet marred her beauty, her childish charm. As, with her head on his knee she falls asleep, the poet muses on what she is and what the future may hold for her:

> Behold the lilies of the field,
> They toil not neither do they spin;
> (So doth the ancient text begin,—
> Not of such rest as one of these
> Can share). Another rest and ease
> Along each summer-sated path
> From its new lord the garden hath,
> Than that whose spring in blessings ran
> Which praised the bounteous husbandman,
> Ere yet, in days of hankering breath,
> The lilies sickened unto death.
>
> What, Jenny, are your lilies dead?
> Aye, and the snow-white leaves are spread
> Like winter on the garden-bed.
> But you had roses left in May,–
> They were not gone too. Jenny, nay,

> But must your roses die, and those
> Their purfled buds that should unclose?
> Even so; the leaves are curled apart,
> Still red as from the broken heart,
> And here's the naked stem of thorns.

At a period when more than ever before Gabriel needed peace and comfort to mend mind and body he was to be shattered by the affair of Robert Buchanan's article, "The Fleshly School of Poetry" in *The Contemporary Review*. The article was written under a pen-name—Thomas Maitland—and at first Rossetti seemed to dismiss it contemptuously. Buchanan's was a lone voice: the *Poems* had been universally praised and had made secure the author's reputation as a poet. In any case, the article was not directed against Rossetti alone: it was a venomous blast aimed at the "Fleshly" school whose verse hymned the joys of physical love. By today's standards such criticism would be regarded as puerile and farcical: even by those of 1871 Buchanan's moralising was pretentious and unwarranted.

> Never spiritual, never tender; always self-conscious, and aesthetic . . . the whole tone of the poem "Jenny" is more than usually coarse and heartless.

If the article in *The Contemporary Review* had been printed at a different time Gabriel might have taken it at its true value and forgotten it. But he was feeling ill. He was tortured by the ill-founded fears for his sight. His insomnia was worse; and it is probable that he came to magnify the affair because of the circumstances in which so much of the *Poems* had been recovered. Grief for his once adored Lizzie had driven him to make a gift to all of her that was mortal: the still, withdrawn body in the open coffin. Was it ambition, was it selfishness, which had tarnished the bright agony of that grief?

Harry Dunn's affection and admiration for Gabriel never wavered at this time and for many months he was to feel on his employer's behalf great anxiety and distress. Buchanan's words contributed to a major breakdown. Rossetti's eventual reaction, after he had time to brood on the affair, was physically and mentally disastrous. He believed himself to be persecuted even by his friends. Swinburne must be banished from his life. Everybody, Browning included, was conspiring against him.

In June 1872, the situation was so serious that Gabriel's sanity was despaired of. It was a harrowing time for all who were close to him. William Michael experienced "one of the most miserable days of my life,

not to speak of his". Three doctors were called, and eventually Gabriel
was taken by cab to Dr. Gordon Hake's house in Roehampton. There was
a dramatic climax: Gabriel swallowed an overdose of laudanum and was
unconscious for two days.

Harry was profoundly disturbed, though all he could find to say when
Gabriel was brought home was, "You must let me do what I can to help.
There's nothing I won't do." But Gabriel was at Cheyne Walk for the
briefest spell before being taken off to Scotland via Madox Brown's house
in Fitzroy Square.

By now Harry had come to feel a very real affection for his chief. He
himself had been bereaved. His father, the respected Truro tea-merchant,
had died in 1870. His sister, Edith's fiancé, James Shepherd, had suffered
a sudden and fatal illness. Both events had found Gabriel immensely kind
and considerate.

Harry was now in his middle thirties, and had grown mature and confi-
dent. William Michael trusted him and was glad to feel that his brother
had a companion who could be relied on to keep domestic and business
affairs under some sort of supervision.

Six weeks after Rossetti's attempt to end his life, Harry was writing:

> Cheyne Walk,
> Chelsea.
> 22 July 1872
>
> My dear Wm,
>   The "Dante in heaven" picture alluded to in your enclosed note of Jerrard
> was had back by Rossetti on acct. of the lettering having all run into one
> confused mass. I had, I believe promised to restore it if he could tell me what
> the original text was and on this matter he seems quite oblivious. So thus it
> stands. Had I better return it as it is with a promise of a future restoration? If
> you think I had please say where the picture is to be sent. The last I heard of
> Lady Holland was that she was living at some place nr. Croydon.
>   F sent for me this morning & I heard from her the contents of yr letter &
> have accordingly given directions to Emma that the house shd be put in
> order. I think it will be as well for Brass to replace the cupboard doors, and
> so fill up the recesses where the Blue China used to disport itself. Upon this
> matter I will consult F ere acting.
>   I do not think it wise that in the event of R's returning to town he shd.
> come to Cheyne Walk. I believe he ought to be kept away as long as possible
> and I also think that his return shd be of the shortest possible duration, just
> what wd. be necessary for the operation you speak of, for I hear the most
> exaggerated acc. floating on all sides of his condition & the most annoying
> part of the affair [is] that it is his friends who spread these things about. I was

told of somebody, a friend of somebody else being in the Solferino Restaurant and hearing Sandys and Swinburne going over the whole matter at one of the tables. Middlemists acknowledgment of the receipt of £18. was one of the things I had intended to mention.

Yours truly,
H. T. DUNN

P.S. If I can find time I will see you for a few minutes at Somerset House tomorrow. It will be about 10.30 or 11 a.m. should I call so I hope I shall not interfere with yr. work.

This letter shows that by the summer of 1872, the Blue China—much of which had been bought at "an emporium in Regent Street, owned by a Mr. Liberty"—had been disposed of. Brass was a builder, who made alterations to the studio and was employed in the packing of pictures and many objects which required careful handling.

Rossetti's search for health took him to many places in the next ten years. Scotland, it was decided, was ideal for recuperation—no doubt because it was remote from associations likely to distress the patient. For a while, Gabriel stayed in Urrard House, in Perthshire, which belonged to his friend and patron, Graham. From Urrard House, he went after a week or so to Stobhall, another place of Graham's overlooking the Tay, and finally, on Dr. Hake's advice, he settled at Trowan, near Crieff, also in Perthshire, and more than four hundred miles from Chelsea and Cheyne Walk. What, the good doctor thought, could be more restful than a Scottish farmhouse, surrounded by mountainous scenery and pine forests, with a river and a lake near by and waterfalls to add to the beauty of the place?

By September, Harry had an opportunity of sharing the delights of Trowan with Gabriel. One could hardly expect a Cornishman to share Dr. Hake's enthusiasm for this wild, Scottish haven. It was beautiful, he thought, but lonely. August, as the following letter shows, found him still in London, working and clearly doing his best to hold the fort in Gabriel's absence.

16 Cheyne Walk
Chelsea
Aug. 10 1872

My dear Willm,

I called yesterday on Miss Wilding. I found her in tears. She had written twice to Rossetti & had had no response. Her letters, it seems, have been returned to Brown as they don't think it advisable that he should have letters sent him. However, his not sending her any money has placed [her] in a very hard up state. R. arranged to give her 30/- pr. week. It is a long while since she has rec'd any money on acct. which up to last quarter day was she says £20. & of course as she knew nothing of the state of affairs she must have her allowance to present date. I have told her she must now take what sittings are offered to her. I should like Rossetti to know something of this & if you write to Dr. Hake ask him if he could not manage to mention it in a judicious manner. F's letters Brown tells me have also been returned whi. will annoy her terribly when she hears of it. At present she has gone into the country for a week or so. On the other side you will see my a/c of monies spent.

Yours truly,

H. TREFFRY DUNN.

			£	
July	27	Stamps & paper	1.	6.
		Emma & Allan	1	– –
	29	Laundress	5.	3.
		Catsmeat		9.
	30	Grocer	7.	8.
	31	Sweep	3.	–
		Ink		6.
Aug.	3	Emma & Allan	1	– –
	4	Carriage of 4 parcels from Crieff	4.	6.
	5	Laundress	8.	2.
		Catsmeat		7.
	10	Emma & Allan	1	– –

4 11. 11.

I shall have to pay £2. for repairing the kitchen range & I have advanced £8. to Miss W. wh. however I have not put in my acct. as it does not strictly belong to it.

H. T. D.

There is a pencilled note in this letter to the effect that two days later eight pounds for Dunn and fifteen pounds for Miss Wilding had arrived from Rossetti.

Had the telephone been available how much illuminating correspondence would have been lost. As it was, Harry wrote almost daily to William who, at work or at home, was only a few miles away. The position of the much-admired Miss Wilding was giving him concern. How could the services of a model who was "most anxiously sought for by Millais and that lot" be retained when the retaining-fee was not forthcoming?

9. "The Beloved" by Dante Gabriel Rossetti.
Fanny Cornforth, with whom Harry Dunn engaged in so many domestic
battles, was the model for the central figure.

10. A drawing by Dante Gabriel Rossetti of his wife, Elizabeth Siddal.

16 Cheyne Walk
Chelsea
S.W.
Aug. 14 '72

My dear William,

Your note of yesterday reached me too late to answer until today. With regard to the letters of F that I spoke of I can only say, Brown told me that they had been returned and I re-mentioned it to you thinking that some arrangements should be made in that matter. As Rossetti shows this desire to return to his work again do you think it will be wise to pay off Miss W. It will annoy him terribly to find she has been sitting to others. Please let me know as early as possible what you think about this because you see she will be most anxiously sought for by Millais and that lot if they find her free.

Respecting the Palmifera I suppose it would be better for me to do it up to my best mark & then let it remain for R's final touches when he feels inclined to give them. This would be more satisfactory for Valpy to whom the drawing I believe belongs. I see by Dr. Hake's letter Rossetti wishes me to write him about it & I shd. like to consult with you as to how much would be desirable to say about these things.

The new monthly's that I sent are wanting in several numbers. R. declares they must be in the house or burnt. I don't think the latter at all probable, but I am pretty certain that I can't find the missing links to the novel. There is a shop, in Wellington St. Strand, on the right hand side facing down to Somerset House where back nos. of periodicals may sometimes be procured. I think it would be as well to get Dr. Hake to tell us what parts are missing & to get them from some such source as that I now mention.

I am
Yours truly
H. TREFFRY DUNN.

Each day seemed to bring its own crises. Within twenty-four hours of the letter quoted above, Harry was reporting to William the unwelcome visit by a representative of Farmer & Rogers, the Japanese and Oriental ware dealers of Regent Street. From Harry's words it would appear that there had been some even less welcome visitors who had made what must have been burglarious "attempts on the house", attempts serious enough for the faithful Dunn to add night-watchman to his other duties. On at least one occasion thieves had climbed to the roof and made off with a quantity of lead which they had stripped from it.

16 Cheyne Walk
Chelsea.
Aug. 15 '72

My dear William,

I almost expected to see you this afternoon, perhaps tomorrow you will be

I

able to look in. This morning one [of] Farmer & Rogers young men seems
to have called & was very desirous to have their account settled. I was out at
the time; he left word to say that he should call again tomorrow. I shall tell
him that I must have the bill first before anything can be done. I have looked
over my file of bills & can only find receipts of Apl. 25 1871, for £20. &
again one of May 8th 1872 for £25. What the balance due is I have no idea.

I have written to Mr. Jerrard, Lady Ashburton's medium of correspondence, telling him that the picture is ready for her Ladyship & requesting
him to say where it is to be sent. My letter to D.G.R. I will try & get written
so that you may see it shd. you call tomorrow.

We have had no more attempts on the house. I have slept mostly since
then in the Studio until it gets daylight then I slink up to bed for an hour or
two for it is surprising how little refreshment one gets from sofa naps.
Whilst writing this note there is a great commotion & series of peculiar noises
right over my head as it would appear between the bedroom flooring & the
ceiling. Not being nervous I put it down to rats but I must try & get the
noises removed in some way because I have often heard R. speak of the
strange noises he has heard here & the continuance of these rat pilgrimages
in quest of grub might awaken all the old unpleasant ideas.

There is nothing more I think to mention so here I'll finish.

I am
Yours truly,
H. TREFFRY DUNN.

(from H. T. Dunn to D. G. Rossetti)

Aug. 21, 1872
Cheyne Walk.

I have told Emma about the noises arising from rats or mice in the studio
ceiling. She hardly knows what to do. Poison leaves them about. Men with
ferrets are all mostly thieves and dishonest characters, and the cat seems to be
too proud.

Dr. Hake's son, George, was in attendance at Trowan, but Gabriel
was anxious to hear the Chelsea news at first hand. "Dear Dunn" was
required to report in person, and William went to Euston to see him safely
aboard the train.

To share Gabriel's wanderings up and down the country was no new
experience for Harry. Four years earlier, when Gabriel's eyes were giving
him trouble, he was his companion on a tour of Stratford-on-Avon,
Warwick and Kenilworth.

By the second week in September Gabriel, though still difficult to
manage, was considerably better and had begun to think seriously about
work. A letter from Dunn to William shows how Harry and young Hake

had to use great tact. Certain topics were to be avoided at all costs, and Harry in particular had to be discreet.

Trowan, Crieff
10 Sept '72

My dear Willm.

Thanks for your note of yesterday and list of monies paid on your brother's acct. This I have not yet shown him, altho he is very curious on that matter & has asked me several times since I came here what tradespeople have been paid. Brass, F. & Dickinson & one or two others he hoped had had nothing given to them as he said they had good instalments in the early part of the year. I think I'll get you if you will to write me another letter & say nothing but what I may show to him because if I show him the list of payments he will be sure to want to see your letter accompanying it.

I have had several long talks with him about home matters, on the house & Wilding question especially. The last time anything was said about the house he declared it to be nonsense for him to be anywhere but in his own studio if he was to paint. He then talked some nonsense about taking down some partition in the room & discovering the whole paraphernalia of machinery wh. had been erected for his special annoyance. I told him if he was going back to Chelsea to throw away his money over such mad ideas he had far better take a house somewhere else.

Rossetti is most anxious to set to work upon some important picture ("The Desdemona") & for that purpose is meditating a move to Kelmscott. Geo. has spent a day in damning & cursing Bradshaw. Of course both you, I and all else will think this move to Kelmscott the worst that could be made but I don't see what can be done to prevent it.

Of work I find a fair amount done & altho he declares it give him not the slightest pleasure yet he is very eager to be at something. "The Beatrice" had been got out of the mucky state in which it was, & now looks a very good copy. I have suggested one or two things whi will improve it in whi he concurs. The predella is now occupying his attention in order that Ford & D. may have the order for its construction as early as possible. I am making a drawing of the frame for them to work from. Such work as this is the only thing I can do, for the weather is of the most melancholy description. It is a continual downpour & entirely prevents my making any outdoor studies.

The scenery & walks about here are most delightful if one could only get decent weather. All the trees are in the finest state of rich green with no signs of turning as yet. The hills from several places on our walks look exceedingly grand & imposing & as far as that goes R. himself says it is very beautiful & much more interesting than that of Urrard or Stobhall. To pass the evenings away we have [a] goodly lot of Books & he likes particularly to be read to. So we get a curious jumble of the Arabian Nights tales & Haydon's lectures on Painting, with a flavour of "All the Year round" or any other work that may accidentally turn up.

Geo & I have to wade thro the atrocious lies of the Arabian Nights by turns every evening until he feels sufficiently tired to go to bed. Rossetti of his own request is having his doses of whisky gradually diminished also the chloral & Geo who sleeps in his room says that 6 nights out of the 7 he gets an average of 6 hours sleep. The 7th night is sometimes bad, & then he declares that he gets no rest. His own statements on these things I find are not to be relied.

He describes his appetite to be of the most coy & delicate description but you would alter your opinion if you saw how he tucks into his meals. We get a most liberal supply of game from Graham so that our meals, in a savage sort of a way are eatable, but there is an entire absence of vegetables whi make them somewhat monotonous. Crieff is one of those miserably squalid towns that one fortunately hears of oftener than meets. You can get hardly anything in it except bad tobacco.

So far my experience of Scotland has been dismal. It commenced as soon as we crossed the border, a heavy London fog seemed to hang like a pall over hill & valley & a raw chillness took the place of the warmth that we had in Town. The 3 men who got in my carriage at Euston Station went all the way to Carstairs whi is beyond Carlisle. They apologised for their rudeness, said they thought you & several others were all going to get in whi alarmed them. Whisky passed around, they fell to playing Blind Hookey or some such ununderstandable game & by & by went off each into a heavy sleep. I had no such luck & continually found the train stopping at the most dreary stations where there was nothing to be had or done. I think to myself this will have to [be] gone thro' again & sigh. I have not space now for much more & so must finish up at once. With kind remembrances for Miss Maria.

I am, Yours truly,
H. T. DUNN.

The move to Kelmscott Manor which had filled Gabriel's two friends with so much misgiving, took place almost at once. He loved the picturesque old place, with its gables, its thick walls and mullions. William Morris had discovered the house in the spring of 1871, and he and Rossetti decided to rent it between them. Almost immediately Morris had gone to Iceland to study the source of the sagas. A few days after Morris's departure, Gabriel was installed in the old house in Oxfordshire by the Thames. "The loveliest place in existence" was how he described it. Kelmscott was secluded and romantic, and neither he nor Janey nor the absent William were the least concerned that there was no town nearer than Lechlade, and that domestic supplies had to be brought from Faringdon.

Gabriel had stayed there for several months: and, remembering how happy he had been there, was determined to return. It was impossible, he believed, to do good work in the Scottish fastness prescribed by Dr. Hake. In Kelmscott lay the cure. "What a Heaven seems to surround me here," he wrote to Madox Brown from Kelmscott, "after the hateful jumble of Scotch crags and brakes."

He was to stay there nearly two years, engrossed in some of his finest work, notably the magnificent "Proserpine". It was during this period that Harry Dunn was left in command of operations at Cheyne Walk, coping with problems, human and economic, and at the receiving end of a torrent of despatches and instructions from the Master.

In Gabriel's absence the battle with Fanny was now joined openly and without equivocation on either side. Already, during Rossetti's first visit to Kelmscott, in 1871, there had been the sad and tangled affair of the fawn. Was it, indeed, a fawn at all—or just a joint of venison? Gabriel wrote of it as the "poor fawn". Paull Franklin Baum, editor of the invaluable *Letters to Fanny*, takes Gabriel's description at its face value. It was a fawn so far as he was concerned. But in the light of what happened, it is much more likely that the "fawn"—Fanny's present which went astray—was a well-intentioned gift intended for the table rather than the menagerie.

The affair led to a famous breach between Fanny and Dunn, who were in uneasy possession at Cheyne Walk. It would, in any event, have been miraculous had nothing occurred to bring their mutual distrust into the open.

Fanny had the notion that Gabriel, down in the dumps, was languishing in some forsaken spot, miles from anywhere, and feeling lonely. She would cheer him up by buying him a present. With her city background it was impossible for Fanny to visualise the country as anything but an interminable acreage of emptiness and boredom.

Not long before—while William Graham had been dining at Cheyne Walk—there had been some talk of adding a fawn to the menagerie, and it would have been amusing to believe that Fanny had really bought him such a beast. (Graham was a wealthy Scottish M.P. a great admirer of Gabriel's work, and was described by him in one of his many letters to Dunn as "the only buyer I have who is worth a damn".)

It is a pity, but we must take our stand with probability and accept the more mundane explanation. Helen Angeli agrees with me that the "present" which was delivered at Number Sixteen, for transmission to Mr. Rossetti at Kelmscott, was a large joint of venison, not in the best condition.

For Harry the incident could not have happened at a worse moment.

"The place is like a madhouse," he wrote, "Gabriel has ordered the studio to be altered and decorated, and the workmen are constantly tramping in and out."

As if this weren't enough, the front of the house was being painted. Ladders were lashed together in a precarious pattern, and pots of paint swung perilously. There was a good deal of shouting and hammering, and refreshments had to be provided for the men. Less than a hundred yards away a gang of labourers was engaged in building the new Chelsea Embankment.

That morning there had been a *cri de cœur* from Kelmscott. Gabriel was, as usual, in need of money. "Please get enclosed cheque cashed, and send me the notes at once by registered letter." There had also arrived what Gabriel contemptuously referred to as "a tax paper" and this, too, had to be sent to Kelmscott. Gabriel's characteristic reaction was "there seems to be no necessity of paying it at this moment, as it seems to be the first".

It was necessary also to break the news that a parrot, purchased on the strength of its being a keen conversationalist, had not yet uttered a single intelligible word. To make matters worse, the long-suffering art-assistant was well in arrears with his own work and he seemed to spend hours every day answering enquiries from friends and business callers unaware of his employer's absence, and all with some problem which, so it would appear, only Gabriel in person could solve to their satisfaction.

It was at such a moment that the bulky parcel was delivered to Harry. There was nothing to suggest to him that Fanny, busy about her own affairs, had the remotest connection with the evil-smelling object. The man who left it at the front door had clearly been glad to be rid of such a burden, and with a triumph of under-statement had remarked that "whatever it was seemed to be in a pretty bad way". Graham had been sending presents of salmon and game from Scotland and Harry assumed that this was one more kind gift which had been just a little too long in transit. Certainly it was in no condition to be forwarded to Oxfordshire. There was only one thing to be done. Harry buried the thing in the garden. Best not make too much of it, he thought. In the next despatch to Kelmscott he would briefly outline what had happened, hoping that the incident would soon be forgotten. He reckoned without the compulsion which made Gabriel write his gossipy letters to Fanny—to keep her happy or just from sheer good nature, for he hated to think of her fretting in his absence. Dunn's hopes that in some way the story might be glossed over were all too optimistic.

Having read Harry's account of the incident, Gabriel either misconstrued it or, which is more likely, decided to gloss over the affair on the peace-with-Fanny-at-any-price principle.

From Kelmscott (in September 1871) Gabriel wrote to Fanny:

> Dunn has told me something about which you must not be angry. It seems that poor fawn that Graham sent was in such a state as not to be worth the expense of sending on here, but that you, like a funny old chumpwump, would have it sent, so it was buried in the garden on the sly and you were never told of it, and I was told to say that I'd enjoyed it vastly. So there is the whole story, you good old thing, and you must not be angry with Dunn or with me.

Then the tempest broke. Sweeping into the house with thunder on her massive brow Fanny confronted Dunn with this latest example of villainy. How dare he not send her present to Gabriel? It had been in perfect condition when she had bought it. Could he not have given her credit for such a tender thought? What cheek! Why, in any event, was she not consulted? The whole thing was callous and outrageous and just what might be expected from Mr. Busy-body-Dunn.

Furiously she took up her pen and wrote one of her mis-spelt and unpunctuated letters to Kelmscott. As he read these outpourings Gabriel must have thought himself well out of it, but even at a distance he was anxious to keep the peace between the two people on whom he relied so much.

"Your poor dear letter has almost made me cry", he wrote to Fanny in reply. The letter had come, he said with affectionate guile, at a time when he happened to feel in very low spirits. The last thing he wanted was for Fanny suddenly to turn up at Kelmscott—where with Janey Morris's companionship he was more contented than Fanny guessed.

"I cannot tell you how grieved I feel", he went on, "to think that your affectionate remembrance of me in sending the poor fawn should only have brought you disappointment and vexation. I wish I was with you at this moment, poor kind Fan, to kiss you and tell you how much I feel about it."

Of course, he went on, he had no idea that the fawn was from her, but thought it came from Graham. Otherwise he would have written "much more seriously" about it in his last letter to her.

"I cannot understand how opinions should differ so as to its condition, as Dunn assured me it was so far gone as to render it no use at all to send it on. I am not surprised at your great annoyance at his conduct, and can only beg you to overlook it, as no doubt he did for the best as far as he thought, and I believe he was under the impression certainly that the fawn came from Graham." He was sure Dunn had the most friendly feelings towards her and deserved to be pardoned for "this over-sight".

Gabriel added a postscript to this story when he wrote: "It seems poor Dunn is going to Croydon—I suppose with the intention of flying from your wrath."

As for Harry, enough was enough.

It was one thing to gaze raptly on the pictures for which Fanny had been the lovely model years ago. Unluckily for him, he had not known Fanny when she posed as "Fazio's Mistress". Was it possible to identify the overpowering Mrs. Hughes with "Fair Rosamund", coral and amber necklaces round her throat and a rose in her bright hair? What had she to do with the magic which thrilled him in "Lady Lilith"? Of course, Harry thought rather cattily, she had been a big woman even then—all curves and splendour and enchantment.

From what he could see now she was portly, viewed from any angle, and likely to become more so. He agreed whole-heartedly with Hunt's description of Gabriel's model and mistress as "the large-throated, dis-agreeable woman he painted so much". Her figure, now more than ample, mocked those idealised figures on the Rossetti canvases. No, the Fanny of 1871 was coarse, unfeeling, and he didn't like her.

Petulantly, Harry wondered what on earth Gabriel saw in her these days. Then, with the self-mockery which was one of his more endearing characteristics, "poor Dunn" smiled. "The truth is, she scares me to death", he told himself. "I suppose it's because she's big enough to eat me alive." Which was the reason, of course, why he had crept upstairs, packed a few necessaries and fled to Croydon.

It was one of those times when it was wiser to make himself scarce. He would be back again in a week or two when the affair had blown over and Gabriel was his old self again. Perhaps by that time the parrot Still-man had brought would have found his voice and would be chattering away nineteen to the dozen.

In a little more than two weeks Dunn brought his self-imposed exile in Croydon to an end. As always, he had missed Chelsea, the jetties, the sailing boats, the splendid variety of cosy taverns. While in Croydon, Dunn carried out a small commission which Howell had obtained for him, and took his sketch-book into the Surrey hills. The change had served to clear his mind of thoughts about the tussle with Fanny. She wasn't called "The Elephant" for nothing, he reflected wryly. She was quite capable of trampling over him for a start. Stretched at full-length in a meadow near Selsdon Park he mused about the odd menage at Cheyne Walk. What on earth had he got himself into?

Of course, it was rough on Gabriel that the organisation (he smiled at the word) of his home should be entrusted to such unlikely individuals as Fanny and himself. He did his best, and had made some reforms: but it seemed to have been ordained that the affairs at Cheyne Walk should invariably be in a muddle, that the servants would always be troublesome, and that Gabriel, highly paid as he was, would always be short of "tin". This was a chronic condition. In no circumstances could he see himself getting on any better with Fanny. An armed truce was the best that could be hoped for. He sighed and resolved as far as lay in his power to do better in the future—and that evening he would be back in his own bedroom at Number Sixteen.

Harry was still young enough for his heart to give a little flap of pleasure as he caught sight of the house, with its simple elegance, looking very smart now that the painters had finished their task. He wondered how long the firm in question would have to wait for its money. Here was one more extravagance for which cash would have to be found. There was a pile of letters on a table in the hall, but he wouldn't read them yet. He noticed there were several from Kelmscott. Gabriel had known, of course, that he would return—to deal with problems all too vaguely explained. The letters would be querulous and affectionate by turn.

He strolled towards the old wooden bridge at Battersea, with its iron railings, the carriage road and the raised footpath on either side. He knew it wasn't as sturdy as it looked, and there was talk of strengthening the foundations and altering the structure. That would be a pity, he thought —just as it was a pity that the new Embankment would change the whole picturesque character of the river bank. The great stone barriers would destroy the intimacy of a picture which had been familiar to Londoners for centuries. It was highly inconvenient when at times the streets and the lower parts of the houses in the vicinity were flooded, but how pleasant it was to stroll on a fine evening by the river's edge under the tall trees.

"Yes, I do think of Cheyne Walk as home at last", he told himself. Harry turned into the Old Swan. It was a shame that the old place must go to make way for the Embankment. But it was agreeable for the time being at any rate to stand on the terrace and reflect that Mr. Pepys had sampled the liquor at the Swan and found it good.

Fanny was as difficult as ever with the servants. They seemed to feel a resentment towards her, due probably as much to her equivocal position in the house as to her peremptory manner. Money, as usual, was short. There were endless instructions from Gabriel. Agents must be interviewed, explanations given as to why this or that commission was unfinished. Harry Dunn, by trial and error, and with naïveté diminishing, came to learn something of the unorthodox principles governing the business affairs of a successful artist. Hints had to be slipped into conversations. There were matters which were to be told to one acquaintance and kept secret from another. If Howell kept out of the way for a while there must be some sinister reason.

Fanny, who regarded herself as being Gabriel's most important model, was showing jealousy of anyone else for whom he showed partiality. One of these was the delectable Alexa Wilding. William Michael described her—and one can detect the note of relief as "a damsel of respectable parentage".

There is no evidence to suggest that Dunn was less susceptible than most young men. He never married, but he had a number of women friends. None made such an impression upon him as did Alexa Wilding —who was always Alice to him. Very soon after Harry's arrival at Cheyne Walk he was seeing a great deal of Alice, who often posed for Gabriel and was the model for a succession of pictures and chalk drawings. If ever Harry was in love with any woman it was with Alice Wilding, and he wrote lyrically:

Hers was a lovely face, beautifully moulded in every feature, full of a quiescent, soft, mystical repose that suited some of his conceptions admirably, but without any variety of expression. She sat like the Sphinx waiting to be questioned and with always a vague reply in return; about the last girl one would think to have the makings of an actress in her; and yet to be that was her ambition. But she had a deep well of affection within her seemingly placid exterior. She was one of the few who journeyed down to Birchington-on-Sea when she could ill-afford it so that she might place a wreath on Rossetti's grave.

Gabriel told Harry the story of how he met Alice and of how he nearly lost her. It seems that one summer evening Gabriel was walking quietly along the Strand on his way to the Arundel Club. He suddenly noticed a young girl who was hurrying by. With her beautiful face and golden auburn hair she undoubtedly qualified as "a stunner". In the busy crowd which thronged the pavement Gabriel found it difficult to catch up with her but at last she turned down a narrow street and he was able to over-take her. "With some amount of nervousness" Gabriel explained that he was an artist and that he was engaged in painting a picture for which she would prove an ideal model. Would she come to his studio and sit for him? She would, of course, be paid for her services. It is not difficult to imagine how the girl felt when a dark, striking-looking man followed her impetuously and accosted her. "At first", says Harry rather naïvely, "she did not seem to understand the nature of his request, but at last she gave a sort of consent and left him with a promise to call on the morrow at the studio."

Gabriel, excited by having made such a capture, waited expectantly with the intention of making a study of her head for "The Blessed Damozel".

"His palette was set, the canvas on the easel and everything in readiness: but she never came. This was a terrible disappointment to him." When weeks went by and there was no sign of Alice, Gabriel gave up any hope of seeing the girl again, and the picture was neglected. But driving down the Strand in a hansom with Howell as his companion Gabriel caught another glimpse of her. He stopped the cab and this time made no mistake. He caught her by the arm, and gently but persuasively led her back to the hansom, determined that rather than risk losing her again he would drive her back with him to Cheyne Walk. As a postscript Harry adds:

> To the poor simple girl an artist's studio was a revelation. She had never heard of such a thing before, and to find that by simply sitting still in a com-fortable room she could earn more money than a week's work at her ordinary occupation of dress-making would bring was a great surprise to her. With very little persuasion she gave up her situation and at a liberal arrangement sat to him entirely....

The "liberal arrangement" was a retainer of thirty shillings a week.

Dunn, with his quick sympathy and easy manners, got on well with most of Gabriel's models and nearly all his servants, and Alice was no exception. A number of times he escorted her to Kelmscott—in fact, he was expected to act as cavalier to several of the beautiful girls who figured in the Rossetti paintings of that period.

These jaunts to Oxfordshire filled Fanny with fury, a fury none the less fierce because she knew there was nothing to be done about it. She hated the idea of any other woman going to Kelmscott while she, for obvious reasons, was unwelcome in Janey Morris's home. Gabriel made it quite clear that he didn't wish her to visit him while he was with the Morrises. When, stung to action, Fanny threatened to descend on him, he wrote firmly: "I am sorry to disappoint you, indeed it gives me great pain to do so, as I should like to see you here, but the thing is quite impossible. Please don't ever press the matter again, as it is very distressing to me to refuse, but as long as I remain here it is out of the question." And that was that.

As Harry could appreciate even more clearly than those who had known her in the days when she held undisputed sway, Fanny was now entering a period of eclipse so far as her reign as the chief model was concerned. That reign had lasted the best part of ten years. As Dunn's now permanent position as secretary-companion came to be accepted, Fanny's place was being taken professionally by Alice and more potently by Janey Morris, though Mrs. Stillman was still retained. For all their quarrels, Harry could not find it in his heart to blame Fanny for resenting rivals who still had youth and good looks.

Most people thought Alexa Wilding the loveliest of all Rossetti's models. The justice of this is clear enough in the painting "Sibylla Palmifera", a title Gabriel chose, he said, "to mark the leading place which I intend her to hold among my beauties". It was out of the question that others should be allowed to share this pearl and Dunn was hardly surprised when Gabriel decided to establish his prior claim by paying Alice a retaining fee—another weekly drain on the shaky economy. Gabriel painted her in "La Ghirlandata" and in "Monna Vanna". She was to be his model for "Veronica Veronese", "The Blessed Damozel" and the "Sea-Spell". Then it was Alice's face which was painted over Fanny's in the celebrated "Lilith" picture—and this must have seemed the crowning insult.

As the squire of Alice and other "damsels" Dunn came in for more than his share of Fanny's venom. If, bound for Kelmscott, he wasn't marching Alice Wilding off to Paddington Station, then his companion was some other interloper—like the model for "Ligeia Siren". This was originally a nude, but public taste was passing through a phase when the undraped figure was considered offensive and in deference to this and with tongue in cheek, Gabriel clothed the figure and decorum was satisfied.

It was from Kelmscott there arrived the first of a long series of letters to Henry Treffry Dunn, letters which passed to the late Mrs. Clara Watts-Dunton and which since her death have been in the keeping of the Victoria and Albert Museum. The first of these is dated 22 February 1872. Rossetti was concentrating on "Proserpine", a picture which gave him immense trouble. (It is said that beside the large number of studies, he started at least seven Proserpines on canvas before the final picture was completed to his satisfaction.)

14

The following letters throw new light on a peaceful and productive period in Rossetti's career. At Kelmscott for the best part of two years he found personal happiness, and pleasure in his work.

The constant flow of comment and instructions and queries show what an invaluable part Harry played in Rossetti's life. "No-one can cut my chalk like Dunn", he wrote, but it is clear from the letters that the Cornishman's duties far exceeded those of a studio-assistant. At Kelmscott, for the first time in many dark and troubled months, life seemed to hold out to Rossetti a promise of contentment and security. He was full of plans for the future. Howell, now in partnership with a Mr. John R. Parsons, was acting as his agent—with considerable success. He was out of debt, and after a few months in his Oxfordshire retreat, Gabriel was able to remark with optimism: "I shall soon be much better stocked with tin than is my wont."

While still at the farmhouse near Crieff, Gabriel was already making plans, and Harry, on his instructions, had worked on the background for a picture to be called "Monna Primavera" (later to be re-named "The Daydream"). He very sensibly determined to complete a number of unfinished paintings which were still lying in the studio at Cheyne Walk.

The Rossetti–Dunn correspondence from Kelmscott deals with the day-to-day problems of a busy artist—points of technical detail, requests for materials, the prices to be asked for pictures, the engagement of models, and a never-ending list of chores to be carried out in London by "My Dear Dunn". From the letters there emerges an absorbing picture of an artist at work. The daily exasperations of a painter's life, his impatience with business matters, the colloquial expressions, the flashes of humour, all give these pages a charm of their own.

The first letter, written before Rossetti's illness and attempted suicide, refers to an early "Proserpine" (for which Janey Morris was the model and which depicts the wife of Pluto, doomed to remain imprisoned in the dark Kingdom).

Rossetti's use of the word "copy" is of special interest as applied to Dunn. There has been much controversy as to how much a nineteenth-century studio-assistant did "copy". Clearly, an artist of Rossetti's reputation and integrity would never countenance copying on a substantial scale, but it is obvious that Dunn's work was not limited to cleaning palettes and preparing canvases.

KELMSCOTT
22nd February 1872

My dear Dunn,

This blessed business with Parsons has now been wound up through Howell, who has received in return for my cheque, the Proserpine picture and the negatives from my drawings, etc. Of course Howell has 100 good reasons why these should all remain in his hands at present, so let him keep them. However, I shall get the Proserpine sent down here before long, as I wish to add to it some accessories which appeared in the other version and which would make it much more attractive and saleable. I expect now before the end of next week probably to be sending for Alice W[ilding]. Do you think you could accompany her here, and stay for a few days, bringing the Proserpine in the cab, and copy these accessories into it from the other picture which is here? I have painted these twice—in Leyland's version and in the one remaining here with me—and don't feel up to doing them a third time.

Ever yours,
D. G. R.

In the eight months which elapsed between this letter and the one which now follows, Gabriel had survived a desperate period of physical and mental breakdown. Anxiously, and with great solicitude, his friends had nursed him back to health. There had been the recuperating sojourn in Scotland, and now he was at Kelmscott, a new man. However, there is little in the letters to Dunn to show that once more Rossetti had a healthy grip on his affairs and was enthusiastically bent on doing the best work it was in his power to achieve. Many of his letters are undated. Sometimes he gives only the day of the week and the year. It was a habit for which his mother chided him, and which has exasperated the entire company of biographers. The letters here quoted are in the order favoured by Mrs. Watts-Dunton.

KELMSCOTT
Friday, November 1872

My dear Dunn,

I have sent the rent by this post and told him to send receipt to Chelsea. So please let me know on getting it.

I never said Leyland had not written. On the contrary, he has written very unsatisfactorily, and seems disposed to evade several commissions given only I fear by word of mouth, and to limit himself to a very small proportion of the work he had asked me to do for him.

Of course you need not mention this at present. I have not yet answered him.

I can hear nothing of Howell whom I wished to see, and am quite irritated by his unaccountable silence whenever one asks for an answer without delay.

I shall be sending Parsons Proserpine to him in a few days.

I am getting on rapidly with the new one, which will be a finer picture than the first and will be very speedily completed, needing no work from nature. You need not mention this copy as there might be some jealousy on Parsons part, though unnecessarily, as I should dispose of it in circles not open to him. No doubt you will proceed with due caution about Dr. H.

I have got a note from Alice W. saying she may not be well enough to come for 2 or 3 weeks! This may prove most inconvenient. Would you kindly look her up and see how she really is.

Ever yours,

D. G. R.

In the same month Gabriel was writing to his brother (on the 25th): "By the bye, I suppose you know that F. has got rid of her incubus just lately?" The words seem almost too casual, since he was to feel that his responsibilities to Fanny were even more pressing.

When on that bleak November day Fanny appeared clad from head to toe in the raiment of mourning, Harry Dunn's heart missed a beat. If what he suspected were true, then his own position would be weakened—at any rate, while everyone became accustomed to Fanny's new condition.

Her first words confirmed his suspicions.

"Mr. Hughes has gone to his rest," Fanny announced, eyeing him with the queerest mixture of propriety and satisfaction. She was dry-eyed.

Harry stammered a few appropriate words and took the hand which was extended to him with such an unexpectedly regal gesture.

"There's a lot to be done, and I shan't be round for a day or two—not until after they've buried 'im, anyway." Then she looked round with the air of ownership he knew, and uttered the words he'd dreaded: "Mr. Rossetti'll be terribly cut up when 'e 'ears about it. But it'll mean I'll be able to spend a bit more time keeping this place as it ought to be kept."

And with an air of subdued and sorrowful triumph, Mrs. Hughes, brave and bereaved, swept from his presence. At last Fanny had acquired dignity and importance. She was a widow.

He reflected on the passing of Timothy Hughes and felt that at last

11. The panels on this Jacobean cupboard, now in the possession of Lady
Mander, of Wightwick Manor, were painted by Henry Treffry Dunn.

12. Swinburne's folding bed—anot!
of the Wightwick Manor treasu:
The panels were painted by He:
Treffry Dunn.

13. Members of the Rossetti circle were models for some of the figures on the
Jacobean cupboard. Swinburne is St. George. William Morris holds aloft the
dragon's head, flanked by Millais and Ruskin.

Fanny's "old man" had done something which was deserving of congratulation: he had taken himself out of Fanny's range. Henceforward he would be remembered, if not with a tear, then at least with the negative tribute—"He was his own worst enemy." Gabriel, no doubt, would now be kinder to Fanny and, generally, things would be more hazardous for Harry.

"Am I an art-assistant or an assistant-housekeeper?" he asked himself, not for the first time.

Hughes was well out of it. Nobody had had a good word for him, least of all the woman he had made his wife. He remains a shadowy, seedy figure in the tale, and Fanny had probably led him the devil of a life.

Harry had seen him infrequently: and speculated on the reasons why a "stunner" like Fanny should have married a "mechanic". The term may have meant that Hughes was an engineer of sorts: he had also been a porter known to the young men who studied at the Academy Schools. Dunn tried to visualise romantic meetings between Fanny and her Timothy, but any possible fragrance there might have been eluded him.

From the evidence it was hard to credit the late Mr. Hughes with any worthy qualities at all. Later, in one of her rare moments when the barriers were down between them, Fanny was to tell Dunn: "Mr. Hughes was a fine looking man when he was young. I suppose you know he sat for Mr. Rossetti and he's in some of his pictures?"

Well there might, Dunn supposed, be some truth in this. From enquiries he made later it did seem possible, as Fanny claimed, that Hughes had been the model for the figure of David in the triptych Gabriel had painted for Llandaff Cathedral. This had been commissioned in 1856, so Gabriel may have known Hughes before Fanny did, and she may even have met Hughes through Gabriel: though this would seem to carry irony too far.

Anyhow, Fanny and Timothy had been united at St. John's Church, Waterloo, on 11 August 1860.

While in Perthshire, Gabriel found time in his own illness, to fret about Fanny's health. She had been complaining of rheumatism, and Gabriel was worried about whether she had enough good food to eat. He agreed with his brother William and with Brown that he should find "a quiet lodger" in the house he had found for her in Royal Avenue, Chelsea.

His feelings towards the ageing Fanny, baffling as they sometimes appear, are endearing, too. The middle-aged protector writes to his

K

middle-aged mistress: "As for myself, you are the only person whom it is my duty to provide for, and you may be sure I should do my utmost as long as there was a breath in my body or a penny in my purse."

These are more like the words of a lover still young enough to write ballads to his mistress' eyebrow. At one point, it seemed to him highly probable that Fanny's creditors might descend on Fanny's humble dwelling and seize her furniture. Or Hughes, while in liquor, might suddenly go berserk, break up the home in a drunken frenzy. To safeguard Fanny's belongings Gabriel made William a "gift" of the furniture in the house (so that it could not be taken in payment of her debts) and tried also to persuade his brother to rent Fanny's house for Gabriel, but in William's own name. William was not taking on any such responsibility. Then came the tidings that Timothy Hughes was dead.

As might be expected, Dunn's fears were realised. Death, as usual, changed much. In his lifetime no-one had credited Hughes with any action which could be construed as caring for his wife. For reasons of character or fact, he had ignored his responsibilities: now, Fanny was a lonely widow, bereft of marital support. When, after the remains of Timothy Hughes had been disposed of, Fanny arrived at Number Sixteen, Dunn thought he detected a new and proprietorial air about Timothy's relict. He held her eye for a moment longer than usual. He didn't like what he saw there.

KELMSCOTT Thursday.

Dear Dunn,

Alice W. writes that she cannot come till after Tuesday. She doesn't say why. I now write her that I will expect her Tuesday if possible or else Wednesday, and that she is to let you know which day she is coming, and that you purpose to accompany her. Also that you will pay her railway fare, etc.

I am glad to hear of your successful decorative work. If it pays well, I should in your place at once make H. and M. take you into partnership in future efforts.

I explained (which you seem to have overlooked) that Howell tells me he is sending the Proserpine here, so here you will find it, I suppose.

Ever yours,

D. G. R.

Howell seems sulky about my proposal to write personally to Marks, so I tell him that if I don't he must see at once himself what Marks can do.

Monday

My dear Dunn,

Having broken off yesterday, I am only too happy to give myself the lie today as to the weather. It is very fine now, and the glass still going up seems to promise continuance.

I hope you have benefited in health by your change. I have certainly done so now, though at first I perceived no great change. I am quite uncertain as to how long I may stay here, but inclined to believe that I am not at all likely to be moving homewards for some time. This, however, is all doubtful.

I am afraid the house expenses are going the old way and have serious thoughts of looking into weekly accounts myself. Can you give me any idea as to what you consider should have been the weekly total for the household here? For the first fortnight, we were only three—George, Watts and self— then Alice W. and Dr. Hake were added, making five—then Watts and the Dr went away and my mother and sister came. Thus we have been five since the first fortnight till now.

I found the other day accidentally to my disgust that a charwoman had been employed almost from the first till a day or two ago when I routed her out and Mrs. Garlicks' explanation was quite unsatisfactory. Surely three servants should be enough in this quiet household? What do you think on the whole ought to be the weekly total?

It is getting horribly cold here. I don't know that there is anything else to say, and I am somewhat hurried,

Ever yours,

D. G. R.

Monday

My dear Dunn,

I got a letter today from Fanny who I find knows all about the H. and Fry business, as to the exchanged cheque, etc. I write to her with this, to take care and open her mouth to *no-one*, else I may be greatly inconvenienced. You did not tell me whether Leyland sent for his pictures or not. Please let me know.

Have you got back from Mincott at any time those white endless papers he sent here and strainers and which I returned. If there is an old case and they could be sent inexpensively (not passenger train or any expense more than can be helped) they might come on, as I am something short of papers for rougher work. If he has not sent them back, never mind.

You never told me how Brass's charge of £28. odd at Xmas was to be accounted for. We paid up all his long old bill. Is this all packing? Good God!

Ever yours, D. G. R.

P.S. I really think you ought to be cautious as to seeing Howell at all. You know his daring tactics, and the difficulty you might have in keeping up the appearance of ignorance with points in question. I thought it necessary to let you know how matters stood, but should not think of mentioning them beyond the circle of my own studio. It will be most necessary also to keep Sandys quite in the dark as to what we know. I do hope you let nothing out to him or anyone else. It should not be mentioned at present even to Watts. I want to see him and talk it over.

Murray Marks was a well-known London agent whom Rossetti regarded as a friend as well as a man of business. Marks gave practical help when "tin" was short, and helped to assemble the collection of "Blue" china. On his part, Rossetti gave Marks some valuable introductions.

The "theft" mentioned in the next letter was one of many objects of all kinds which were often "missing" during Gabriel's tenancy of Cheyne Walk. This was hardly to be wondered at in a big house in which the servants entertained their friends, cash was left in an open drawer and articles of value were carelessly left about the place. Howell was known to remove items to which he took a fancy—although his "borrowings" could never justify the word theft. Fanny might occasionally take articles to wear, or perhaps to sell when more than usually hard up, but she took the view that she was too much a member of the family for such a habit to be regarded as stealing.

                                                    KELMSCOTT Wednesday.
Dear Dunn,

   You probably know now that I have written to Watts and heard from him in reply about the theft. Mrs. M's idea that it occurred in this house is *quite impossible*, for reasons I need not dilate on to save time. Remember always that Mrs. Morris did *not* pack the hamper—it was her servant Sarah who did so. Thus there can be no need of her being called as a witness, nor myself either, who was not present when Philip unpacked. So please *recollect* this, as otherwise trouble might be caused. Of course, neither she nor I can personally be incommoded in the matter. If that were needed, it must be dropped.

   A little early Italian picture has been sent here. I know not whence or why. It is a Resurrection—fine colour and interesting. I suppose you know nothing of it? For background of this Roman Widow I shall be wanting some lightish *green* marble. I don't suppose it would be easy to pick up such, but you might *at convenience* look in at the artificial marble works in Pimlico and see if they make anything of the sort. I mean in Pilgrim Place—Jones's, I think. Verde Antique which is dark wouldn't do. It would have to be a green tint about the depth of the grey you sent.

   The young Robertson in question is no doubt the man. What has his success been? No hurry about the crockery—suit your convenience.

                                                    Ever yours,
                                                         D. G. R.

                                                    KELMSCOTT 187?
                                                         Wednesday.
Dear Dunn,

   I can't at all make out about the copy of my Poems you sent being the only one at Chelsea. There certainly *was* a later edition there. Who can have taken it? I have got the carving and the wing has been of great use to me, enabling me to complete the painting. I enclose a sketch for the binding of my new Book, but it needs enlarging to the full size of the cover which is that of the thin bit of paper enclosed. Would you enlarge it for me to this size, copying it *exactly* in *pencil only* at first, then send it to me and I would suggest any modifications. It must cover the surface as much towards the various edges and corners as the sketch does, and as far as possible bear the same relation in every way to the space. I suppose this can be managed by increasing the spaces equally everywhere. After I have seen it in pencil, I shall probably get you to draw it in pen and ink.

There is another thing I want—to wit, a dragon-fly or two to paint in my picture, you know they are quite blue and I want one with his wings spread upwards as they do when they fly or sometimes when they stand. You might, if possible, get me 2 or 3 set up in different positions. I am wanting them as soon as possible. Also you might get me a few blue or blue-grey butterflies. These also to be set up in action flying or resting. Are there any of Miles Halliday's remaining and suitable? I used to have a lot in a flat box which he gave me. Also you might send me at the same time that little blue bird there is at Chelsea. Will you try and let me have all as soon as may be and safely packed.

I wrote to Graham yesterday about the big picture. The one I am doing for him now is not Blessed Damozel but that figure playing on the queer old harp which I drew from Miss W. when you were here with her. The two heads of little May are at the top of the picture. It will really be a successful thing, I am sure now, and is getting fast towards completion, but I have not yet got the frame. It ought to put Graham in a good humour and I am glad he is to have it as he is the only buyer I have who is worth a damn.

I am glad Brown is getting on well with his Cromwell which I think promised to be a vast deal better than any of his latter things—in fact, the best perhaps he ever did. The painting is all clear and masterly as far as I saw it.

You don't tell me what you are doing yourself, nor does George seem to have seen any picture of your own you may be doing.

Ever yours.

D. G. R.

P.S. I think it might be well if you sent me that reduced chalk drawing you were doing from the big picture. I mean, send it now and so save time when the picture comes, as I would look at it for any suggestions which I could doubtless make from knowledge of the work, and let you have it again before the picture reached you. I should also like at the same time to have a set of photos from an old Flemish missal which are somewhere and which I had from Marks in a little portfolio. Also it might be well to send down when convenient, one of those two book-stands with cupboards underneath which Stennett made—the larger of the 2. Are the spaces below large enough to contain those portfolios of old pencil drawings of mine which are at Chelsea?

(undated)

Dear Dunn,

Thanks for insects, etc. The dragon-fly is not blue—so no use to me. Blue ones abound here—much longer than the one you sent. But do not show except in hot weather. Accordingly they are very scarce this year, but I must try and get one caught if I need it. Meanwhile, I won't trouble you to search further unless I write again, for this or anything. The sketch seems all right unless I alter anything. I will see to it.

I send you an order for the big picture from Graham. Of course F. and D. must be employed to fetch it (perhaps superintended by yourself if you think necessary). I have written to W. and N. for the large easel again, as we must have frame as well as picture, in case I come to town at all and want to show it, as I may possibly do for a few days on completing the Ghirlandata for Graham before sending it to him in Scotland. Do not of course send the Stennett case or anything else till I write again. I must return you some more packing cases. Graham is still desirous to have the smaller Dante's Dream instead of the larger one "if I am likely to complete it in a twelvemonth or so". Thus it will perhaps be best to push on with it as well as maybe. I would like you to get the reduced outline exactly correct first, after which you might proceed to lay in the background in oil, but the whole of the figures would have I think to be done by myself, as well as the colouring throughout, as this would in reality be the quickest plan and meanwhile if then feasible you might go for me to Wales.

Ever yours,

D. G. R.

P.S. I got a letter today from Graham acknowledging with enthusiasm the arrival of Beatrice. I write by return to request tin on account of other work in hand, so I suppose I shall be all right in a day or two.

About clothes for *Found* which I shall be taking up, could you look in second-hand shops? The woman should wear something with a pinkish tinge I suppose, to balance the sky—also a mantle of some sort—pretty showy, but seedyish.

P.P.S. I am looking through proofs of my poems in the Tauchnitz edition, and want the English book here. I think there are 2 copies at Chelsea—one the last edition and the other the penultimate—5th I think. I fancy it is *this* and *not* the last that has pencil corrections in it. Will you send whichever contains these?

Miss Wilding sat for the Ghirlandata of which Rossetti thought lightly. Gabriel wrote to his mother in September 1873: "Little May Morris appears twice in the picture, as a couple of angels." Little May was the younger of the Morris girls, and was then eleven. Jenny was a year older.

Wednesday.

My dear Dunn,

I suppose you had not my last when last writing to me. Mine explained that I need not trouble you further about dragon-flies etc. Also that *nothing nee d be sent on at once*. I thought *I had also* explained that the large picture can be sold at once to Valpy (as Howell tells me) for the same price given by Graham, as soon as the replica is ready for delivery to the latter.

The scale of the drawing you were making is correct. I hope this has not been lost. Is it perhaps in that oak chest in the passage? Or in your room? Or in the lumber room. The replica was I believe to be ½ size nominally—that is, the height of the figures (without question of modified proportion afterwards) would be half the height of the original figures, and the area of the replica would thus I believe be a quarter of the original.

Ever yours,

D. G. R.

By the bye, the enclosed about easel from W. and N. is most awkward. I am writing them again, to press the matter, but if one cannot possibly be got there you would have, I suppose, to try Barbe. I don't think Robertsons keep such heavy easels, do they?

I think it might be very desirable to ask A.W. if she is willing now to see to the mending of the gold thread in that white sacque dress and petticoat, previous to making them up in another form. What house is she moving to? She wrote me that she had given my name as a reference, but I have heard from no-one as yet.

About the sky, it would be I suppose a sort of pink and green in streaks, or anyway characteristic of dawn and having some warmth in it.

KELMSCOTT March 1873

Re "Found"

Dear Dunn,

Please post enclosed. I have always forgotten to ask you to make me, at your earliest convenience, some sketches of skies at dawn for that calf picture, as I am quite determined to take up and finish it this coming winter.

Ever yours.

D. G. R.

Saturday 1873

Dear Dunn,

Will you at your earliest leisure look up Howell? I have been writing and writing to him on matters needing answer, and wished to see him here on business if he could come, but absolute silence is the only result and I can make nothing of it.

Perhaps you have sent that Davis drawing to Brown, but if not, please send it with a frame you will find about (either in china room or passage I suppose) the sight measure is 24¼ and 23¼. It has a black bead outside and a gilt moulding inside. Whether it fits the drawing or not, please send it. If the drawing is sent, however, Brown will probably send for the frame.

Ever yours,

D. G. R.

Brown and wife are coming here Tuesday, so the things should go to him if possible before then.

KELMSCOTT 1873
Sunday.

My dear Dunn,

Thanks for your letter. The chair has not yet appeared, but probably will do so tomorrow. I am in no special hurry for it. Graham has written wanting his Ghirlandata picture. Will you write a line to Ford and Dickinson to fetch it and charge me with expenses when they make out my next account, as it was borrowed by my wish.

I am writing to Graham that you will see to this.

Have you heard anything of Howell? Has a report reached you that he has got into a row with some dealer about a spurious D. Cox and that judicial proceedings are mentioned? Perhaps it is not true?

Give my love to Fan.

Ever yours,

D. G. R.

KELMSCOTT 1873
Sunday

My dear Dunn,

Thanks for all your intelligent care and pains. The things all reached in splendid order. If still time, it might perhaps be better to register the silk gauze, as it is so valuable to me.

I ought to write to that old lady—Mrs. Maenza at Boulogne—but have forgotten her new address. Could you look up a late letter of hers, most probably lying in the basket or else on the desk, and send me her address. Also the other I asked for—Miss C.

I am writing to A.W. to come down on Tuesday evening or Wednesday.

I hope you will enjoy your change in the country. Here the weather has mostly been most unpropitious and as soon as there is one day's glimpse of daylight the darkness and rain recommence on the morrow.

Thanks about the chair. It may certainly be needed. Blue cheque book safe to hand. The only things missing in the packages were the 2 crosspieces of wood you made. However, now that the canvas is being shortened, it is possible I may not need them, or I might recollect enough of their principle to get them made by Charles.

Ever yours, D. G. R.

George says Edmond has notice from him to pay you the £5.

The "blessed picture" of the next letter is one of the various versions of "Proserpine". It was despatched by the frame-maker to Kelmscott, and unaccountably vanished on the way. Another version was badly damaged in transit. No wonder Rossetti was so insistent on adequate packing—even though he grumbled at the bills.

KELMSCOTT Tuesday.

Dear Dunn,

From what you tell me of calls, I suppose I had better send this further cheque. It is difficult to make out from yours enclosed whether F's taxes are £25. or £2. 5/-. I suppose it must be the latter as the former seems impossible. No news of the blessed picture. Today George has been to Lechlade and got the station master to set enquiries on foot—or to say he will do so. It is a pretty go. At any rate, if I have to bring an action to recover damages, I can prove having received 800 guineas for a precisely similar picture from Leyland.

Ever yours,

D. G. R.

P.S. I am writing again to Merritt today. All he has done as yet, it seems, is to enquire at the booking office!—where they say it left them alright on the 4th. I am now urging him to make proper enquiries at Paddington and to follow them up, and should be much obliged to you to spur him on and join in, as I think he seems rather helpless.

KELMSCOTT 1873
Friday.

Dear Dunn,

Here is a little job in the boat and staircase line. I want something with a little design on it to paint as a top for that harp-instrument in the picture I am doing for Miss Wilding. Something like the enclosed might do, if you could cut it quite roughly out in wood. The height of it from tops of heads to points of lower wings should be about 6 inches and the width between the points of the expanded wings about the same. The expanded wings might be slightly hollowed I think. The birds to be crested ones perhaps—not so much like ducks—but still good solid headed birds. I suppose the round tops of the folded wings must project sideways as knobs a *little* more than I have made them do, as I perceive in the instrument, a few of the strings seem to be fastened round the corresponding knobs in the awkward ornamentation at the top. However, the knobs project but little more than the wing-tops in my sketch. I should be glad of this as soon as you could let me have it, as part of the composition of the picture depends on drawing it in.

Thanks about Bd.Dl. Also Dr. H. whose note seems satisfactory.

Ever yours,

D. G. R.

I suppose the wood should be darkened a little and varnished or gummed.

The light-hearted reference by Gabriel to "a little job in the boat and staircase line" reminded Harry of some practical help he had been able to give on an earlier occasion. In addition to his other duties, Harry became carpenter and property-master, and constructed in some detail a model boat from which Rossetti was to paint the vessel in his unfinished picture "The Boat of Love".

> I took a great deal of pains to construct a mediaeval ship or rather open boat for which a book of engravings from the frescoes in the Campo Santo at Pisa was consulted. Rossetti watched the building of this boat with great interest from the laying down of the keel line, the constructing the ribs and planking of the timbered sides and partial deck, to the final little chambered poop set high upon the stern and rudder post. It was built on a very roomy scale but he had so many figures in his design comprising the boating party that it would have been impossible to have crammed them all in with ease and comfort to themselves. . . . Over this boat building I worked down in one of the cellars of the house, a massive brick groined roofed place. It was a very narrow place owing to the thickness of the foundation walls cob-webbed from floor to ceiling and limited in space because of the chaos of disabled iron grates with their projecting dogs for fire irons, lumber of every kind.

"The Boat of Love" was one of the pictures which caused Rossetti endless trouble and was in fact never completed. The other was "Found". "The Boat of Love" never emerged from the stage in which it was a large monochrome in oil.

The "big picture" or the "big daub" was "Dante's Dream": and thanks again to Mrs. Troxell we can read an account of this in Harry Dunn's own words. In the original manuscript of his *Recollections* he writes:

> 1869 opened with a commission from Mr. Graham to paint him a picture of large dimensions, the subject for it to be taken from the *Vita Nuova* of Dante.
> The germ of this largest and most famous legacy left to us by Rossetti was a little watercolour drawing painted as early as 1855 and purchased by Miss Heaton of Leeds who with great readiness let him have it for a time to re-design and make fit for a large seven foot canvas. Graham had but limited room in his house and the utmost space that could be given for this new commission was seven feet and no more and Rossetti's original intention was to adhere to it, but the cartoon which was prepared and perfected ere transferring to canvas seemed to have an india rubber expansive quality about it for it grew and waxed larger until at last it reached ten feet by seven much to Mr. Graham's alarm for he knew it would be impossible to hang it in the place intended for it.

Mrs. Graham, Harry tells us, strongly objected to having the picture in her dining-room. It was accordingly "relegated to the staircase . . . where it hung like Mohamet's coffin midway between Heaven and earth". Eventually, Graham persuaded the artist to take back the original and paint a replica of more manageable proportions. "The task of designing and arranging first one and then the other seemed endless," wrote Harry, "and I despaired almost of seeing either of them finished."

Monday.

Dear Dunn,

Please send me the wood carving *as it is*. I would not on any account give you any further trouble with it. I merely meant the roughest cutting out of the softest wood and that you would do it in a day. As it is, I have been obliged to fill the space in the picture, as I could not do the surrounding parts till this was in. I have concocted something from that bird on the Indian instrument you brought here, but could avail myself of the spread wings in yours if you would send it me.

I must be writing to Graham forthwith and agree with you that it would be well to try and get at the big picture now.

Of course the writing on F's sketch must be sketchy or it will kill the Elephant dead.

About the screen, no doubt my statement as to receipt was correct, but I cannot answer at this distance of time that it may not have been one of those cases when the things have remained at the station awhile before being brought on.

The paper of your letter is of the block I've tried—the horridest of all papers to me. Look at the water mark of this, but the best papers are Whatman's, of which you will find samples in the little sample book of that large stationery place in Garrick-street.

Yours,

D. G. R.

While Alice Wilding was proving more unreliable than ever, Harry was busy dealing with a fusillade of requests from Kelmscott. There were errands to be run, odds and ends to be found or bought, journeys to be made to the bank. He was also busy preparing for the smaller version of "the Graham picture".

In his riverside retreat, the "heaven on earth" about two miles from Radcott Bridge, Gabriel worked on "The Beloved" (or "The Bride") in oils. This, William declared years later, was thought by many experts to be Rossetti's "very best work".

KELMSCOTT 15th March 1873

Dear Dunn,

There is in some drawer at Chelsea a little black Mem. book of above size, new and blank. I bought two, have carried one ever since, and the other must be there. I wish you could find and send it by post. There must be also somewhere a walking stick with knob covered with thongs or basket work of some sort—I wish you'd send me this in next *convenient* parcel.

I am wanting a big showy looking jewel of the diamond kind (or yellowish would do, but I suppose glittering white would be best) to paint in the nigger boys cup in the Beloved. I daresay a theatrical jewel such as you could get for a few shillings in Boro Street would do quite well. It would be nice to have it heart shape, but that might be hard to find. Could you look me up one *at once* and send it. I suppose you and Howell went to poor Allan's funeral.

I suppose I shall immediately be sending for Alice W. now in good earnest to begin a picture from her. Her last account of herself was "ill in bed". Do you know how she is now?

Ever yours,
D. G. R.

P.S. About size of replica (of which I had written him) Graham says "the replica of the 'Dream' will be a very manageable size—5 ft × 3 ft. 6 ins." I have not a very good eye for dimensions but I did rather expect it to be somewhat larger than this. But the fact is I feel quite confused about the size of pictures till I see them actually painted, and I feel quite sure the replica will be all I could wish on whatever size you have scaled it. So we had better go on as we mean to go on, since to do it a larger size would be a new bother of a serious kind.

"Poor Allan" was the ineffectual husband of Emma, a servant, who so often took advantage of Gabriel's tolerance. He had been in the Army and his death was accelerated by a combination of tuberculosis and alcohol. Emma and Allan accompanied their employer during his convalescence at Urrard House in Perthshire and Gabriel reported, with a note of surprise, that the man was behaving himself. With characteristic generosity, Gabriel paid his bills and overlooked his faults: but with the best will in the world it is hard to picture them as likeable or trustworthy.

The way of the tenant is often hard. On balance, Rossetti seems to have had rather more than his share of exasperations so far as Number Sixteen, Cheyne Walk, was concerned. If "the men" were not busy on the face of the building, they were altering the inside of it. Decorators, builders, renovators, carpenters were forever in and out of the place—whether Gabriel was in residence or not. A certain Dr. Hawksley, a neighbour, initiated certain alterations which swept Gabriel and Harry into a fever of protestation.

Harry was expected to present Gabriel's case as being, wrote his employer, "the only person who could speak re the matter".

Sunday

My dear Dunn,

I enclose £5. Shall be sending home the Proserpine this week and then have money. We are already suited with servants here—Mrs. M. having got some in London. The difficulty with Emma seems to continue, and if necessary I shall have to part with her. If F. writes me particulars I will write to Emma if required.

No doubt you will keep a strict eye on Dr. Hawksley.

Watts assures me it is quite out of the estate-architect's power to over-rule my voice in the matter while I hold the lease. I will write to Dr. H. myself if you think it necessary.

I spoke to you in my last about Howell who is becoming quite a mystery to me.

As to Alice W. I shall have to write her a serious letter as soon as I absolutely need her, which will be very shortly.

Ever yours,

D. G. R.

1878.

Dear Dunn,

This Miss H. is the most inquisitive old bore in the world. I enclose an answer which you might copy and send off. When she comes, and bores you with any questions, just don't answer them. As to the ownership of the picture, you can say it belongs to Graham.

About Dr. H. I suppose he can make his balcony if *entirely shut in* at the side next my house—not otherwise.

Ever yours,

D. G. R.

16, Cheyne Walk,
Chelsea,
July 30, 1873

My dear Dr. Hawksley,

I am sorry to again call your attention to the fact that the alterations you are making on your premises are different to the plans you submitted to me. Last week when our experiment respecting diminution of light was made, the elevation of your outbuilding did not come above the top of the second pane of glass in our staircase window which was shown in the sketch sent to Mr. Rossetti (and you assured me it was to go no higher). Today I perceive that it is carried up into nearly two-thirds of the 3rd pane. Now it is very evident that every inch you carry up an erection of this sort, past a certain limit, must be prejudicial to the lighting of our staircase; therefore, on those grounds and in Mr. Rossetti's behalf, I protest against these departures from the plans which were shown me and which I understand would be strictly followed.

I am yours truly,

H. TREFFRY DUNN.

KELMSCOTT 1873
Thursday.

Dear Dunn,

I return the card from a heap of oil-saturated papers just going to the kitchen. Last night there was a disaster with that lamp, hung from the ceiling of the tapestry-room (which is now my studio) and then lit for the first time. The flame caught the thing it hung by (being wrongly put up) and down it came on the table beneath. It is a miracle the place was not set on fire. As it was, nothing of importance suffered. By the by, the light, instead of equalling 3 gas lights, does not appear equal to 2 candles.

The costume book and draperies came all right.

About Dr. Hawksley, I thought, on your telling me you had sent him my letter, that this was perhaps a little rash, as I remember saying something about litigation being out of the question and perhaps after that he does not care what he does. Do you think I had better write to Valpy and get him to drop Dr. H a letter? Or would this be prematurely hostile? I suppose, if we did go to law, *my* evidence would not be needed as I was not there the whole time, and *you* are the only person who could speak re the matter.

Please give enclosed to the Elephant, if she is not yet gone out of town, but I hope she is, as I am sure she must need it. In that case keep it for her. It contains *cheque*.

Yours, D. G. R.

Wednesday.

Re Hawksley.

My dear Dunn,

You have done wonders to make the building matter intelligible to me, but still, out here, it remains a little puzzling. I suppose the staircase window is the *only* one affected—(if it *be* affected) not *your* room also. The difference between such light as this from light weather (in which I find *I* can read a little without spectacles) and a dark winter day is so enormous, that, while the light might not be sensibly affected *now* at all, darkness might possibly be the result in winter.

Is not the estate architect willing to interfere (if needed) on his own responsibility. I certainly can't think of litigation but encroachment ought to be avoidable without this surely, as Dr. H. by his letters seems a reasonable man. Will you give me your further views by next post. The agents themselves are lawyers, and can't I should think wish such a house as number 16 to be spoilt for the sake of such a house as number 17.

Ever yours,

D. G. R.

15

Arguments involving Gabriel seemed to have a way of becoming prolonged; and the trouble about the alterations to Number Sixteen proved no exception. Taking his ease in the lovely old garden at Kelmscott, Gabriel must have thought that London as a headquarters was less and less desirable. He was bored by the anxieties of running a large house which he now seldom saw and was no longer using as a personal residence. For some time it had seemed desirable to escape from Cheyne Walk altogether, and to Harry's other tasks, house-hunting was now added.

Howell's various sins of omission seem to have been forgiven when he turned up at Kelmscott, as voluble and entertaining as ever. He showed his goodwill by buying a picture and, true to form, was planning to make his own and everyone else's fortune. It was Howell, no doubt, who propounded a remedy for Leyland's "grumpiness".

1 July

Dear Dunn,

These advts. (copies from the Daily News) really look to me more than usually promising. It would be doing me a real service if you would go and see the places and report on them. You know that absolute enclosure in its own grounds and immediate accessibility of perfectly retired walks are among my primary requisites. Some sort of goodish accommodation for painting would be necessary also, but I should reckon on having to improve or create this for myself. I am very anxious to get a place nearer London as soon as possible, and give up the others. The Hemel Hempstead place seems the most promising (though unluckily the dearer) as being further removed (not *too* far), having larger grounds of its own, and the place not being, I find, near a station. What the station to reach it *is* I am ascertaining, so George is writing to the agents mentioned to send you by return the name of the station and a card to view. The Tottenham place seems good but perilously near the station for quietness in such a cockneyfied neighbourhood. Pardon haste.

Ever yours, D. G. R.

I see at Hemel Hempstead they offer a photograph, so George is telling them to send you that too. If it were something supremely hideous, perhaps I had better see it before we think further.

My dear Dunn,

You have done your "spiriting" as regards the houses in the most thorough and friendly way. After your ample report, I consider Hemel Hempstead on various accounts quite out of the question, and George returns the photo to the agents today. Tottenham is quite another matter, eligible in many respects, but the fact of the best aspect (the one fit for painting) being to the front and that front the main street of a very cockneyfied place, and the other fact of constant railway noise and smoke at the back, are very serious objections. I shall reflect on this place, but on the whole I fancy that better might be found.

P. P. Marshall is an old Tottenhamite and might have been helpful had one settled there, but just at this very moment he has left the neighbourhood for good and removed to Southend. You do not say to what extent the attentions of the Hebbs of Hemel Hempstead were carried in your behalf. Champagne was certainly apropos after a hot railway journey. Many thanks for your exertions.

Howell has been here since Saturday evening and has just left. It was the only way of getting to an understanding on various points to have him down here and talk them over. The Lucretia he brought with him from Christies (it did not appear in the sale, he assures me) and I have now offered it by letter to Rae, but shall not send it "on approval". Howell's wonderful stories were as endless as usual. One was that he saw a man and a boy at a hotel in Leicester Square with perfect dogs' heads, and that they are either exhibiting or about to be exhibited in London, and that all London is placarded with their portraits! Is this true? If not, to tell such a story (so easily disproved) shows that Howell is really mad at last in the most literal and medical sense.

Valpy, as I think I told you, is disposed to pay £50. a month from this time forward on account of the large picture which he purchased for 1500 guineas. On delivery he would pay up arrears, or would disburse larger sums whenever I was chiefly or wholly occupied with it. I was thinking that there ought to be a written agreement between him and me (in case of either dying, etc.) but this seems very difficult to manage, on account of Graham's position as real owner of the picture till the replica is painted and delivered. Therefore, I suppose the idea must be given up.

Howell has bought for 250 guineas that head of the Blessed Damozel on a gold ground, and is prepared to disburse as soon as I let him know that the picture is ready for delivery which a few days work would effect. This is convenient. He said a good deal about the Agnews and said that Wm. Agnew would come down here at any time with him if I had an important picture such as those of Leyland's and Graham's which I could offer him. H. talks now of buying Colnaghi's business (having, it appears, good opportunities to do so) but what the whole scheme may really be worth I cannot say. However I must say it did not seem all moonshine to me. If done, he would command fine exhibition rooms of which I could avail myself. The baronet has come back, and given up drink!! I give the second part as an *on dit* merely. I suppose you have returned F. her money ere this.

Ever yours, D. G. R.

Tuesday.

Dear Dunn,

Thanks for your vigilance in re Hawksley, etc.

In a day or two I expect to be sending you an oil head—Blessed Damozel, being that one on a red ground which you know, now cut down to a small single head picture, as I have begun the large version over again.

What I want done is that you should get Ford and Dickinson's gilder down to Chelsea and make him gild under your directions the parts where the red ground of the canvas is left, both dress and background. This would require nicety round the edges, and where these seem dubious I will mark them with a white chalk line. When gilded, I will get you to re-pack it as it came and return it to me at once to paint on. I will write to F. and D. myself as soon as the picture goes to you. I really think I had better send you a small cheque for yourself now that it is to be had. However, the things in hand seem to promise the probability of keeping the wolf from the door in future, and I hope Howell will be able with leisure to enlarge my market. Graham is still well-disposed I am glad to find, and the best remedy for Leyland's grumpiness will be that he should find the pictures settled elsewhere without delay. He will then probably be glad to get things and not grumble so much about back debt.

The weather here is divine at last. Poor George seems to find complications in his case and it has not turned up yet. I sent him your good wishes. His address is 53 St. John's Street, Oxford, if you can think of anything to amuse him in a letter.

Peace never reigned for long below-stairs at Number Sixteen, and Emma in particular was proving refractory. One cannot help thinking that Gabriel thought himself well out of the various "breezes" which blew up at frequent intervals. Miss Wilding was as elusive as ever. Gabriel, one might think, could quite easily have made the short journey to London and cleared up some of his manifold domestic problems in person: but he was content to leave Harry Dunn to resolve these as best he could.

Those all-important cheques arrived in an erratic manner. The household finances resembled an accountant's nightmare: but Harry must be given credit for his efforts to keep the boat from rocking too crazily— especially as his own modest salary seems to have been one of the last items to be given attention.

KELMSCOTT 1873 Friday

Dear Dunn,

That blessed Alice writes me in a fix. All I can possibly send is £5. Indeed,

L

this is a difficulty. Will you consult with her about her d—d house. Surely she *must* get rid of it. I have paid her, I find by my cheques, nearly £60. over what was due to her since we re-opened accounts in September 72, and there is of course no prospect at all of her ever being otherwise than far behind. Perhaps if she had lived in lodgings she would have had these £60. by her now.

I believe I have nothing else to write about today. I trust to send you some tin very soon.

Ever yours,
D. G. R.

I suppose Marks is in London. I am thinking of asking him to bid again at a sale.

The first sheet of the following letter is missing.

You can be sure I have no intention of buying in all pot boilers that may come into the market. As I shall have to write details to Marks (*if* I do bid in this instance) it is no use my writing twice. He will explain the thing to you when he gets my letter. The case is quite peculiar.

Thanks for the links. One of the gold ones was lost. I dropped it out of sleeve into the water, I believe from the boat.

I should be much obliged to Mrs. Burthe to see to the dress. Indeed it is important, when the embroidery is mended, I would send directions for re-making the thing. Of course, whatever she charges I will pay; and when I get it in working order again, can speedily paint a paying picture from it.

Please let me know as to Marks' whereabouts. If suiting me best, would you accompany him here just for one or two days this week? I can then explain to him viva voce, and save writing. Thus I ought to know at once where he is. Also about A.W. as soon as maybe and I will send cheque if necessary on your enquiry. I write her a line to look you up or let you know when to see her.

My debt of £70. to you makes you much less like your name than I fancied must be the case. You must have managed wonderfully with what I have sent, to meet the house expenses and so on so far. Suppose I enclose a small cheque on account. Whistler will be going sky high now no doubt.

Ever yours,
D. G. R.

Brown has got another bloke to paint—the 4th.

Saturday

Dear Dunn,

Thanks about F. I have written to her as to her most absurd proceedings and am getting an order from Leyland to withdraw the picture.

Will you send on by post a book called "Alexander the Great", *not* any other book.

Ever yours,
D. G. R.

There seems to be no clue as to which of Fanny's "absurd proceedings" was giving Rossetti concern. Had she, perhaps, offered for sale a painting for which she had been the model? When pressed for cash she would never think twice about any step which seemed to her a good idea of raising the wind.

KELMSCOTT Thursday

My dear Dunn,

My silence has depended first on no particular news I had to write and next on worries and uncertainties with work. I hear little from Howell—nothing from others who ought to write. I sent Leyland his chalk drawing (Bd. Daml.) on Friday last, and I have not yet heard from him. I kept it by me, after finishing it very carefully, for the purpose of laying in a picture from it, which I have done.

Thanks about the head-dress. Fanny made up something. George does not think the 3/- for the case extortionate, as it was not *empty*.

The Lamp is all right, the oil having come separately.

Thanks about your organ, which *may* prove very useful, but I am not yet certain whether I shall need it.

I answered your most unsatisfactory news of Emma in a letter to Fanny which I daresay she shewed you as I asked her to do. As to Graham's picture or the Llandaff one, I will write again soon.

Ever yours,

D. G. R.

The Emma affair now reached a critical stage. Against his better judgement and the advice of his friends Gabriel had been remarkably lenient: but some incident must have brought him unwillingly to the point at which dismissal was the only course.

KELMSCOTT
16th June 1873.

Dear Dunn,

Enclosed contains a cheque.

I have been writing to Miss Wilding, but without answer as yet. I want her as soon as she can come. What has become of her? Could you come down with her if desirable? I may as well enclose cheque to you also.

The question of Emma must be wound up soon, and I begin to incline strongly to a belief that she will have to go.

Ever yours,

D. G. R.

P.S. I find I must defer sending you a cheque till I get a new cheque book (which I have written for) as the one in enclosed note exhausts the present book.

P.P.S. Please get out a roll of yellow Chinese satin with circles all over it (entered in your inventory of the wardrobe) pack it *carefully* and send it by Parcels Company (paid) to

> Mrs. Morris, Horrington House,
> Turnham Green Road,
> Chiswick, W.

KELMSCOTT
26th June 1873

My dear Dunn,

I am sending with this a letter to Emma dismissing her, and I enclose copy to you in case she does not choose to show it you. The cheque from which her wages can be paid is enclosed. Will you pay her up to now and a month more in advance, and show her off. I do not of course wish to hurry her off if she would alter and behave properly, but I cannot judge at this distance what prospect of the kind there might be, and it seems rather hopeless.

My mother and sister are here now ... Brown and wife gone but returning about Monday next. Howell beginning to telegraph, so I don't know where it may end.

I am extremely sorry about poor Fanny's teeth, but I suppose she is relieved in consequence ... I am very sorry to disappoint her by not running up to London, but really it is impossible just now ... will you give me the exact dimensions of the base of that leather and brass cabinet now in the drawing room? Its stand is not genuine and I want to see whether an old one in this neighbourhood would fit it.

Would you send up that screen of mine I use in painting—a three-leaved thing, black on one side and red or green on the other, with a sort of canopy top. I should think it could be packed in some rough but safe fashion without expense—no case needed.

Ever yours,
D. G. R.

"The Roman Widow" was based upon a somewhat gloomy subject—the figure of a woman in a mortuary, playing on two harps. Opinion was divided as to the merit of the picture, for which Leyland sent a couple of hundred pounds on account. Some critics thought the work uninspired. William Michael, on the other hand, thought it "quite unsurpassed ... for pathetic sweetness and beautiful simplicity. If he painted one supremely lovable picture it is, I think, 'The Roman Widow'."

KELMSCOTT, LECHLADE
FRIDAY, 11 July 1873.

My dear Dunn,

The screen only came yesterday, the wings some days ago. I showed George the passage in your letter about packages, and he said he would look up his memoranda. Today he is gone to Oxford to have that lump cut out, and will not be back I suppose till Wednesday. After that I expect Mrs. M here, and kids. The Browns will leave on Monday. You will be surprised at one piece of news. In Italy, William proposed to Lucy Brown! I suppose they will soon be married, you can tell F.

My mother and sister leave here Wednesday. Christina has benefited surprisingly and both enjoyed themselves very much indeed. Alice W. has also shown more faculty for enjoyment than I ever saw her display before. She and my mummy and sister have got on very well together and like each other much. Alice has sat daily almost and much better than last time, though the first day she looked alarmingly ill. The picture I am doing of her has been sold over Leyland's head to Graham for 800 guineas. I am to have the cheque in a day or two. I am also making a study from her for a picture for Leyland—Roman Widow. By Howell's account he now seems horribly fidgety at having missed the other. I think he is likely to have the Proserpine which is here—not Parsons but my new one, for 800 guineas. Besides this I have a new picture well on, done from little Annie, and another thing or two besides, so I expect tin will flow in.

About the servant, if F. still thinks her Hannah advisable and *if it will not bring a brood into the house* and a man tramping in and out from work, you might try her if you think fit and see no better.

I heard from F. but she says nothing of country prospects. I feel sure she ought to be getting a change.

Ever yours,
D. G. R.

Tuesday.

My dear Dunn,

Your calculating Elephant is really splendid.

I think it will be no use your hunting for the card case if F. wots not of it. It must have disappeared somewhere. I don't remember seeing it for ever so long. However, it barely *might* be in some part of that high black and gold cabinet in dining room.

I think you are quite right about frame of Annunciation which must be hideous and will see to it after Graham gets it. I have written to him "to be persuaded". I should like to know what the Shields (No. 18) the Burton (No. 78) and the Eastlake (No. 121) fetched at the Sale.

F. & D. are making the frame for this Leyland picture and have promised it me faithfully by the 15th May. There is a tablet for the inscription

Dis Manibus

and much trouble would be saved if you would kindly just write it on the tablet at Wardour Street. This question would also enable you to egg them on about the frame which is most promising. I could only order it quite lately because not till then was I precisely certain about measurements. On second thoughts I write with this to them to send the tablet to you at Cheyne Walk, that you may write on it, which will be more convenient to you. But still you might try to keep them up to time when possible.

I am greatly in want of marble for the background. It must not be Verde Antique nor Malachite which is fussy.

When Rossetti made one of his rare excursions to London the greatest secrecy was observed. Nobody was to be told. The journey was made with the greatest circumspection. What on earth was "My Dear Dunn" to make of the following guarded instructions? Perhaps he just smiled, and told Fanny to air the bed.

KELMSCOTT, Wednesday.

My dear Dunn,

It may possibly be necessary for me to come to town tomorrow (Thursday) though quite uncertain as yet, and if it were so, I don't yet know what train I should be taking. I suppose you can manage to make it possible for me to sleep in my usual first-floor room, though the proper mattress of that bed has been brought here; and as I should be starting hastily, could not well bring it along with me. Do not mention the matter to anyone whatever—not the old couple or anyone. I am writing a line to Fanny and in case of my coming it will be quite possible to get ready the little that will have to be seen about after that. However, it is just as probable—perhaps more so—that I shall not come at all. Do not give yourself any trouble about the matter, and do not telegraph to me.

Ever yours,
D. G. R.

George would of course come with me.

Kelmscott 1873 Thursday.

My dear Dunn,

Really, having had all this trouble with Emma for the sake of reducing expense of servants, do let us now manage with one servant in my absence. All my early years we had but one servant at home, and she used to go out when possible and not when impossible. She must stay in when you need her and go out when you do not. Hannah, as far as I recollect, is the daughter of the woman who robbed Fanny. With her I think we had better have nothing to do, nor do I want a slatternly young family about the house on any account. The house must be kept decent as it always was. Were I to come to town again for any time myself, I should, I suppose, bring my own servants here (a German mother and daughter who are satisfactory) and therefore in such case I should be provided.

I wish I had sent you more empty cases, or that you had asked for them instead of having a new one made for those wings about which there was no hurry. Please do so for the future except in important and immediate matters —as I do wish to stop this packing case expense as far as possible.

I believe Howell will be asking you to write a name on the frame of that

Beloved picture before it returns to Rae. His Baron turned out to be no good for the present.

My picture goes on fast and well.

Ever yours, D. G. R.

The screen top I remember now I took off myself. Emma is getting a place at Wandsworth.

Wednesday.

My dear Dunn,

I am heartily glad you like the little picture so well—vexed about the accident—I said tracing paper should be used but that as new paper of the kind was running short, an old bit drawn on would do as well. However, it seems other paper was used. I hope you will be able to set all right. You probably know that Watts is going to bring Fry to see it, pricing it at £500. If he buys, it will meet a cheque for that sum just received from him and need not then go as a third advance on the Venus Astarte, which would be nervous work. Whether I come up tomorrow, (Thursday) evening or not, I'm still uncertain. Of course, you will be kept informed and money sent if there is delay.

With thanks,
Yours ever, D. G. R.

P.S. It is by no means impossible that there may be a delay in our coming up. I have got to doing the flowers in the Damozel picture and find myself fully employed. When we do come, we shall be late and would be asking you to meet us with a brougham at the London Bridge Station (most likely as the late trains do not go to Victoria), thus when you get a telegram as to day and hour, you will understand that this is the plan to be adopted without specifying in telegram.

Kelmscott, Monday.

My dear Dunn,

I forget whether you told me you had got out the Magdalene subject on the scale of the Dante replica, as I once asked you kindly to do. I have a great desire to set about working that out as soon as I may, so ask the question. I felt a reluctance to tell Valpy at once that his picture could not be found so (having failed myself to get any answers from H. on former points) have now got George to write him a friendly line asking him whether he can explain this question in any way. If he doesn't answer in a day or two, I must just write Valpy according to your report.

I shall no doubt be returning soon, but as yet find scraps of work which can be done here, and moreover have lost today and yesterday in enjoying the fine outdoor weather previous to returning to London. The Blessed Damozel has now a very forward look. I have succeeded in doing the veil quite well from the green beginning in which it had been carefully done from nature, assisting myself with a piece of the stuff for the colour. Thus, the wings of the angels and the lilies and roses will be pretty much of the out-standing material when the drapery is done. You do not tell me what you have done of your own and whether you have sent anything to the R.A.

yours ever, D. G. R.

Kelmscott

My dear Dunn,

I write in post haste (for the post passes here on Sunday at one o'clock) to say only that I shall certainly not be later than Wednesday next (at latest) in returning to London, and that I shall therefore be very glad if you kept your intention of leaving yesterday as it would be most inconvenient to me to be quite alone in the house. Thus it will be no use my writing further till I hear from you again, as I do not quite know where you are.

Ever yours,
D. G. R.

Wednesday.

My dear Dunn,

The pencils from Robertson's do not seem to be right. They are marked No. 4 and are not I should think, made for artists. I am returning them to you, together with one of the right sort, and *at your leisure* would be much obliged if you would call on R. & Co. and ask them to send me the right sort instead. The letter should be HH. I cannot think what could have become of the several doz of these pencils I have lately bought.

Neither can I guess at all what has become of all the mediaeval costumes I used to have. For instance, I remember distinctly one woman's dress—cotehardie, open up sides and kirtle to go under it—of white velvet quartered with yellow. This is not in your list and there were a number of men's dresses I know, not one of which seems to be extant. Are you sure that none are mislaid in your room upstairs or elsewhere. The thing to send would have been the "white velvet mediaeval woman's dress" in your remainder list, not one of the kind you sent is anything but a fragment. However, I have had to do without it now, so no need to send it on.

I now see there are two of the dresses in question in your list which are probably the ones in question. Why ever not have sent these? Really they had better still come, safely packed, and together with them the "Crimsony red Silk dress used in Rosa Triplex".

The roll you sent I do not unpack, but will bring it back with the many lumps that are here.

I could not possibly realise at this distance from the picture what the diagram meant, nor would it be any use if I could. Many thanks for your valuable labours in the matter. They will determine me, I suppose, to dismember that unfortunate canvas again if such a thing be feasible. Nevertheless, I would almost feel inclined instead to see if the hands could be successfully reproduced before I did so, in which case I would substitute the reproduction. What say you to getting out a correct diagram of the whole in true proportion and perspective, a half size, longer than the original. I would then when we had looked together at it, get you to trace it on a canvas and paint the heads myself from the old ones. I should then see if I could make them as good as these, and if so, probably substitute the enlarged replica. In any case, it would be the commencement of a very valuable new version for sale.

Even in the seclusion of Kelmscott, Rossetti was still a man of moods. One detects a certain testy sarcasm in some of his letters. All the same, Harry was a man of intelligence and it seems probable that his instructions were not always as clearly expressed as they might have been. As for Gabriel himself the following letters are written by a busy man who was enjoying his work and anxious to lose no time in the execution of it.

There were still "vexations" to write to Dunn about—for example, the alleged breakage of a blue jar in Fanny's possession. Some commentators have taken as fact the suspicion which occurred to Gabriel himself—that Fanny had sold the jar and spent the money, and then made up the story of its being broken.

Friday.

Dear Dunn,

Cheque after all. Haste. But I must see to replenishment. You perfectly delight me if you are *sure* that the crimson gold shot drapery which I painted in "Palmifera" is now at Chelsea. However, I fear you merely speak from not finding it in your list of things sent, and having *now seen* it in the wardrobe. So sure am I and George also of having seen it arrive here when that crimson yellow lined jacket thing (since lost on the railway) was sent. The Palmifera drapery had never been asked for, and I was thus surprised and annoyed to see it arrive and spoke to you at the time on the unwisdom of sending things that, not being needed, lay about liable to loss or theft. Surely you must remember this circumstance. Thus I cannot conceive how it should be back at Chelsea. If by beneficent miracle it is there, of course let me have it with the rest. It will save infinite trouble and expense in seeking and buying substitutes and moreover is far better than any substitute could be.

This is most vexatious about the breakage of that blue jar at F's. If it is not merely an Elephant dodge to keep it at home (and the breakage thus a fiction) please let Marks *junior* (who has written me) take it at once to a good mender and get it mended *wihout delay*, as it forms a necessary part of the balance of my proposed picture. If this unhappily impossible, then Marks might say if he knew where to get a similar jar which I would buy. But it seems to me it cannot be so spoilt as to be unmendable.

Ever yours,

D. G. R.

My dear Dunn,

I have sent the coal merchants a cheque in full for their account and told them to send receipt to Chelsea. I enclose £30. If you like more at present I can send it easily. I daresay you would like a further supply *yourself*. If so, please let me know at once and it shall reach you.

I have so many profitable things on hand and in hand that I am in no anxiety of tin running short at present. Graham (Proprio motu) sent me a cheque in full for the Ghirlandata (£840) which is well advanced.

Your account of housekeeping at Chelsea is most cheering. What *can* have become of all this waste money? It seems as if Emma did not get it or at any rate keep it, or why is she in such a hurry to find a fresh place?

My mother, sister and Miss W. leave today. The last-named has sat very well, and is to look you up for sitting as soon as she gets to London. She has greatly benefited in health I think by her stay here.

I will speak to George about the railway matter when he returns here on Monday next. The operation and results have been a much severer matter than he expected and I expect to find him a good deal pulled down, but no doubt he will soon pull up again.

I am glad poor "Miss Clive" is better. I wrote to Sandys lately and received an affectionate answer. I fear Miss C's engagement must be sadly thrown out by her illness. It seems she had somehow secured unheard of terms—£30. a week (Howell says) besides other advantages.

Is there a pair of canvas pincers here? If so, I cannot find them. Unless you can tell me where they are, please send another pair. Also my address book should come, as I often want it. There is also a wing of a pee-wit (lapwing) (or a pair of wings, I think) which are somewhere.

I am sending the rent with this to L.P.R. & Co. and telling them to send receipt to Chelsea.

In one of the pictures I am about, I want something of a spotted russet colour—somewhat like an Indian "bandana" handkerchief, to serve for *an apron*, something yellow and red and amounting to a sort of russet. Could you find anything of this sort in the drawers?

I find in your list: something Chinese, *yellow and green striped*—this if I remember is a small jacket or pair of trousers or something. I also find "some scraps of green Chinese figured silk". This, I think is rather satin than silk. I find also, a Yellow Chinese cape, silk and small—about this I am uncertain, but I wish you would make a packet of all these and send it me by passenger train at once. There is also—part of an old dressing gown, modern English. This I think has a very reddish obverse side. You might include it, and perhaps might get the wings of the lapwing into the parcel.

Ever yours,

D. G. R.

One day all is sweetness and light. The "tin" is rolling in, and Dunn is carrying out his mixed commissions with admirable efficiency. The next, the clouds are lowering, the pencils are of the wrong type, and Harry is given a lecture on passenger trains and "balance and exactness" being "the soul of order". This, from his employer, was a trifle rich!

KELMSCOTT Friday

My dear Dunn,

I do wish you would kindly read my despatches as carefully as I write them. You have now sent me an old rag of a figured silk counterpane. I asked distinctly for a *linen* Indian counterpane covered with a *light yellowish or brownish pattern in embroidery*. There could be no possible mistake between the two things. The one you have sent did cross my mind, but it seemed *quite* useless to say *that* was *not* wanted, as mistake was impossible after reading my description. However, here it is by passenger train, and I may still wait for the other one. Please now send it at once by passenger train, and with it that small brass spice box with birds on it which I last saw on the mantelpiece in the drawing room.

Again about passenger trains. You ask anxiously this time if it is worthwhile sending these small and inexpensive packages by that conveyance, when I said specially I wanted them *at once*. On other occasions I have witnessed with anxiety the arrival of heavy goods by passenger train when I have said there was no special hurry about them. However, no mighty disaster has occurred, and I don't want to bother you with grumbling, but balance and exactness are the soul of order!!

I have reflected that when last sending you a cheque, there was only £15. available for yourself. I therefore enclose another £15. in case you need it.

Ever yours,
D. G. R.

No counterpane of any kind had been sent on former occasions.

KELMSCOTT Tuesday August 1873.

Dear Dunn,

I wish, my dear boy, you would read my letters carefully. Today I have to telegraph to prevent a cabinet stand from lumbering down here. What I asked for (as you will see on referring again) was a memorandum of the *dimensions of the base* of the cabinet, to see if it would fit a stand which is on sale hereabouts. I trust my telegram will be in time to stop the afflictive phenomena arriving. If not, I must just send it back. In case you are sending today, I am including in telegram a request for a pair of pelican wings and another pair of some other bird which are at Chelsea and which I need for painting. They would require careful packing.

I am glad Emma is gone. About Llandaff we will see in due time. Is the Tax paper the *final* application? If so, I will send you a cheque. If not, it may stand over awhile. Howell never gave me the Pandora. I am writing him and expect him back here.

My picture from A.W. goes on swimmingly (in spite of two November days created on purpose for the start of it) and will be the best I have done of her. She sits well, though on the day of her arrival she looked so deadly pale I thought she could not sit at all. She has evidently been very ill.

Ever yours, D. G. R.

I got F's letter all right and will write her soon.

Sunday.

Dear Dunn,

The sample of canvas you took being obscured by the red ground, I send another cutting to show W[insor] and N[ewton]. You will want *dry* Light Red and Raw Sienna to lay it with. It may be better not to lay it so dark that a red chalk tracing will not tell on it, as the white chalk is very fugitive and awkward. Perhaps you might put a little more red in the mixture than the sample I gave you, but it should tend decidedly to orange.

Ever yours,

D. G. R.

Gabriel enjoyed discussing with Harry the technical details of an artist's work: his comments on the use of light must have a special interest for professional artists and critics and, indeed, for all who have tried to master the difficulties of suggesting sunshine and shadow.

The following letters provide an intriguing glimpse of the secrecy which was often observed in the art-world. While negotiations for a sale were going on it was advisable for certain people to be kept in the dark. Even the whereabouts of a new picture might not be disclosed. A direct reference to the scope of Dunn's work is unusual: writing of one picture and how it should be placed, Gabriel says: "This will also be the proper light to enable you to copy it. . . ."

29 August 1873

Dear Dunn,

W. & N. write me today saying that they fear they see no chance of hiring one of their easels for me, but could sell me one which (they say) would in reality be the most economical plan if needed for long. I believe there is some truth in this, so if you think best, get one from them only *take care it is as large as the one I hired formerly*. I have myself a smaller one, as you know.

I believe the purchase by Valpy is virtually concluded—at least it is quite so far as he is concerned, but I think it necessary to await answer to some further points from Graham. Of course you need say nothing about the matter as yet. I have told Howell the picture is at Chelsea, but have said also that I think it better Valpy should make no pilgrimages till further notice. About the dawn sky, there is no sunlight in my picture, as you will remember —this is no sunshine casting definite shadows. The light is an ordinary sun-less one. Thus the sky must not be of the order when the sun would cast shadows, but a very quiet dawn as warm and varied as maybe within such limits. I cannot see that the point from which the light comes is then of any consequence. It is diffused.

About the wedding, I suppose it will be done quietly, but I don't know when. I will bear in mind what you say if such a question were put to me.

I hope that cartoon for the replica is not lost, as we had settled several questions in it as to modification of proportions.

I suppose you posted all right the letter I sent you for F. at Brighton.

George proposes to get the station people here to keep and send him always an exact mem. of the arrivals of parcels. Thus we shall I trust know better for the future.

The picture of Jones' of which you send me a sketch is (if in oil) a replica— I suppose enlarged—of a good sized water colour called "Chant d'Amour" which he did some years ago.

Ever yours,

D. G. R.

30 August

My dear Dunn,

The picture cannot remain as you have placed it. Gibbited in that way against the light, it is simply ruined, and an occasion might probably arise for my wishing someone to see it—Valpy or another.

Did W. & N. tell you they had no easel to let out only, or none to sell either? I see that in their book the "studio easel" is priced at £10. 10. My impression is that the one I had from them (*my own*) cost £9. and this I suppose was the one as above with the artists discount. A larger one therefore (such as the one hired before) would cost I suppose some £12. or £14. I don't know whether the longer one mentioned in their enclosed note would be large enough. If so, it will be the shortest plan (and probably the cheapest in the long run) to go in for it. Just please call on them unless you have since found they really have none large enough, and tell them to send the proper size easel to Chelsea at once on *sale* to me.

If there is any delay in getting the easel thus, the picture must be at once, in some other way, put in the light in which I used to show it—that is, with its back to the fireplace, and turned quite sideways to the large window, between it and the small window of which the shutters should be closed. The green curtain of the large window should be kept closed, and the green blinds put to the height I used to keep them at. Thus, if anyone comes in to see the picture it can be seen: and it should be kept there habitually and the table etc. put quite out of the way. This will also be the proper light to enable you to copy it, and where you have placed it you would be perpetually in your own light, besides being unable to see the whole picture at once.

If the easel cannot be got at once, the wooden steps could be backed up to the fireplace and the picture fastened to them as now, with weights added at the back part of the steps if a counterpoise is needed. Or else it would even be better than at present, if you took it out of the frame and place it in the proper position on the W. and N. easel I have, which is the one it was painted on. When the new easel arrives it could be framed again, and fastened on that.

Ever yours, D. G. R.

P.S. I write with this to W. & N. telling them you will call about it, and saying I will *buy* the easel.

P.P.S. It might be better to receive in another room such people as you judge I should not wish to see the picture at present as, till we know exactly what arrangement is to be made about it, there is no need for the generality to know it is at Chelsea.

Friday.

My dear Dunn,

I find it is possible that Howell may be taking someone to see the pictures at Cheyne Walk as a matter of business. If so, he has my sanction eventually, I believe, though it will be necessary first for him to go and arrange them properly and with your co-operation. I have written a line to F. to ask her to clean the glasses, as your time ought not to be taken up with this, and it must be needed. Would you ask her to clean *all* glasses—including duplicate of Beatrice, Lilith and all.

Ever yours (in haste) D. G. R.

P.S. I have written a line to Stephens asking him to get the Athenaeum Nos. containing his article on the pictures and my sonnets, and post them addressed to you at Cheyne Walk. So please let Howell have them if he comes.

Sunday.

Dear Dunn,

I have told Howell to send you six copies of a printed description of the big daub, which will save you word of mouth in case anyone calls. In each case let me *implore you* for the future to take care the picture is in the only proper light.

I think on reflection that if Miss H. calls and pokes her nose (as she is sure to do) into the question of ownership, you had better just tell her plainly that I am exchanging the large picture with Graham against a replica which he can hang more conveniently. It would not do perhaps to let it get about on my authority that the large picture does not belong to me, in case I want to dispose of it.

Ever yours,

D. G. R.

16

One can imagine Harry Dunn, temporary master of Number Sixteen, sitting at Rossetti's desk, reading the letters from Kelmscott, and making formidable lists of articles to be bought, letters to be written, and matters of business to be attended to. He was loyal and industrious. Gabriel's interests were paramount. But this is not to say that the Cornishman did not enjoy himself while his chief was at Kelmscott.

He was gregarious, fond of the theatre, liked good company. To think of him as a lonely, timid figure, working weary hours in the studio, browbeaten by the tartly robust Mrs. Hughes, is wide of the mark. I have no doubt he carried out Gabriel's orders to the best of his ability, and painted in the studio while the light lasted. But as twilight gave way to night, Harry departed to spend agreeably convivial evenings with his artist friends and the Heatherley colleagues who had long outgrown their student days and had studios of their own. But Number Sixteen and its problems were his abiding interest. Gabriel's letters, in which he leaps from a technical point to some household crisis, leave us in no doubt of that.

My dear Dunn,

I fancy it is quite unfeasible for you to come as Howell proposes so am glad that you have settled to defer it. Besides Leyland and the Howells, I expect Watts and Brown—or if Brown does not come, Sandys is likely to be here, so that all space would be occupied.

Thanks for your most careful plans as to the Dante frieze. However, I can tell you beforehand with certainty that the Indian Red is the proper laying-in if on *white*, some purplish tone being indispensable in painting gold or silver. Whether in laying-in or on the *red* I used this only, or drew in the stronger lines with Bt. Umber, I cannot recollect, but the thing itself would probably show when closely examined.

Rae has sent a cheque £126. today for that eternal Borgia, which I push off to Birkenhead and the deuce with much satisfaction. I enclose a cheque £20. You must tell me if more is absolutely needed.

The attitude of the Elephant is idiotic and ridiculous to the last degree. I shall have to call her over the coals.

As to your coming here at all about that drawing, of course I shall be glad to see you at any time, but must see further whether or not it is necessary on that account. The drawing is the one I made for the Ghirlandata, and failing the picture to copy, I suppose the sleeve and drapery in the drawing will have to be drawn again from nature, as well as some leaves for a background. But it strikes me that perhaps you could go to Graham's and make a sketch of what is needed from the picture. I am sure he would be agreeable—which would on the whole answer better. But we can see about this. In exchange for this drawing and another—a mere profile of A.W., without background, Howell cancels a bill of £70. odd due for things purchased by me through him (I identified the items) and is to pay me besides £37. cash.

I don't know exactly what Lucy means about housekeeping, but this letter is already long and I have several others to write, so must conclude. Many thanks for all your labours.

Ever yours,

D. G. R.

P.S. In ordering the canvas, better have ⅜ of an inch extra all round for the frame to cover.

(KELMSCOTT 1874)
Thursday: Re: "Annunciation"

My dear Dunn,

Thanks for your trouble with the blue pot. The Elephant writes in a rage but I have sent her a settler. I do not know how to thank you enough for all the extreme trouble and care you have taken about this replica, but believe me, I am sincerely grateful. Few indeed would have laboured thus for the sake of another's work. As to the frieze, I think the Indian red alone will be sufficient (with white mixed in the tint where needful) for the laying-in—leaving the value of the red ground, of course. I find a difficulty in getting *good* Indian Red. It is either too laky or too bricky. I fancy Eastwell is best.

I thought your book of anatomy was a special one of Knox's, but find it is only a translation of Fan. which I have here, with additions. I think I shall try and get through Ellis the original work by Jean Cousin, from which Fan quotes

It must be valuable and curious.

F. and D. have at last sent the frame—and I think though the picture is a shadowy one in a certain sense, I never painted anything so *luminous* and it is without glazings. The frame seems to melt into the fair mellow tone of the picture. Thanks for inscription. I think for the future, the initial letters had better be the same size as the rest.

I have got the Annunciation—and really think there is a certain inspired quality about it which sets it at the top of my work. Alas to say so at 46! It is quaint enough and rickety enough in small ways, but not so to be minded. All I have done is to stipple into the faces without alteration but so as to even the surface which (from inexperience and difficulty, no doubt) was broken and queer. This has been a great gain, but nothing is changed. I shall make Graham get a new frame—the present one is too hideous. Perhaps I may make one addition to the picture—i.e. of a little white jar standing by the embroidery frame and containing a tallish very slim green plant of some sort which would grow up partly covering the waste of white at that side. I remember there used to be somewhere at Chelsea a few classically shaped little white vases of the kind made for what is called potichomanie (i.e. covering white pots with patterns pasted on to imitate coloured china). Do you know whether these are about, or is there anything else white of at all a suitable shape?

Ever yours,

D. G. R.

P.S. Surely A.W. will now get rid of this mad house of hers. But how could even she be ninny enough to get such a set in at all? Surely the whole thing must have been a plant of some sort. Did she get her money?

KELMSCOTT 18th September 1873

Dear Dunn,

I only bought of Rolfe one picture—Judgment of Solomon—which Scott now has. Perhaps he might buy others from R. but at present he is at Penkill. The Pompeian subject I will buy for £1. 5s. to be of use to the poor devil— or you can do so, whichever you please. I certainly never offered £5. for it and a fellow, indeed in R's letters he says "for a pound" or is it "for a panel"? £5. is a simple lie—I never dreamt then of giving such prices for such pictures.

By the bye, between you and me, they would be a better investment than the Britten at £20. *This in confidence.* Of course I said what I could to the artist in reply, and am not in the least disconcerted as I bought it solely to serve the young artist. But, my dear fellow, you paint 1000 times better yourself. It is slovenly and foggy to the last degree. And the style followed seems to be that of Leighton's, clumsy imitations of (G.F.) Watts such as he has produced latterly. How B. will manage to paint like Holman Hunt I don't know but (without thinking H.H. the king of painters) certainly the severe discipline of so positive a style ought to be of use to B. I confess if anyone had shown so much willingness to serve *me* as I did with B. at that stage of the profession, I should have tried to do him the best justice I could. However, this is all *in confidence.* I daresay he was pressed for time and tin.

I enclose £25. which please apply to your own needs or mine as the call occurs.

I suppose Wm. does not now visit Chelsea.

D. G. R.

KELMSCOTT Thursday
November 1873.

Dear Dunn,

Your letter shows you had not got mine posted on Tuesday, which seems strange. You *must* be done up indeed if you've been without fires till now.

M

But it is possible enough to light a fire behind a big picture. Thanks for all your labours. No doubt I shall hear from you tomorrow in answer to mine of Tuesday.

If a book has come or should come for me called "The Shepherds' Garden" will you send it on?

Ever yours,

D. G. R.

I have read Nolly and I think him really miraculous for his age and exceptionally excellent for anyone.

Saturday.

Dear Dunn,

This blessed Knewstub thing used to hang about the passage near the garden door. It is likely there still. It never was here. I need no other studies except what I asked for. George Ness sent you some cases. Merritt's picture has never turned up yet! How about the endless tracing paper you were to send me?

Ever yours,

D. G. R.

KELMSCOTT Friday,
12 December.

Dear Dunn,

You need not send me Brass's blessed bill. I will send you a cheque towards it as soon as convenient and must certainly consider whether at the same time some step could be taken towards establishing the stable matter more clearly.

About cooking when I come to town.

F. will have to lend me her girl I suppose. It would be quite inconvenient to bring up this woman for a few days only—besides she is no cook at all.

Thanks for the Fan's Anatomy. But I wish at the same time you would have sent me your Knox. On loan as you proposed to do. Please do so now if you can spare it, and at the same time my French dictionary—a large volume—which George wants. The two books might perhaps be put inside that large brown great coat of mine with a velvet collar, as I want this sent *at once*—always supposing the moths have not made a meal of it.

No news up to this writing about Merritt's picture which was sent by him on the 4th. What can such devilry all mean? I am writing him to make enquiries. Perhaps you had better see him. There must be some mistake about what I said to F. The picture is not at Lechlade yet.

I have got into the tapestry room again after many changes and much patchwork, and hope it may now be habitable. It is much lighter than the other.

If you speak to Marks, of course be very cautious. I've written again to Howell expressing my surprise at his ways. If money comes in—as is now probable—freely from other quarters I really ought not to sell the big picture for 1500 gns. at all.

> Ever yours,
> D. G. R.

Tuesday.

Dear Dunn,

Please tell me what is the width of the frame of the big picture? It seems the space Graham has for it is 88 inches long. Thus, if the picture, as seems likely, is about 77 inches long, there would be $5\frac{1}{2}$ inches to spare on each side for the frame. Let me know about this at once.

Have you forgotten those notes you took about various things needed? It seems the two anatomy books might as well come with the Dictionary.

I have heard at last from Howell—most unsatisfactorily as to the big picture. All he says is that Valpy is back and is collecting money to buy it!!! I must insist on further explanation.

I find Graham considers that large Dante boat sketch as his. I shall put it, when finished, at 800 guineas—being big and full of work, and then he can let me have something now on account for it.

Howell tells me Graham is very eager to have a companion to the Ghirlandata and complains that I have said nothing further about it. However, at present I shall have to be very attentive to Leyland's work who is not to be trifled with any longer.

I hope F. got safely a £10. cheque which I sent her.

I have just got a very affectionate letter from Graham who seems to want everything I can let him have. So I don't think bankruptcy is quite at the door just yet.

> Ever yours, D. G. R.

P.S. Merritt's picture not to hand yet—not having been sent by passenger train.

Kelmscott 18th December 1873

Dear Dunn,

You have probably learned by this from Merritt that the picture was sent off by North Western Railway, Camden Town! He writes me so only this morning. Whether he means that this is a metropolitan line which took it to Paddington or whether it has gone by a wrong line altogether, I cannot yet tell. Yesterday George went up to London on purpose to enquire along the line, but now telegraphs me that he has learnt nothing—no wonder if it went by a wrong line!—but will see Merritt and return here this evening. A hopeful state of things! Pickford's must be mad if they really took it to the wrong station.

It is impossible to hear a word from that devil Howell. You say Marks "retired altogether from the business". But *what* business? Does he mean as connected with a project of engraving, or the far more important question of selling the picture at a high price to Armstrong—and if so, at what price?

Can you find this out, letting him know of course that all must be quite confidential at present. I should be quite willing, I suppose, to treat through him if advantageous to myself. As for Howell, it seems no use thinking further of him about anything.

Ever yours,

D. G. R.

K. 1874. Monday.

My dear Dunn,

I am getting very anxious about Merritt's picture which shows no sign. Today I finished the other Proserpine which is to go to Leyland. Would it be practicable for you to come here one day and write that by-sonnet on the new frame? The one you did belongs you know to Merritt's picture. If you came, and if it were necessary for someone to make enquiries along the line about the missing picture, you might perhaps manage this at the same time. What can have become of it is a perfect mystery. Merritt wrote on the 4th that he "had *this day* forwarded it".

Leyland told Marks to get that little Lucrezia Borgia which is at 23, Queen's Gate and now belongs to me and send it on here. Is Marks ever going to do this? Would you ask him and say I wish it done at once.

Ever yours,

D. G. R.

Shall have more tin immediately I trust.
You said something of rates so I send cheque.

Sunday.

Dear Dunn,

In your inventory of things at Chelsea I find an entry—"a quilted coverlet, salmon coloured and intricate pattern". I don't remember exactly what this is, but think it might possibly do for something I am needing. Will you send it on *at once*? Also at the same time please find and send another counterpane thing—a sort of Indian linen covered with a faint browny yellow embroidery —which for a long while was used in the first floor bedroom, but got in holes I think. F. could find it. Also, please include in parcel several pieces of Indian muslin or linen embroidered with gold ears of corn. There must be three or four I think, though I only see one noted in your inventory.

Ever yours,

D. G. R.

P.S. There is a silk remnant (not enough for a dress but pretty fair size) I think bought by Fanny. I don't know if it is the one described in your inventory as "a remnant silk (blood red)"—my impression is that it is rather crimson brown shot with tawny. I daresay it is the same however. Would you include this in the parcel, together with "Chinese brown silk robe with gold circles on it"—and "a silver blue scarf with purple fringe".

I am writing a line to Marks in case he knows of any draperies.

Wednesday.

Dear Dunn,

Four things are needed for a new picture of the object-painting kind which I want to do quickly. They are four things which will need very careful packing to prevent accidents, viz

1. One of the two low folding firescreens covered with peacock feathers under glass. The one I want is the one which has the best design and firmest fretwork beneath the feather part. This is the fretwork I mean, but I forget the design. The one I do *NOT* want has had to be mended two or three times in the fretwork and would probably look gummy thereabouts and have a tendency to be still loose, so you might tell the *other* by its not having these defects.

2. That large purple blue jar which Emma broke and which is now in a mended state at F's.

3. A sort of blue green garden pillar of glazed ware which I fancy may be lying in the lower part of the corner cupboard in studio.

4. The little blue green pot with black stand which is on the drawers in first floor bedroom.

These things you will perceive, will be troublesome to pack. If necessary, write Marks a line asking him to see to it and to oblige me by charging for the trouble. It would be a 1000 pities to send the things and get them destroyed.

The picture I am projecting would have absolutely needed that crimson drapery with the gold thread woven in, which is so unhappily stolen now through being sent here when never asked for. Failing this, the loss of which is a misery—I am seeing what I can do in town by trying to buy velvet or something else approaching the colour—but nothing would ever equal that in quality.

I am vexed to find that you have to travel to the bank to get a £5. cheque changed. Had I not better in the future send sums by bank notes registered?

Please consider well the packing question. I tremble as to destruction or loss.

Ever yours,

D. G. R.

P.S. As a kernel to the parcel please introduce a candlestick which is somewhere I think in the drawing room.

KELMSCOTT 1874 Sunday

My dear Dunn,

Several points induce me to stay on here just now, as I have work I can get on with for awhile. I am in correspondence with Watts about the Chelsea house, and he is exerting himself actively to get the claimed sum (in lieu of repairs) reduced. He tells me it will not be as much as the half of what was named as probable—£1000—and thus my resolve respecting the house must be suspended till this question is decided. It would be payable on expiration of my term.

Would you let Fan know that I am not likely to be returning just now, as her mind may be anxious on this subject, and I am so hard up for time in writing today that I cannot well write her also.

Ever yours,

D. G. R.

If any books or newspapers come, please burn all such, and don't let F. see them—least of all take them.

Tuesday

Dear Dunn,

Would you send the materials of my bed (first floor) at Chelsea *at once*. Pardon haste. Postman waits. I'll explain later.

Ever yours,

D. G. R.

Harry, a competent artist, was at this time doing some work on his own account. He had some minor success, but was finding it hard to break into the charmed circle of painters who were considered a good investment. With the example of Knewstub in mind he pondered the wisdom of setting up on his own account: but to do this he had first to make some impression on the critics, and on the agents. Gabriel was sympathetic, and ready to give helpful advice.

Rossetti's letters continue to be friendly and cheerful—with occasional shafts of irascibility: the illness of the forbearing patron Graham was giving him some concern. "Dizzy", to whom he refers, was a terrier belonging to George Hake. Gabriel so often "borrowed" him that George eventually made him a present of it.

Kelmscott 9th Feb. 1874

Dear Dunn,

About the silks, what I [meant] was that you might *possibly* hear from Miss B. but the matter resolved itself without troubling you.

Graham has bought the Bower Maiden—the picture of little Annie which is now finished—for 650 guineas. Thus I shall now offer Parsons his money back instead of exchange work, save myself the worry of getting the picture sold for him through Howell, and have some £80 profit. Of course not a word of this to *anyone*.

I suppose you have been stuck in election mud for a fortnight. Of course Howell got Dilke in! At least, he says so.

You will be sorry to hear that Graham has been very seriously ill, and is now only slowly recovering. He did not go in for this election at Glasgow. He is my only rock of defence, and if he drops into the billows I may as well go over too.

You do not tell me how your picture fared at Dudley.

The children have got the measles here. But don't tell F. or she will get uneasy.

Kelmscott 12 Feb. 1874

Dear Dunn,

I enclose £20. Am extremely vexed to hear of your renewed ill luck at Dudley. However, Knewstub took a turn at last, and so will you. If I were you, I would set to work at a drawing or picture now—not *too* ambitious but calculated to show your knowledge and skill with some nude if possible—and give *every* spare moment to it during the whole year. Thus you would produce something really complete, and what *is* complete undeniably I believe commands attention. What I last saw you doing had excellencies but was begun too late.

As to election bores, just lock the iron gate and don't open it. I suppose you heard it was Howell got Dilke in!! ;

Graham goes on only pretty well I fear. The last letter was in his daughter's hand. I have received the price of the picture from Glasgow, but in *pounds* not *guineas*! This knocks off half my profit but I shall not complain now Graham is ill, and as the picture is not a very important or laborious one.

Tell the good old Elephant that I shall write soon, but that there has been nothing to say.

I must see about Brass,

Ever yours,

D. G. R.

P.S. (Monday) This has somehow not got posted till now. I suppose the Chelsea election is at rest, is it not? It seems Dilke only got in by 45 votes, so I daresay he hates me for not voting. I am anxious about Graham, who I fear gets no better and do not hear from him since I last wrote.

Howell will be getting that Proserpine from Parsons and it will be sent to Cheyne Walk. When it comes, do not even unpack it but just leave it as it is. *No-one must see it.* At some moment before long I shall be asking you to send it on here, but not at present. Jenny *fille* and I shrieked "Creepy" in one of Dizzy's ears and "Crawley" in the other at the same moment while May drummed on the top of his head. He turned round howling and bit my nose, which has been patched up since!! It is all right now.

Kelmscott 19 Feb. 1874

Dear Dunn,

I am writing to Howell who will I suppose tomorrow wind up the Parsons business, as well as the picture of Proserpine, and I have told him he had better take or send to Cheyne Walk the negatives of my things (about 30 including those portraits taken from life in my garden) which are in Parsons' hands and which I may now reclaim. When they come, please *lock* them in a safe place and take care *no-one* meddles at all with them as they are very liable to damage. I am also writing to Mrs. Cowper, who has the other negatives taken by her brother Thurston Thompson.

I have taken up the Triple Rose, traced it from your water-colour on a new paper and painted the three heads straight off from little May successfully. You see I could not conveniently get Alice W. down here just now for the Roman Widow, and as this other thing had to be done I set about it from May who did charmingly for it. By the bye, was not a roll of Whatman's White Imperial paper sent here? I was greatly inconvenienced by finding none to paint this thing on, and could not have done it, had I not luckily found just one of those stained chalk papers which was white.

Ever yours,
D. G. R.

It might be as well for you to be in tomorrow (Friday) for the probable arrival of picture, etc.

Kelmscott 29 Feb. 1874.
Dear Dunn,

I think I said—bring the picture when here I will get it up into my studio before opening it, as I don't want its return to be spread abroad.

What a jolly thing to know the claimant is a convict at last.

Ever yours,
D. G. R.

Kelmscott April 1874
"Roman Widow" etc.

Dear Dunn,

I am thinking of making a drawing for a new picture before Alice leaves if I have time. Could you get me one of those reflecting globes one sees in gardens and in shop windows? The enclosed sketch which please return will show you the sort of size it might be. It would be best if a little dusky so as to darken the landscape about as much as a camera obscura.

Is there any Indian muslin quite thin at Cheyne Walk? I want some for the head-dress of the widow, which progresses very successfully—as good at least as any I have done. Head, hair, neck and one hand are finished. Tomorrow I do the second hand.

Ever yours, D. G. R.

Globe might come at once by passenger train if you can get it.

P.S. The picture is now, as I said, likely to be delayed for roses. What I want for the large festoon under the arm (which are needed first and *now*) are those warm white roses with the slightest flush towards the centre, such as I painted in Lilith and the Ghirlandata. I suppose there would be no possibility of you or Alice bringing me these from Covent Garden or elsewhere.

I have sent the rent and suppose you will get receipt.

Euston Square,
Wednesday

Dear Dunn,

I expect to sleep tonight at Chelsea. Would have let you know before but movements have been hurried.

Ever yours,
D. G. R.

Kelmscott
May 1874, Sunday.

Dear Dunn,

I am asking Alice W(ilding) to come here Tuesday evening, and expect to keep her Wednesday and Thursday. If you could come with her for this short time it would be a pleasure to see you and I could show you the picture which is getting towards a finish, but your presence is *not necessary* if inconvenient to you.

Thanks for the mounts. A lot must have been stolen as there were many.

Two of the dearest, and fluffiest, of infant owls have been caught. They sat on the breakfast table and were fed with hard boiled eggs.

All right about Queen Anne letters for title, Brucciani it were well to pay, and do so if you think best. At present funds are low till I get more, but I will send you small cheque by next post if necessary, and if I don't see you. Indeed, on second thoughts, I had better send £5. now for travelling expenses and am telling Alice to look to you for hers.

Would you kindly look up a perch or two—I think there must be more than one—that owls and parrots used to sit on at Chelsea. I want a good one for these little owls, which being young can be brought up quite tame. I will write word when to send it unless you or A.W. can bring it.

Graham has been to Madrid whence he wrote me the other day. He must now be back or nearly so. I have written him about Agnew's picture of which A promises him (at my request) the first offer.

Ever yours,
D. G. R.

Regnault you shall have when free. It is now at Turnham Green.

P.S. I hear with great concern that Boyce has broken his left arm. Would you call on him with my love and enquiries.

KELMSCOTT
June 1874—Sunday

Dear Dunn,

Many thanks for despatch. The things got here safely yesterday evening. The crimson drapery is simply a stupefaction to me. I swear I saw it here at the time that jacket was sent for.

It is a great nuisance the Elephant won't give up that pot. I *did* write her about it and have now sent her a picture of an elephant burying it in the garden. I *must* have it or else buy another.

Thanks about mulberry leaves.

The picture I am projecting is not yet begun, but it will be made up of colour and materials like that of Annie and the Marybuds.

Graham has bought the Annunciation from Agnew, but seems fidgety about the price, though A. only charged his buying commission, i.e. £425. in all. The picture is coming here for me to revise. I wish you would send me the exact title publisher and date of that book on Anatomy by Knox which you have. I want Ellis to get me one.

Graham asks about his replica. Have you yet got it on the canvas, and if so, can you give me an idea of the way you are proceeding as to method?

Ever yours,

D. G. R.

P.S. Graham is always talking about wanting a black and gold picture, together with the Blessed Damozel when that is fairly launched as the Venus cannot be done yet.

Another thing I ought to have without more delay is the 3 leaved screen. If you are still in town you might write to Bertram to see to all these at once under your own eye, but if not I must write to him and manage through Edmund. I suppose in all probability you will be back again at Chelsea before it becomes necessary to send the things for the Venus; but the canvases would I suppose come on straight from W. and N. and besides that I can't remember that there is now anything needed except your smaller cartoon which had better be put in one of the cases already bespoke if this reaches still in time. With love to F. to whom I shall write forthwith.

Ever yours,

D. G. R.

P.P.S. It is probable I may be sending very soon for A.W. and have written to her. If you are still in town and can call on her and see how she is situated as to coming, it might be well.

P.P.P.S. I judge by your not saying that the easel has yet been sent off, that such is not the case. I am much needing it. I find I don't need the old book, as I have a Mem. on the point.

K. Friday, June 1874.

Dear Dunn,

I have received a vague enquiry as to whether I wish to sell my lease at Chelsea. I have asked Watts to see the writer for me (without the least idea whether in any case I should sell or not) and have told him that as he, Watts, may probably wish to see the lease (or copy of lease) which is at Cheyne Walk, you will show it and if necessary lend it to him (Watts). Thanks for the China pot which arrived safely.

There was a toilet glass sent to Euston Square which always lacked one little ivory handle to a drawer—a thing about as large as this (sketch). Mike Halliday kindly turned me one to supply its place, and this must be somewhere at Chelsea. I thought it was probably in the little trinket case here but can see no sign of it. It is a pity it could not be stuck into its place. I daresay F. could lay her hand on it in some corner of the house.

I had better enclose cheque £10.

Ever yours,
D. G. R.

Saturday

My dear Dunn,

This is unaccountable about the sale. I forget if I told you that the work of mine in question was the little Lucrezia Borgia—the original, not F's—which I had taken back from Leyland in an exchange and which I had got him to put into Christies as his (with the others he was sending) as a ready way of disposing of it without trouble to me. A reserve price of £100 was to be put on it, and I had asked Marks to bid it up if things looked likely, otherwise to let it go for anything over the £100 it would fetch. This morning, just after your letter, I got a mysterious telegram apparently from the Elephant who should be represented working the telegraph. Telegram is from "Hughes" and says "Leyland has withdrawn the picture from the sale". What does it all mean? I am writing to Leyland for explanation and to Marks telling him of the result. I am also writing to F. enclosing the telegram.

Are your wits wool-gathering about the Signorelli picture? The enclosed, sent me by you, says bluntly that it was bought for the gallery. The one Leyland bought seems to have been a subject of Coriolanus. About A.W. you do not say what she said as to her immediate troubles and how soon she will need tin. Please keep an eye on her, for I don't want her to skedaddle. If she is much wanting tin I must manage to send her some, but may probably be asking her down here for a new head almost at once.

Ever yours, D. G. R.

p.s. About this Sale matter. I am writing F. for the same reason as before. The sum would be smallish—£160. and I have asked her if she gets it to place it in your hands in notes—not pass it to my account. I would then write Marks, so please let me know if he is away.

K. Tuesday.

Dear Dunn,

Weather divine here now. I'm writing Marks a line asking if he would come down here by 2.15 train from Paddington to Lechlade tomorrow, or else by 5.20 train. I've told him (if he likes) to look you up or telegraph you, as you say nothing as to if you can come.

I find I forgot to enclose Alice's last letter to you. It is mislaid however, but what she said was that she would reflect whether to "go into a family and travel"(!) and let me know the result of her reflections.

I may likely be asking her down here very soon indeed to begin another picture,

Ever yours,

D. G. R.

P.S. Barker pictures seem to have gone only very shadily as to price, when compared with the huge hauls for modern rubbish.

Wednesday

Dear Dunn,

I may probably be writing to F on a point of importance tomorrow.

I did enquire into the house point through Watts, and it is still in question, but am quite uncertain whether terms will suit me. You may be quite sure I have my eyes well open to all objections. The people seem eager, and possibly if they give £3000 I might turn out—not under that most assuredly. Indeed, I don't care one way or the other even then, as I hate the premature bother. What one would have to do would be to warehouse the furniture. Get a Newman St. studio or something of that sort for the large picture, and wait for a permanent place to turn up, while my lease runs out here which will be in about 15 months.

It is a real privation not to have seen the Barker pictures of which I have heard endless talk.

Of course, you won't name anything of this house matter to anyone.

Ever yours,

D. G. R.

I send you Reynault's by book post. If Watts brings anyone to see the house, of course it will be with my sanction and they can do so *in his company—not without him*. Of course, in such case you would take good care they saw no work of mine—especially the big picture. I don't mean, of course, that it could not remain in the studio, but must not be visible to examine.

One thing to do now at once is to cover the picture from Christies unless indeed it is still wandering in railways like half a dozen other things I have done. I write Marks to enquire. My name of course does not appear in the matter, the picture was sent in as Leyland's.

Please at leisure you or F. get me two or three pairs of common shirt sleeve links—pearl or something—quite cheap, but *double* links, not the stupid other kinds which can't be used. It is no use buying gold ones—they only get lost.

7th June.

My dear Dunn,

I enclose A.W.'s answer which is incomprehensible. After all, it wouldn't suit me that she should leave at all, and if nothing but housekeeping will give her occupation and keep her easy, I suppose she will have to do it. I wish you would have a serious talk with her and find out her intentions. I suspect she is in a fix and disposed to go to the devil with this probably good-for-nothing fellow of hers. You see if she hasn't a house of her own she probably couldn't receive him, and this may be the real reason she sticks to housekeeping. You know my engagement with her is for 30/- a week. What I have paid her since September/72 is at the rate of £2. a week with some £12. over. If she would try to live within expenses, I would give her £2. a week as her regular salary. I wish you would talk to her. You see if she left at present, she leaves much in my debt; and though I should not think for a moment of pressing this point, she would be behaving very badly if she did not consider my interests. If there is any immediate necessary outlay to get her out of some scrape, I will try and meet it in moderation. Please find this out and tell her (with due precaution) that I will not leave her in a mess. A *little* money has come in since I last wrote you.

I think it will be better at this moment for F. to meet all the expenses you name, keeping due account of them, and I will reimburse her.

By the bye, I find Brown brought visitors in to see the big picture. It can't be helped, but I wish he hadn't. As to the application to buy the house, Watts thinks a *large* premium would certainly be obtainable, but whether *so* large as to render my turning out worthwhile, I don't know yet. Of course, if (as evident) a rich person, they would expect to pay a much raised rent later.

K. 1874. Saturday.

My dear Dunn,

Damn this big haul for taxes! Are you certain they must all be paid now?

I have received the Triple Rose drawing safely. I must see about Brass's bill. I suppose I must write Watts a line to call on him, but it is such a bore explaining everything. Brown was here two days lately—left Sunday last quite well, but is since, I fear, very seriously ill. I trust he won't be long in mending.

I am doing the picture of little Annie with the marybuds and it is fast getting done.

Is enclosed cheque sufficient.

Ever yours,
D. G. R.

P.S. I just got a letter from Brown who is getting right again. I wish you'd get me a little pocket sketch book—*not* block-size as below or as near as maybe—*not* larger. Paper—Whatman's, *not* thick. Send it by post. I hope your own picture goes on all right.—but I suppose its sent in now.

Leyland dogged about Proserpine but pleased, I believe. Graham most kind about Bower Maiden, but I see rather disappointed at its being so realistic.

K. 1874 Saturday.

Dear Dunn,

I now find Howell *has* sent the picture to Chelsea, so no doubt you will bring it with you on Wednesday, which day I find will be soon enough for me. Please tell Alice.

Ever yours,

D. G. R.

K. 31 December 1874.

My dear Dunn,

By all means send the cartoon and drawing of Triple Rose. Only I have been looking everywhere here for the photo and cannot find it. I think you brought one down once, but did you take it back? At any rate, I shall need one, so if it is lost, please get another at once from Hedderley who has the negative, if not obtainable elsewhere.

You will be astonished to hear of another Proserpine smash! The one that went to Leyland is returned to me scratched all over by the broken glass, and the frame a complete wreck. I have repaired the picture satisfactorily but it is despairing work. However, Leyland has paid up . . . it seems the railways will not be answerable for more than £10. on any damaged picture unless specially rated in transport. So I suppose this must be done for the future.

I am sending £25. to Alice W. but my memorandum states that the last £25. (sent 13 September) settles up to 20th Jany.—not *first* week in Jany. I do not know how the account stood in September when I sent it, but have no doubt at all that my note is correct.

Ever yours,

D. G. R.

17

There is little in the foregoing correspondence to show that Gabriel was not in reasonably good health. But by the spring of 1874, the story takes on a sombre note. Gabriel once more became nervous and tense. He suspected the motives even of his closest friends. The winding up of Morris's firm—Morris, Marshall, Faulkner & Co.—disturbed him greatly. The bonds of friendship with some of his friends weakened. The kidney trouble, which had already given him pain and anxiety, returned to plague him, and he tired quickly. His answer to this was chloral, and more chloral.

A distressing incident occurred one day when Rossetti and George Hake were strolling by the river, and came upon a party of anglers. There was some shouting—probably good-tempered enough—and Gabriel grimly determined that the fishermen were insulting him. William, describing what happened, thought it unlikely that the men intended to be offensive—or, indeed, that they had taken much notice of anyone passing by. But Rossetti approached the men in a fury and there was a disturbing scene. George Hake did what he could to smooth things over, but the story was told in and around the district and lost nothing, you can be sure, in the telling.

Later in the year came another hammer-blow which for a while stunned Gabriel—the death of Oliver Madox Brown, a brilliant young man to whom he was greatly attached. There was a conspiracy, he felt sure, to make his life miserable. The "Heaven on earth" with its boathouse "and all things handy" (Morris's description) lost its magic. The golden days at Kelmscott were ended. The days of the half-light began.

Rossetti returned to Tudor House and took up the threads of old friendships which had suffered by reason of his long absence. It was no good. He was restless. He took both whisky and chloral in increasing doses. And 1875 found him in Aldwick Lodge, Bognor. Deeply concerned, his mother, his sister Christina, and Janey Morris visited him: and once more the stream of instructions flowed from Gabriel's pen to "my Dear Dunn".

Bognor, Thursday.

My dear Dunn,

I was much vexed to find that George omitted to telegraph early in yester-day to you as to my change of intention. I am afraid it must have caused you and F. inconvenience which would have been avoided had the telegraph been sent as I asked him to do early in the day. I am going to try to add some details (while here) to the *first* beginning of the Venus Astarte, which I abandoned for the second, i.e. principal head of same in a finished state, and turning it into a picture by itself for sale, which might soon be done and let us hope bring grist to the mill.

Leyland writes in much satisfaction with his pictures which he has hung at Princes Gate. There is a good deal of botheration occurring with Graham who is showing a good deal of impatience about the work of his remaining in hand. He is not otherwise than friendly, but dissatisfied and impatient. I should like as soon as possible to take up the "Found". What is doing with it? I feel reluctance now to open your parcel sent here and containing dia-grams as it is so well packed and would soon have to be packed again for return.

Ever yours,

D. G. R.

I wonder if the Cowper Temples would be at all likely to buy the Astarte head in question. Have you seen them at all?

Bognor, Tuesday.

My dear Dunn,

This place is getting frightfully cold, and I find has a reputation for being so. It has crossed my mind (only as a wild idea as yet) whether it might be feasible to push on to that place at the Undercliff, I. of Wight, which was described as a tropical paradise in winter. I should like at any rate to take the first step of ascertaining if it is still unlet. Neither George nor I can remember the name of the man at Lewisham who was applied to about it and owns the place. Could you look up among letters (presumably in that basket under my writing table) the letter or letters which referred to this place? I believe they will certainly be found. I don't know whether some of that kind may have got into the two centre drawers of the inlaid bureau next the corner window.

Will you impress on F. to keep the studio most strictly locked while you are away.

My third month (at 7½ guineas per week) terminated just a fortnight back, but from that date it is to be 6 guineas a week, which is still very high but one is in for it. However, if I get good work done I shall no doubt be gainer by good air, and shall not repine.

Ever yours,

D. G. R.

Bognor 1875 Tuesday.

Dear Dunn,

It is possible that Leyland is not at Speke where I wrote him on Saturday—

14. Rossetti himself (behind the monk's right shoulder) and some of his friends are also recognisable in this panel from the Jacobean cupboard (painted by Dunn). Top row—Tennyson, William Morris, Millais, Ruskin, unknown, Rossetti. In front, possibly Woolner, Mrs. Rossetti, Christina Rossetti and Swinburne.

15. A Max Beerbohm drawing inspired by the notorious "menagerie" in the garden of No. 16, Cheyne Walk. The figures may be identified as follows: behind or on the wall, Swinburne, Theodore Watts (later Watts-Dunton), and Hall Caine. Whistler is in front of the wall and next to him, Meredith. Facing the kangaroo is Burne-Jones, while the bearded, declamatory figure under close observation by a pelican is William Morris. On the right, Holman Hunt, and in front of him, Ruskin. Rossetti himself sketches in the foreground, and the lady is described as "no one in particular; just a vague synthesis". But students of the household at No. 16 will make a shrewd guess.

still one would think the letter would have been sent on to him in London and got answered by this morning.

I see he has made a pretty haul out of that stupid Leighton. I should think he would buy more Leightons—and sell them.

Ever yours,
D. G. R.

Bognor Oct. 1875 Sunday.

My dear Dunn,

I should think that the height of the right measure of canvas had better be still further reduced, now that I have made up my mind not to include the lower hands: as the shorter it is the more convenient in working. If it reaches a little below the right elbow of the Venus (the elbow belonging to the upper hand) this would be sufficient—the rest could be turned over at back. Would you kindly see to this? I will write again almost immediately about forwarding things.

George has put your letter in his pocket and gone on the tramp, so perhaps I may omit some desirable point of reply.

About Brass's box, really I will take no such thing. It is absurd to suppose that London cannot produce a moderate priced box to hold my tin-pot plate, but we must send to Sheffield and spend £5!! Was ever anything so absurd? Charles assures me that he never dreamt of any such thing as ordering it, and that less than half the money ought to have procured it. He says the right measure of the box should be about that of an ordinary dinner tray. As Brass has chosen to have this box made without asking further questions, he must either return it to the makers or sell it to us at a moderate price.

Dizzy's first sight of the sea resulted in violent and indignant barking at the aggressive billows. He then shook a piece of seaweed like a rat, and seeing that nothing subsided, he almost choked with rage. He then walked on a little way, refusing to look at it again, but shortly subsided on his haunches and had a spasm in which it was thought he would expire, but he survived. He now walks in a little, and staggers about, spitting the salt water from his gullet: and the general result is that his usual doggy smell has a twang of Tidman's Sea Salt.

There was an alarm of the Euston Square baby—nurse and all—being shot here, but I took prompt measures and it has blown over. Thanks for the books sent on. Both are excellent and very cheap. The History of Shipping, a fine old stodgy book of its kind—plates very good and the earlier ones sure to be useful.

I really should be glad if you could look up Howell. I have had no word from him or Valpy either since that letter of V's to which I replied: but two days ago I got a most full and particular series of enquiries. I should like to know how the married couple in the house get on. Do you find them suitable? You know the man engaged to get the garden right with a little assistance, and I am very anxious this should be done.

On second thoughts, I think the easel and fittings had better be sent *at once*.

N

Howell was in disgrace again. The truth of the matter can be found in Howell's own volatile and egocentric approach to life. When Gabriel was in London and a cab to Cheyne Walk was the simplest of matters, he could concentrate on the Rossetti affairs. When he was away in the country, it was a case of out of sight, out of mind. His man was the client on the spot.

Thursday.

My dear Dunn,

I don't know whether after reading Fry's letter which I enclose, you will think it better to call at Fulham or not. Fry's first and longer letter brings, as you will see, very serious matter indeed to bear against H. The £200 cheque extracted from Fry in exchange for one afterwards dishonoured is no joke at all. It must surely amount to obtaining money under false pretences, or indeed to positive theft.

I should like to send you with this a copy of my letter in reply to Fry's first and which produced his second very satisfactory note. You will judge by its tone how completely I set myself right with him; but I am unable to send you a copy of mine, though one was made by George, for the reason that George scrawled it in pencil over about a quire of paper which has since got scattered all over the house. I send you a copy I retained of my answer to Fry's second. You will see that I did my best to avert his just wrath from H. I wrote yesterday to H. himself most seriously, telling him (though not the details) that Fry had written me of his misdoings, and insisting on the exchange matter between him and me being *at once* wound up, for which perforce he must furnish me with items and total up his account, against which I will set work *at once*. I told him I should charge the pearl pin at my own price to the account, as he has evidently pawned it or put it somewhere out of reach, and I demanded the St. George drawings to be sent to Chelsea at once. I told him if silence should prove his answer as usual, I should put the matter without delay in a lawyer's hands.

After payments made by cheque and £50. sent here in notes from the bank for current expenses, I find there is but £230. left in the Bank.

Ever yours,

D. G. R.

Please return enclosures and seal your letter in doing so.

Bognor

My dear Dunn,

I thought George had returned the "Found" diagrams. As they are still here, I shall now take a good look at them, but every minute gets run to nothing somehow—though I seem to get little done. Thanks. Will you give my love to F and tell her that I have slept better the last two nights and am feeling somewhat better altogether. The worries you speak of *are* worries and may be great ones, but it was not those which caused me restless nights, as I began to suffer in that way long before I heard of the matters in question. This cursed Howell ought really to be put out of every decent house. What *does* he mean? He is, I suppose, likely to be seriously in for it. I am writing a line to Watts, and shall name the pearl pin to him.

Ellis being Marks' backer is a new fact to me, though I had surmised it as possible. Did he see the Proserpine? I ask because I possess a replica in a forward state as you know which I *may* be obliged to part with. Do not mention this in any way at present however to Marks or anyone.

The mattress I wrote about is thus. I have been sleeping lately on the only one which can be sleepable on in my present bad-sleeping state (all of the others here I had experienced till lately and they are abominable). Someone is coming now who will need the only available mattress, and hence my note of one from Chelsea. I suppose it can easily be sent with safety, can it not? I hope now to be getting on to some extent with the Astarte.

I suppose you received—did you?—an impression that Ellis was really pleased with the Bella Mano, and not discouraged by its being still on his hands.

Ever yours,

D. G. R.

Bognor, Wednesday.

My dear Dunn,

I cannot be certain after all about any throne being needed. Can you send me the dimensions of the one at Chelsea? Nothing need be sent on just yet in the way of easel, high chair, Cartoon of Venus etc. but I will send word in time. A tracing of the Venus cartoon with red chalk outline at back, would have to be sent with it.

It pours here like anything, and there is no seaside walking at present, the tide being always high at manageable hours. The house is agreeable, but never was there such a bad one for painting. Every window of the least importance has a heavy hood projecting which makes the room quite dark. I don't know how I shall manage eventually.

Ever yours,

D. G. R.

You send me the bill from Jameson. I told him, if he does send a receipt, to send it to you at Cheyne Walk.

Friday, ALDWICK LODGE, Bognor.

My dear Dunn,

Thanks for the care of my belongings. You are the best of fellows and my guardian angel. If I show any impatience pray pardon. Do about Bertram just what you think necessary. I should be glad to hear that the man in the house, being a gardener, was doing something in the garden as he proposed, and should be willing to pay a cheap assistant, which was his plan. Indeed it much depends on this being done now, whether or not the expense with Winsett is to prove of any permanent use. I am sending a cheque to the Elephant, and enclose one to yourself, as no doubt you need the same.

The green dress I name with others in my last is *not* the dark one I painted in the fiddle picture, but one of the same material as the curtains of the large window in the studio.

Would you lodge Miss Boyd's picture safely in the studio before you go away.

Ever yours,

D. G. R.

Aldwick Lodge, nr. Bognor Sunday

My dear Dunn,

I daresay you will soon be back in Chelsea now, but judge that you must at present be at Broadlands. All personal matters go well here. Alice Wilding has just returned this evening to London after my getting the head and hands successfully done in Graham's picture. My mother and Christina have been here some days and are both well. The gales are tremendous since last evening—the sea higher than it has been known altogether for eighteen years, and havoc on all hands. A fine elm, the central feature of the large lawn, lies prostrate, and the cows are feeding on its branches. How long the gale will last I know not, but it shows no sign of subsiding as yet in any decided degree.

22 Dec. 1875.

Aldwick Lodge, Bognor

My dear Dunn,

I enclose cheque for use, out of which please pay A. W. £20. as she has written for money. I suppose she will be glad to get it before Xmas Day, and write to her with this that I have asked you to give her same. We have hardly written to each other lately: probably things have been as stagnant at Chelsea as here. Graham sent £300 on account of the Blessed Damozel picture—thus there is something in hand for the present. Tell me if I shall send you some on your own account. I was glad to hear from F. that Leycester wanted you to paint his portrait.

Howell goes on humbugging as usual. I suppose if he brings Baron Grant (who is the big buyer he talks of) to the studio they must be let in: but I am writing to H. that I won't have the man there unless he is as sure to prove a buyer as Fry was. Moreover, the pictures must be put in proper viewing order before he comes: and this devolves on Howell to see after.

I don't know whether or not I shall be returning to town immediately after New Year's Day. It will depend on chances of further work here. My work has been scanty enough as yet: still the Blessed Damozel's head and hands are quite a success and I see that picture can be very readily finished. The other one gives me anxiety, though the head and shoulders (which were all I could get done in the time, so arduous were the sittings) is certainly not otherwise than successful—only I want it to be *so very* successful. This picture also is a quick going one, the heads once secured.

You probably know that my mother, Christina, two aunts and some of George's family are coming down here for Xmas Day.

I suppose the Hakes will go on the Monday—the others, or at any rate, my mother and sister, will stay on probably till the New Years Day.

All good wishes of the season, my dear Dunn, from Your affec.

D. G. ROSSETTI.

P.S. I was omitting to say what however you probably know—viz. that the Bride of Nettleship has definitively come to hand in the person of a Miss Hinton, daughter of a retired artist—herself a sculptress. So he writes me. Did you ever hear of the lady as an artist?

Kelmscott Sunday 1875.

My dear Dunn,

I'm very sorry to hear how much you have suffered with your inflamed eye. I have myself once or twice in my life undergone the like torture, which is among the worst of nuisances. I hope you will have now got over it.

I heard today from Howell, who shows no special sign of dilemma, though in this and former letters he speaks as usual of money pressure. He says he has sold works for Sandys—a picture and three portraits—at £1,000 apiece, whether to Fry I do not learn.

Mrs. M. has just left for the present—perhaps to return after Xmas, if I am still here. The sittings were inevitably short ones, and I only got the head and neck done, not the arms and hands which remain to do. But a beginning is made and I hope a good one.

I forget how far the life size version of the Sphinx design was carried. Would you tell me? I want to take it up on that scale as soon as I can. Did Valpy send for his chalk drawing?

Howell asks whether Marks has yet done anything with La Bella Mano. I suppose it is still where it was, is it not? What a rum 'un he is!

Would you send me those two little Vols. of poetry by Dixon—one called "Christ's Company"—I forget the name of the other. I think they are in the studio—otherwise in my breakfast room.

I hope Fan continues well. I have felt very anxious about her during this severe winter. Things are now somewhat improving down here. George has been in London yesterday and today. Perhaps you have seen him. I will give him your note. The fish from Walkers I stopped at one time: but I suppose it is just lately that some may have been got again.

Ever yours,
D. G. R.

P.S. If it is still feasible when you get this, I think it would be well to include in one of the cases a couple of pieces (in good condition) of the silk gauze material I use so much. The whole lot is in that little cabinet made by Stennett, now standing in the back hall. I suppose the key is among the other things in the usual drawer. I habitually carry it in my pocket but cannot find it there at present.

P.P.S. Since closing this letter I open it again to say that Mrs. Conway 2 Pembroke Gardens, Kensington, has written wishing for her pictures and proposes to send her son for them. If you can conveniently take them in a cab to her yourself or send Bertram tomorrow (Saturday) I think it would be a desirable civility on my part. But if this is not practical, I have told her that after that day she had perhaps better send her son for them. I should not wish anyone but Bertram to go with them except, of course, yourself.

Bognor Sunday, December 1875

My dear Dunn,

Many thanks for your letter and the new particulars about the wondrous Lucas. He is evidently far from taking a mean rank among mortals, and this renders it all the more curious that he should be able to persuade himself of such oddities as being facts. All you say about exaggerated tea drinking is most true, but how to deny thy friend when he asketh for a cup of tea?

The Valpy letter *was* found among a mass which George had brought down here to put in order. If he had originally told me he had this mass I need not have troubled you before looking through it. We have now heard again from the owner and the house is still unlet—£4. a week for the winter months and £8. for the summer ones—much cheaper than this. George will probably go to look at it.

A letter from F. crossed mine to her. Will you thank her for the paper containing account of this strange story about Shelley's death. I incline to suppose it certainly is true, *if* the *confession* itself is a fact and not an empty rumour.

Coming primarily through so very fanciful a person as Kirkup it seems to me some prudence would have been exercised in waiting a little before it got into print. Shelley's son must be much pained by it.

I was extremely glad to hear from you that the old gardener had done his work so well, and shall view him as my debtor for an Xmas box, otherwise it might really have cost another big sum to make things tidy. What sort of people are he and his wife?—at all possible, do you think, for permanent servants? Can the wife cook at all. And is she inoffensive?

My Astarte progresses favourably: head and hair are now done.

Ever yours,

D. G. R.

Monday 1875

My dear Dunn,

Charles has just found your trousers here and they are going at once to you.

I am very anxious at finding that *one* at least of the black morocco covered square ms. books is missing, among the lot which I brought here and which I suppose to be all. I believe I gave *all* to George who packed them either in the studio or front room, but I judge may have left one out by accident, or else one may still be lying in the bottom drawer nearest the angle in the upper part of the black and gold cabinet in the corner of the studio on which the Clytie bust stands, that being very usual and proper receptacle. Or else one might accidentally be lying on the desk near the window or elsewhere in the studio. As well look in the other drawers, too. I shall be very anxious till I learn something about this ms. book as it happens to be just the one containing drafts and schemes for new work, and without it much would be lost. I know I have seen it quite lately, as I remember reading part of its contents.

If, as I hope though with some misgiving, you find the ms. book in question it had better come with the above things in the same case, as this I think safer than coming alone, but please let me know by return whether you can find it.

Yours ever, D. G. R.

P.S. Another thing you might enclose is the blue leaved bank book which I use in making remittances to the bank. I think I told you that Fry had paid the £500. Curiously enough he had sent it spontaneously (in a letter which you sent on here) and my request crossed it.

18

The friendly note about Harry's trousers is a reminder that clothes were frequently interchangeable—especially when Rossetti and his associates were younger. In a letter to William his brother once wrote: "I know not whether you have to go anywhere tonight, but just today you have put on the only pair of breeches in which it is possible for me to go to the opera tonight. Unless you *do* want them yourself, I wish if possible you would manage to be home by 5, in order that we may make a transfer. . . ."

There is also a domestic and somewhat appealing touch in Gabriel's: "My Dear Dunn—your dress trousers are, I believe, in the drawer near the window in my bedroom. I saw two pairs lying there lately and I believe I only possess one. . . ."

The year 1876 was an unhappy one. In November Rossetti was profoundly distressed by the death of his sister, Maria. She was forty-nine and for three years had been a professed member of an Anglican Sisterhood.

Then the dubious methods of the "ruffianly" Howell became too much for him: and their connection ended. William was careful to point out that Howell had never "wronged him in any money-transactions": but the agent's ideas of integrity were very loosely defined, and he had been raising money on the strength of various Rossetti drawings he did not own.

Also in 1876 a Mr. Levy threatened to take legal action against Howell, and a dress which had come into Rossetti's possession was involved. The artist's honour was never at any time in question, but he paid Levy forty pounds to ensure that he would not be called on to give evidence in the distasteful affair.

In the following year Rossetti was justifiably incensed when some drawings said to be his work turned up in a London art-dealer's shop.

One picture, examined by Rossetti, was patently a forgery, and he wrote to *The Times* to make his position clear. Howell was an excellent facsimilist ("ingenious" is the adjective William Rossetti used) and when other works appeared, while Gabriel was still alive and also after his death, his friends drew their own conclusions.

Sunday.

My dear Dunn,

You may as well be posted up in the Fry correspondence, so I now send you a copy of my answer to Fry's first letter, which answer elicited his second very friendly note. I think the request for the pen and ink drawing in his first was rather sharp practice, but I suppose he had been induced to suspect that I had been possibly making a covert profit out of him in concert with Howell. D—n that fellow! In his second note, he makes no reference to my reply on this point of the pen and ink drawing. Please let me have the copy of letter back *by return* as I may need it. It would be better to seal your letter.

I have answered Skelton's letter and you need *not* send his back on.

Of course, you would let no word out to Howell on any point of detail. I have written him at full length demanding a settlement but he does not answer. No doubt he could give me trouble about the exchange transactions, but not successfully I think. The mere fact that he planted the transaction, or a part of it, *as an exchange* on Fry, transferring my liability for drawings to him, would be a clear proof that such was the real nature of the bargain, and Fry would of course give willing testimony. Besides this, I should have George and you quite cognizant of this matter.

Ever yours, D. G. R.

P.S. There are various accounts—lists of goods furnished to me and also of drawings I have promised to Howell as against such goods. These must be about the studio and I would be much obliged to you to look up all such.

Sunday 1876

My dear Dunn,

I am writing to Watts about this filthy Levy. Would you send his exact address to Watts at 2, Danes Inn, marked *Immediate* on envelope. I enclose cheque—am short, but have written to Graham for the rest of the money on his picture—£250. as the only thing to do. I am getting on with it but there is still a lot of work. The draperies came alright. Thanks.

There was not, however, a female mediaeval dress of the kind I mean. I referred to those which are made for a loin girdle. If you conveniently can, you might send me one—with sleeves in of the long hanging kind—but don't send anything of value unless well protected.

The muslin thing belonging to the La Pia dress is an outer dress like the one in that Botticelli portrait of mine—but this I do not need at present.

Ever yours, D. G. R.

I have now sent money on account to Liberty £50; Middlemist £36. 2s. Thresher & Glenny £7 14. 6d. Chas Ellis £50. 13. Bell & Co. £15. All these except Ellis have been directed to send receipt to Cheyne Walk.

Thursday

My dear Dunn,

You see I did not make my appearance and suppose I shall not do so at present. I see by chance that Brass is down on your list of Xmas bills for something near £30. What is this for? I thought I paid him up lately. Has packing things to come here reached this huge expense? Some packages seem more costly than needed. The last draperies, which were chiefly little better than rags, were enshrined in a capital case which could not be made for nothing. A hamper, it seems, with a rough cloth sewed round it so as to prevent its being easily opened, would answer as well in cases of this kind. I begin to feel quite depressed about so many liabilities, besides having other anxieties to depress me too.

When you write again please answer me as to whether Ellis saw the Proserpine and how he seemed to like it. I told you my reason for asking. The Levy business promises of course to come at least half on *my* shoulders, short of getting subpoenaed which would be a worse outlay and bother in reality. Howell has now reached a pitch of undisguised ruffianism.

I suppose you realised clearly that Ellis is Marks' backer and did not merely come with him to look at pictures.

Ever yours,

D. G. R.

Thursday, 1876.

My dear Dunn,

You did not mention what F. tells me—i.e. that the Cadogan people had sent to enquire about the repairs. How about this? I have let Watts know the fact. He is seeing about the Jew business. Thanks for package (not yet here) and for the list sent. Graham has sent £250, closing account for Blessed Damozel. This would enable me to pay what is most necessary of the Xmas batch. What do you reckon to be so?

In haste for post.

Ever yours,

D. G. R.

Bognor, 1876 Wednesday.

My dear Dunn,

Your reduction of the sketches arrived safely. Thanks. I shall be glad of some news of you when leisure serves.

Above is the size of a little memorandum book you must have seen me use and which has just got filled. It exactly fits my waistcoat pocket and has a sheath for a pencil to slip into inside. I think I once bought two (now both filled) for 1/6d. the pair. There is a somewhat similar notebook blank as yet, in some corner at Chelsea—perhaps in the table drawer or in a drawer of the black cabinet, or in the envelope case. Would you send it me if found. But it is not so good as the two I have used, so if in passing a stationers shop you could get me several of that kind, they would all get used if I live.

I shall be getting ahead now I hope with the Blessed Damozel picture—indeed, I am fairly launched in it now. Have made two studies of Mary (housemaid) for angels at bottom of picture and shall get them both painted in a few days. —also have done a complete study for the background arrangement—can do the drapery from the old laying-in with help of a bit of the gauze for colour, which I have here. When all this is in the picture it will look more than half finished and really be so—indeed more like two-thirds, and I make little doubt of getting so far in a fortnight, after which I shall have an opportunity of taking up the Astarte again here. I hope to good purpose. So I shall be staying on here at present.

Bognor, 21 March 1876

My dear Dunn,

Many thanks for your beautiful sketch of Donatello's cherub. I enclose a cheque for £50. having received this morning one for £500 from Mr. Fry. I wrote to him on Thursday last to ask for this advance and received on Saturday a letter from him informing me of the direct misdoings on the part of the accursed Fulham wretch (Howell) who had somehow mixed up my name with some of them as usual. I wrote in full explanation and today get an assurance of Fry's utmost confidence together with the desired cheque. I will probably send you the correspondence which is curious. Today or tomorrow I shall write finally and very seriously to Howell against whom Fry (who felt much interest in him) is now much incensed. In acknowledging Fry's cheque by this post I tried to say what could be said to mitigate his wrath against H. but the position of the matter has grown very serious.

I write to A.W. today telling her that you will let her have money in the course of tomorrow. I find noted in cheque book £50. in various payments to her since September last. She is doubtless much overdrawn. It is necessary no doubt to let her have this £25. (I suppose tomorrow) on account of her rent. That will make £75. since September last. Pardon the trouble.

I judged rightly that you have been quite unable to get anything out for yourself of the scanty supplies I have sent. You are most good and patient. Will you take some out of the present, and let me know if any more needed on your own account?

I must now proceed to pay something on account of Xmas bills but it is too late for the post tonight. I will send, however, to the coal merchant at once.

Ever yours, D. G. R.

Bognor, March 31st 1876 Friday

My dear Dunn,

The housemaid, Mary, is leaving and will call for her things at Cheyne Walk on Monday about 12 or 1. I should be glad if she were prevented from gossiping with the old people in the house, but made to take her things and go promptly. It strikes me as possible that since she has sat to me a little here, she may take it in her head to become a model and might possibly ask you for directions how to do so. If she does, please decline to give her any.

F. seems again out of sorts in a most absurd manner about nothing. I fear her health must be queer. I write to her with this as to the housemaid leaving.

Ever yours,

D. G. R.

Funds are running low, of course, and all things conspire downwards with me. Of course, you will have due notice of my running up.

One question I have always meant to ask, have you seen Miss Boyce.

P.S. Probably I shall get at once your answer as to whether Leyland has removed his pictures yet. I wish to know. I did quite understand about that Japanese mandolin. Howell, I believed, proposed to buy it himself from Liberty and put it to my account in the exchange transaction but I suppose Liberty's mem. means that Howell has never paid and he wants to know who owes for it.

Saturday

My dear Dunn,

I need hardly say if you do see Howell and he fishes for details about this correspondence or any other points I have mentioned, of course you know *nothing*. I did not let him know what Fry's charge was.

Would you look carefully at the pearl pin and see whether it is alright. The story now (as told in a note by Mrs. H. which I shall not answer) is that she broke it at a party and the jeweller who had to mend it has kept it till now—for some 9 months. If deteriorated I shall return it to him and charge it at my own price to the account.

Ever yours,

D. G. R.

P.S. No doubt neither Fry nor Valpy—both the kindest of men—would prosecute H. criminally. Probably with harsher customers he has kept more on the right side of the law. Else he might really end like his last friend Hogg.

Bognor Tuesday

Dear Dunn,

It is possible though quite uncertain that I may be in London tomorrow (Wednesday). I am not quite sure whether I should come to Chelsea to sleep or go to Euston Square, but would like things to be right at Chelsea. If not that evening, you would doubtless see me next day or next evening. Better not tell F as all is, as I say, quite uncertain and I can send to her when I get to Chelsea if I do come.

Ever yours, D. G. R.

Dear Dunn,

I send you a letter from the now jubilant Valpy. That large chalk—the one of which you joined the strainer at the back—is *not* at Chelsea is it? Did you really perhaps after all overlook the oil head in question called Beatrice—just a head of Mrs. M. with a scrap of green background—or is *that* also not there?

The Kingden sketch is, of course, not here in any case whatever.

Ever yours,

D. G. R.

P.S. It strikes me—did the fellow H. manage to plant this oil head in the house somewhere on the day he called and found you away? I suppose and hope the studio is kept locked at such times. Did you look for the oil head in the glass case.

P.S. Continued. If you do find the oil head just ask if H had anything in his hand the day he called and if he went into my room.

Tuesday

My dear Dunn,

You are right a thousandfold about that cursed commission, and you of all men have every right to rate me. It was done in a rash moment when I thought my incomings would warrant it, and though I have now for some time regretted it as unfair to others and perhaps undeserved from me by its object, I have nevertheless thought it best to clear it off and not have it continuing to hang on me. Pardon me, my dear Dunn. I was very foolish to do it, but I thought myself not unjustified at the moment. Take every care that F. does not know it, or there will be a final row with her.

I wrote to Fry to enquire if he had heard further about H. and enclose his reply—a pretty affair this second case! Please let me have it again under seal. By the bye, where did you get your seal of Hercules, or whatever it is?

Ever yours, D. G. R.

P.S. I am answering Fry (not without the need of long explanation) that I cannot show the Astarte to Herkomer or anyone just now. I am enclosing also a letter from Carr which may interest you. Please return it with the other, and of course do not mention the subject. I have given no final reply, but written leaving the question open. I send the cheque owing to the bank.

(Notes in margin) Three bundles of letters sealed in 2nd drawer below cash drawer in the bookcase in studio. Two top drawers full of letters unsorted.

Aldwick Lodge, Bognor, 2nd April 1876

From Dr. Hake:

My dear Dunn,

Accept my apologies for not having written to you before. I can only now say that I will attend to everything you draw my attention to in your letters. Would you kindly pay Mary £2. (two pounds) when she calls at Cheyne Walk at 12 tomorrow and get a receipt from her to the effect that it is in settlement of all claims. I paid her all else: had no further change. I am sorry to have to trouble you on this matter but as I will write and explain tomorrow the whole affair of turning Mary away was so sudden not to mention "*fads*" of the moment that I was completely upset. I will write and explain all tomorrow.

Believe me,
Faithfully yours
GEORGE.

Aldwick Lodge Bognor
4 April 1876
Dear Dunn,
I will write and advise you of all movements. At present the barometer points to "worry" most persistently. I assure you that my nerves are not worth the purchase. Excuse this short letter. Worry! Worry! Worry!
GEORGE.

Bognor, Thursday, April 1876
My dear Dunn,
I send a cheque for £30. which please cash at your convenience and on way home call on Morgan & Sons, 20 Hanover St. Oxford St. and pay £22. 15s. keeping remainder for yourself towards our accounts. Let me know what you may need in this respect. When going to Morgan please put his bill in your pocket and make him receipt it. Will you also see if he has hot water plates—full size like what I use. If so, I will take as many as half a dozen if he has that number—but should be glad even of one or two.
Ever yours,
D. G. R.

Bognor, Tuesday, 1876.
Dear Dunn,
On getting yours I looked up the d—d Jew's address among letters and sent it to Watts. I have written F to ask if she got alright the cheque I sent her on Friday last.
Does there happen to be a copy of Swinburne's "Erechtheus" lying for me at Cheyne Walk? If so, I do not want it sent on, but ought to acknowledge it to him. But I daresay he has not (very rightly) sent me one, as I never wrote in order to acknowledge Bothwell.
Ever yours,
D. G. R.

Do not trouble to answer about S's book if not at C.W.

Bognor Sunday re "Found"
My dear Dunn,
I don't know what time you have at present that is not required for present

work of your own, as you are probably getting something ready for the Exhibition. But whenever you have time for my work, I would be glad if you would enlarge the Magdalene subject to the proportions of the Dante replica (i.e. figures of that size) using as your guide the nude sketch you made for perspective planes. I want to get the subject out on the scale I mean to paint it on, so as to be available at any moment when I may wish to take it up.

Another job which has been haunting me is the necessity of ascertaining by perspective measurement whether that calf and cart in that beginning of the London picture are on their proper plane, or whether it will not be necessary to move them higher up. But for this worry, I might possibly have tackled the picture again before now.

There is somewhere (I fancy in the lower drawers of the black and gold cabinet in the studio) a pen and ink design in which the cart seems in its right place, and that is higher than in the picture. If this is absolutely wrong, it will I suppose be necessary to take this long suffering work of art to pieces again and re-patch and re-line it. Could you make such a diagram as will enable us to ascertain the fact about this point, and then if necessary I must call the liner in once more; but if it can stand, I shall thank the gods.

I don't know exactly what my next moves will be. There is such a lot to carry on one's back since the things came over from Kelmscott that one must not think lightly of a move back before one is quite sure one means it.

My impression is that the Grant business I mentioned is all moonshine. I suppose you have seen no more of Marks nor probably of Howell.

Ever yours,

D. G. R.

Bognor, May 1876, Monday.

My dear Dunn,

It was only yesterday morning that I heard from Watts of the monstrous "legal" outrage attempted against me. You acted most wisely in saying nothing about it. George went up yesterday to town and saw Watts and Marshall and I am assured that proper steps can be taken to render the outrage quite abortive. George has just returned here (afternoon) with this report. I am sure the matter must have weighed painfully on your friendly mind and am very sorry about it. I daresay you kept poor F. in ignorance, but if she heard of it, pray re-assure her at once. If I learn that she knew of it, I will write to her. It is a very good thing I did not leave this place earlier.

I don't know if you are aware that the repairs question has just reached a climax. George brought the news from Watts this afternoon that it was necessary to decide it *today*, by telegram to him. He had got Pemberton and Hunt down to £300. to be paid at end of term: and as I did not know whether they might not probably expect me to go out *at once* if I elected that course, and as there was no time for consideration, I have telegraphed to keep on to end of term and then pay the £300. This seems the better course.

You have not I think heard of a place in Surrey—rent £100—old-fashioned and promising in description but I fear with no good painting room, which

George spotted in Debenham's list and which we are in some treaty about. I don't know of course whether it will come to anything but am much inclined to find moderate country quarters if possible, and wherever I went, should probably have to set up a studio of some sort.

I daresay funds are low with you. So they are with me. Nevertheless if unavoidable you must let me know. I have *some* prospects of improvement.

Ever yours, D. G. R.

P.S. Fry seems to have come to some compromise of some sort with Howell which will (if duly met!) prevent going into court about the cheque business. I have put Watts into relation with Fry who he assures me, is ready to buy to any extent, but these things are only really known when brought to the push. I have been going on satisfactorily with the picture made out of the *first* commencement of the Astarte now turned to a smaller and different thing which may bring grist to the mill.

Bognor, 1876, Sunday.

My dear Dunn,

My return will be either tomorrow (Monday) night, or else Tuesday or Wednesday. I judge not later. Do not mention this too freely, but of course I wrote a line to Fan. There are several necessary worries connected with my return.

Leyland has written wanting his pictures and I now write with this to Bertram to fetch them and take them to Leyland's new house in Princes Gate. I can't remember the number but it is the house that used to be Lord Somers, and Leyland's name also must be known as having taken it. I *think* you will find the exact address to Leyland's name in my address book. Of course, it is not the old house in Queen's Gate, but the *new* one in Princes Gate. In any case, Bertram will be able to find it by enquiring quite readily.

The pictures to go are the Fiddle, the Proserpine and the Roman Widow and the Lilith. The new unfinished picture is to remain. The glasses should be cleaned before they go.

There is the most vexatious question of the surveyors still pending. I write to Watts with this to try and get them over the house before Wednesday at latest, if not possibly earlier. It will be most irritating if they come while I am there.

You know there is a quantity of furniture here which came from Kelmscott. All this will have to go back to Chelsea and it is not easy to know where to put it. I propose to turn the bed up of the first floor bedroom and put it in the side breakfast room and then use the present first floor bedroom as a breakfast and evening sitting room, putting the Kelmscott things in there. It would be much better if this change could be made before I come. I rather incline not to employ Brass, but if you think it best, let him do it. Otherwise Bertram might perhaps be willing to do it. But probably Brass will be best if you superintend.

I should propose I think to sleep in your present bedroom myself, as I

16. Dante Gabriel Rossetti reading his poems to Theodore Watts-Dunton at No. 16, Cheyne Walk. This picture by Henry Treffry Dunn hangs in the National Portrait Gallery.

17. A self-portrait by Henry Treffry Dunn, painted towards the end of his life.

18. This Celtic cross, designed by Ford Madox Brown, marks the grave of Dante Gabriel Rossetti near the South Porch of All Saints' Church, Birchington, Kent. The inscription reads: "Here sleeps Gabriel Charles Dante Rossetti, honoured under the name of Dante Gabriel Rossetti, among painters as a painter, and among poets as a poet."

19. A full-length photograph of Henry Treffry Dunn taken in the early days of his association with D. G. Rossetti.

always did formerly, and that you should occupy the side room next to it. The new first floor room would have to be kept in case of a visitor I fancy. All this may need reconsideration but at present such is my view. It would be a great boon if this could be done *before I come*, so as not to have endless noise overhead when I am there. The thing to do is to clear a space in the present breakfast room for the bed from the next room, put it up there (I suppose with its back where the *oak* chest is at present—i.e. next the fireplace —to put it where the other pictured chest is would need the removal of that troublesome black and gold corner cupboard) but if this seems best it would have to be done, or else the bedstead laid in the breakfast room simply in pieces, and the other things left there for the present. Perhaps there is only time at present for this, as the bedstead may not be at once wanted on my return; but it would be best if possible.

It is possible I may be sending some bedding on before coming, if I don't come by tomorrow. My plan would be to come up with George and the things involved in my work. Then for him to see about the packaging people in London, and come back here with them and a proper conveyance to fetch away the rest. I am writing in great haste. Pray pardon.

I have been far from well for some days. The train I shall almost certainly come by is very late and only gets to London Bridge at midnight—not coming to Victoria. Thence we should go on by cab and be at Chelsea about one or a little before.

About servants there will be no need to consider anything till I come. George will get in some cold provisions which will be quite sufficient for a day or two.

Ever yours,
D. G. R.

Thanks for finding the hot water plates. Of course don't send them here.

Wednesday.

My dear Dunn,

After all I shall not be coming up for some days yet. One or two things make it more convenient to stay on a little. Pardon uncertainty. I will write further as to movements at Chelsea and things I may be sending on.

Watts writes me that the surveyor nonsense is at an end. He (W) and Hunt are to settle to give a sum to be fixed by me at end of my term instead of doing repairs. Our own surveyor turned out no use and has been cashiered. I suppose you know that Pembertons are now still disposed to forego repairs or payments if I will go out; but this seems hardly feasible with nowhere to go to. Still one must consider.

Ever yours,
D. G. R.

George proposes that you should take his room and he sleep on the studio sofa.

o

Tuesday.

My dear Dunn,

I make no doubt of coming up tomorrow (Wednesday) by the late train I mentioned. I suppose I must rob you of your room even if the bed is still up on the first floor, as the bedding for that bed is here and cannot well be brought back so late.

Ever yours,

D. G. R.

Saturday.

My dear Dunn,

If there is no lacquering (or whatever the colour matter is called) visible on the frame now, it has been washed off or else the frame re-gilded. The reddish colour was very visible, stagnated in all the hollows and the mouldings when it was here. I cannot but fancy that perhaps you did not examine it in a good light. If you look especially at the upper outer edge of the frame where there is a slight indented pattern, it is most visible at first sight if not altered since. However, if you approve the gilding I will so far take the frame (as I judge it must have been regilt) but the pattern on the flat *must* be set right. If that is done I will take the frame (seeing that you approve the gilding) but not otherwise. Of course, I suppose this would involve regilding the lower part of the flat.

You will see by enclosed letter (the first received from B. after the difficulty arose) that he there undertakes to make another new frame if necessary and charge me only for the flush strainer. Thus if he now proposes to turn nasty, you see he cannot unsign it. *Pray keep this letter carefully in case needed,* and also not let him get possession of it.

However, it is evident that F. & D. are the only frame makers. I enclose you a bill of theirs and would be very much obliged if you would see Williams about it. Is the first item the frame for La Bella Mano? If so, that is to be half paid for by Marks or Ellis. And what is the second frame referred to? Is it one for the last unfinished Damozel & Dulcimer picture? I cannot now remember whether this was framed or not before I left. But there is no other frame at Leyland's that I can remember answering the description. In seeing Williams you might make some approach towards my giving him another order, but in a light and trifling manner, and try and get from him some expression of regret for the cause of split. You see it will be quite necessary to get a frame *at once* instead of the one botched by Bertram if he will not set it right. The picture cannot be kept unsold.

Ever yours,

D. G. R.

P.S. Do *not* let Bertram know I am coming to town. I expect to be returning almost immediately but will write further. Please *seal* letters. Intimate to Williams that I will send a cheque on account as soon as convenient when I understand how matters stand.

London, May 31.

Sir,

The case was safely delivered to me at 8 o'clock last night. I have the frame now before me and fail to discover the slightest fault in it every possible pain was bestowed on it from beginning to finish, there is not one spot of lacquer on it and is not gilt with inferior gold but the very best procurable. The punched design on the flat I consider the best I have ever done in my life, in fact, the frame is a perfect specimen of good workmanship and materials of unsurpassed quality; if it was actually necessary to alter and regild as you desire the simpler plan would be to prepare a fresh frame altogether, this I would willingly do for *you* but in the first place I certainly could not produce a better one, secondly, I do not like to venture another frame being thrown on my hands. I do not suppose I shall ever sell the frame as it is not a regular size, but I can show it without fear as a specimen of my work of which I feel not a little proud and conscious. You cannot get a better go where you may. I express to you my unfeigned regret at not being able to please you. I shall only have to charge you with the flush strainer which was not returned with the frame.

I am sir, your obedient servant,

L. BERTRAM.

Tuesday,

My dear Dunn,

Thanks for your note. Watts is here and will probably write you a line about a print or two—at any rate he will see you as soon as he returns to town, probably about Thursday. I fancy I am very likely to be up in town myself about the end of this week, but you need not mention this of course to *everyone*. I will write again shortly.

Ever yours,

D. G. R.

P.S. I have been taking steps through Watts to get a man servant into the house temporarily. He also has his eye on another who may answer permanently. You need not mention this, but I name it to you lest you should think it necessary to raise the question by letter. Of course eventually men will have to be got in.

Among those concerned for Gabriel's well-being was his good friend William Cowper-Temple who was later to become Lord Mount Temple. One of the first letters he received on returning to Cheyne Walk after his stay in Aldwick Lodge was from the Cowper-Temples asking whether he would visit them at their magnificent home, Broadlands, Romsey, for a change of air. Gabriel did not think twice and in August 1876 he was writing home to say that everything was "extremely favourable for walking or strolling about" and that on a clear day one could see the Isle of Wight looking like a cloud and "floating above a halo of light—the sea".

1876. Sunday.

My dear Dunn,

Many thanks for all your exertions. I now enclose £20. as for house and your own needs. The dreadful rent question is a complete puzzle. I remember so clearly (George the same) that at Bognor after the repairs question was settled to my advantage, I said to him: "Now there shall be no cause for complaint as to delay with the mid-summer rent", and then and there I sent it them before application—that the whole seems a devil's trick to help one to ruin. If the counterfoil (to Lee Pemberton) cannot be found about that date, does there happen to be a blank one there? (Perhaps I think wordless, or would it not be well to ask for the pass book?). Moreover my impression was that I asked you at the time if they had sent receipt to Chelsea and you said *yes*.

Our movements here have been so uncertain that I must ask you to pardon vagueness of telegrams. My present impression is that we may be leaving Tuesday evening but hardly before. Nevertheless we *may* be staying later and will keep you informed. I hope the studio will be habitable by my return. It will be wise if possible to set at once about carrying out your excellent idea of a shelf to the height of drapery hanging and those green Utrecht curtains might be hung in front (a pair at each side of hearth) and look sightly, then canvases, etc. could be stored *on* the shelf which should be pretty solid. This could not cost much, and something must be done to give a set off for the dummy wall.

They set about finding my babies for the baby head in the "Damozel". First came a workhouse baby—I spent a day in drawing it but it wouldn't do. Then they found me a truly noble little fellow, son of a parson near here. Of him I at once made a successful drawing (which I have promised to the delighted parents), and yesterday painted his head right off into the picture at one sitting very successfully. It is as good as anything there. Sweet Mrs. Temple has been quite a refreshment to me in her ineffably womanly goodness and Miss Munro also a most welcome old friend, full of intelligent conversation and practical helpfulness. I must not forget all Mrs. Temple's thoughtful and inspired kindness. At present the house is filling but Miss Munro says that the coming and going during the next four days will be no joke. All the parsonic tack.

I hope some news of F's return may not be long delayed, though I am truly glad she is getting some enjoyment.

Ever yours,

D. G. R.

Your reduced cartoon of the "Damozel" is at Chelsea come from Bognor. Could you just make me a tracing of the top of head and stars round it as it would enable me to trace them in the picture and paint them. Fortunately I put in my pocket your sketches of cherub authorities.

Thursday.

My dear Dunn,

I am somewhat dismayed at the passage in your letter to George which says you are going to make a list of my requirements. I have been daily hoping to see the easel which I asked you to send *at once*. Please do get it sent off *as soon as you get this*. I write to Bertram *with this* to come and fetch it *tomorrow* (Friday) and see that it does go off by train. I have been trying to get a common easel in Bognor but cannot. The other things I asked for were:

1. Green Blessed Damozel.
2. Your cartoon of same.
3. The tracing for background of same (in drawer of gents case).
4. Red lined canvas.
5. Cassandra photo pencilled over.
6. Mandolin and bow with flowered childs dress for picture of Mary.
7. Grey nigger dress which Alice often wears for sitting with yellow pattern round neck and on shoulders and sleeves lined with crimson.
8. Crimson silk dress made low and without sleeves, only puffs at elbows. Also dress similarly made of maroon velvet, with long hanging sleeves used in Bella Mano. These dresses I did *not* mention before but think might be useful if sent. Also green velvet dress which I think is hanging up outside back studio door. The other I fancy must be in wardrobe. There is no special need to send anything *quite immediately* except the *easel*. Bertram must see to that tomorrow (Friday) and I have told him to take your orders about the other things which I want *as soon as possible*. Of course they will all require careful packing—the dresses notably so—but I suppose we probably have cases in the garden shed or elsewhere which would suit all. If absolutely not so, they must be made, but don't encourage this if it can be helped. They should be packed under your own eye if possible.

Is Morris the gardener doing anything to the garden. I much wish this seen to.

Ever yours,

D. G. R.

It is possible I may have named other things in my former letters. All must come.

Monday

Dear Dunn,

The only man's dress sent—a sort of sage green long thing—has sleeves which stop halfway down the arm, and the sleeve was just what I most wanted. If you have not yet sent off the dress I wrote about yesterday, you might send another man's dress or two with it. I know there are several. It does not need to be long. I fancy Fan made a tunic man's dress from a pattern one of Jones's. If so, it might come.

Ever yours,

D. G. R.

Kelmscott,
22nd August 1877

Dear Dunn,

It is my *express wish* and order that Ellen Wilbee be discharged at once
with a month's board wages and a good character.

Yours truly,

D. G. ROSSETTI.

19

Gabriel's physical condition grew worse. In the summer of 1877 only an operation could save him and this, says Watts-Dunton, "was performed with all Marshall's usual skill".

The operation left him pitiably weak. His family anxiously agreed that sea air was essential, and Madox Brown took his old friend to Herne Bay. The journey was taken against Gabriel's wish, and William Michael suggests that the move from Cheyne Walk had to be made almost by force.

From Herne Bay itself Gabriel went quickly to the village of Herne, with its lovely church and its clusters of quaint dwellings. He stayed, with the hired nurse, in Ivy Cottage, a brick house built twenty years or so earlier and which had little quaintness or charm. It was knocked down in 1962 to make way for the building of a housing estate.

This part of the Kent coast was familiar to the Rossettis as a family. Mrs. Rossetti and Christina were holidaying at Herne Bay in 1847 and Gabriel was talking of going there the following year with his friend Collinson.

The letters Gabriel wrote from Herne Bay show him as very much the invalid. His hand, he complained, was unsteady, and he had restless nights. He was bored. "The absolute want of occupation is rotting my life away hour by hour", he wrote to his mother. "Brown is the sweetest and kindest of companions, but such a life is almost unbearable."

Fine weather and the clean air gradually gave him vigour. He walked or drove around the countryside each day. But he had a slight attack of shingles, and the querulous note crept into a report to William: ". . . the day is cut up with necessary exercise, and moreover, the sun floods the only room I can paint in."

At last he felt strong enough to work and began "a successful drawing of Mamma's head, quite up to my mark", and the old confidence returned. In the only traceable letter he wrote to Dunn from Hunter's Forstal he writes of working on the background of "Rosa Triplex".

Hunters Forestall
Herne Bay Monday October
1877

My dear Dunn,

I am expecting for certain to leave here this week—most probably Friday.

I don't rightly know whether you have returned yet to Chelsea, so send this to Watts to forward if necessary. As Watts told me that on starting you meant to be only a week away, I daresay you will in any case not be more than a few days longer before you return. I am of course much better, but still far from thoroughly well or strong, and it would be very helpful both to my mother, sister and self if you would meet us at the station (Victoria I suppose) and kindly see to the luggage for us. Watts would I dare say come also. Of course I would write further as to precise day and hour.

I hope you have been successful in your work if you went to Mr. Leycesters. I myself, after doing a couple of drawings of my mother and sister, have now made a joint one of the two together, which I fancy is one of the best things I have done.

I hope you are well, and with kind remembrances from all here, am ever yours.

D. G. ROSSETTI.

I suppose I wrote you that Wm. and wife with Brown and wife were here for a few days. Howell and wife are likely to be here next Saturday to meet Leyland who is coming—I fancy to stay till Sunday morning. His picture is finished and I am at work on the dog rose background in The Triple Rose.

As if Gabriel had not enough to contend with a new set of personal problems arose.

Fanny, whose eye for the main chance never wavered, chose this time to make herself a new life and a new home. She did not, perhaps, deliberately vanish. It was just that she "went", and did not bother to tell anyone where she was going. Gabriel's friends, realising that her disappearance would worry him, tried to find her. Harry, it is hardly necessary to say, was called to a conference, and deputed to do everything possible to locate her. On September 24, 1877 he wrote to Watts-Dunton:

F's move is a surprise to me. I don't know what to make of it. I discovered that the furniture had been carted off by Taylor of Pimlico so I called there and found them very loth to give me any information as to her whereabouts, but by representing myself as a party anxious to deliver a picture to her, they gave me her address at 96, Jermyn Street. This I find to be the Rose Tavern.

The entire business, he added, was "a series of conundrums". If he had not been suffering from a bad attack of lumbago he would have run down to Putney to discuss the matter with Watts-Dunton.

Fanny at last had come to comprehend the virtues of security. To be forbidden to visit Kelmscott was bad enough; especially as the reason was no secret. Gabriel's family and friends were ranged solidly against her. The "sneering" Dunn was clearly her enemy, or so she believed. There had been a series of decidedly awkward questions about articles missing from Number Sixteen. Rossetti, though he still wrote affectionately, was ill and might not recover.

She found an ally in the widower who was to become her second husband—John B. Schott. Fanny did not conceal her friendship with Schott. He not only met but made himself generally useful to Rossetti. Schott carried out various small commissions in connection with the sale of pictures, and by various means, obtained large supplies of chloral from different chemists.

Under Schott's wing she was installed as manageress of the Rose Tavern, with "three servants and an accountant". There were arguments as to whether or not Fanny was entitled to certain pictures she took with her, and the familiar and dismal round of recrimination and withdrawal went on.

The truth is that Gabriel could not get Fanny altogether out of his mind. He was quite unable in his thoughts to shake himself free of her.

When eventually he left Ivy Cottage for Cheyne Walk he asked for the latchkey (the curt demand for which had given Fanny so much grief) to be returned to her.

Gabriel now became desperately anxious that certain correspondence still stowed away (not too carefully) in Cheyne Walk should not reach unsympathetic hands. A number of personal letters had already been removed, but more still remained "in the drawers of the large bookcase and of the black and gold cabinet near the door".

Writing to Watts-Dunton, he expressed doubts as to the safety of the letters in question:

Herne Bay
Oct. 13 1877
. . . As to the letters, I wrote to Dunn as well as to yourself the precise receptacles in which I know all were safely lodged at the time of my departure. I impressed on him the necessity of removing *all* the letters to the iron safe—a work of a quarter of an hour at the utmost! and I hope he has not neglected to do so. The matter is a good deal in my mind.

1877 October.
Monday.

My dear Dunn,

Since I have heard of your intention to leave Town, I have been worrying myself about the letters which exist in the studio. There is a drawer full next the money drawer, and I think some packets in a drawer below that, but am not quite certain. There is also a batch of letters from various people in one upper drawer of the black and gold cabinet near the front door of studio. And besides, there are the contents of the basket. I would be much obliged if you would take all these now and lock them in the iron safe outside the studio. The unaccountable wholesale disappearance of large batches of letters some time back makes this move advisable, though I am well aware that you are cautious in keeping the studio locked. I write in some haste for post, and am ever

Yours truly,
D. G. ROSSETTI.

If other letters found elsewhere please include them.
P.S. I hope your lumbago is taking itself off. My nurse here recommends a new flannel to be applied to the part and ironed over with as hot an iron as can be borne.

Wednesday 1877
October

My dear Dunn,

I judge from what you say that all is alright: but should have been much obliged for an explicit answer to effect that *all* letters had been found in the various receptacles as described by me, and that *all* had been locked in the iron safe.

I enclose another letter from Brown which I fancy does refer to the same house you mean, and in which he particularises as to means of making it answer. You do not say anything as to the Hampstead house. It would need great temptation to draw me out there, as it is pretty well beyond civilisation, and one might also as conveniently be in the country altogether. I hope you have not had the trouble yet (I judge not) of packing the little Kelmscott picture, as I hear from Rae yesterday that he is likely to be in London in a week or ten days and then would go to see that and the "Proserpine".

Unluckily the letter is a discouraging one as he says he has been spending thousands in buying a new house and is not likely to be buying pictures at present. I suppose in these circumstances I must nerve myself to ask you an unpleasant question—What is the exact balance at my bankers! The chances of realising the next remittance from any visible quarter seem more and more hazardous.

Ever yours, D. G. R.

P.S. I wonder what has become of my Chelsea latch key. It is not in my pocket, as I have observed ever since coming here. Are you aware whether it is at Chelsea? Of course, if not there it might have somehow got into improper hands, and all the trouble of new lock to the door would go for nothing.

To suggest that in the last three or four years of his life Dante Gabriel Rossetti sank gradually into a decline is to give anything but a true picture. The physical decline, yes, that was all too evident: but although his social life was greatly restricted he worked hard, and with results, in poetry and painting, which were brilliant.

He claimed at Herne that the doses of chloral had been reduced and that he "sometimes" took only a third of the amount taken when he first went to Ivy Cottage. At the same time, it was accepted that the drug, in some quantity, had become essential. But he finished the "Venus Astarte" and worked satisfactorily on "A Vision of Fiammetta". In 1878 the "Donna della Finestra" was completed. Large sums of money came in, debts were discharged, and professionally the future looked bright enough.

There were the inevitable anxieties. Janey Morris was ill (and it was the safe-keeping of her letters which caused him concern). Fanny had gone her own way, and was independent. And at last, Harry, pleading in vain for arrears of pay, had to find alternative methods of raising the wind. He was skilful enough to earn a living by portraiture, and by working in the new Cathedral at Truro. For many years he had served Gabriel loyally, and there is no reason to suggest that his occasional absences—certainly those between 1878 and 1880—were not solely due to the necessity of earning some money. Until the break in 1881, Harry was always ready to return—when he could afford it!

Written almost in despair and clearly under great nervous strain a letter from Dunn to Watts-Dunton gives some idea of his own efforts to help in some of the darker days.

16, Cheyne Walk,
Chelsea.
S.W.
Thursday [date on
env. May 9 1878]

My dear Watts,
    Tomorrow morning a man will put on a new bell handle so that the rapper may be removed when you deem convenient. R. is in an exceedingly irritable state & I am in a wretched. He is taking fast against me again, says that I am continually seeking an opportunity of using rude & censorious language

to him, but the fact is that I have been endeavouring to explain & smooth over what he calls the neglect of his friends.

The chloral dosing is on the increase & that with the warm weather will of course account for anything that happens. It came out yesterday that he considers me very unkind not to walk out with him of a night—this idea comes because I have said I believe that I like a walk home at night but my walks are very different to his—if I walk it is always to see some of my relations or friends whom I probably shouldn't meet from year's end to year's end, so tied by the leg am I & unable to ask them to come here.

I believe some scheme is afloat for some one to walk with him—as any idea that I can do is out of the question. I promised to take a walk on Wimbledon Common next Sunday with Mrs. Mason but I really don't know what will occur between this and then. A single knock has just brought him suspiciously to his studio door; it turns out to be Photos from the Auto type Co. five minutes later, another single knock: fortunately he doesn't hear this time, for an umbrella directed to you is left. This I have unpacked and put in my own room until you call. You see from this, the necessity of immediate action in the matter of the Rapper ere outside influence is brought to bear.

When you next have an opportunity I wish you would try and calm his mind with regard to what he calls my censoriousness & coercion but it is a case in which mild remonstrance wont do & in reasoning with him I have put before him what a sad effect upon his relations there wd be in case of anything happening to him thro' his want of moral strength in not trying to resist the desire to increase the nightly dose of Chloral. If a drowning man is to be saved its no use speaking to him from the waterside he must be grappled with & lugged out & so here he mustn't suppose his best friends are enemies because they speak seriously & strongly on the matter.

Unfortunately being R's junior, any strong remonstrances from me are termed want of respect & courtesy to him. I believe anything said by you tho' has its due effect & if by any means you could introduce an allusion to your own self sacrifice in that wh: I mentioned to him the other day & try to make him feel that he is a man who has had an unusual number of self sacrificing friends.

At present he seems to be consumed with the idea that he has done everything. I had quite a wrangle about B (37 Fitzroy Sq) & told him that he ought to ascertain the reason if he thought there was any coolness in that quarter &c &c. Excuse such a long letter but I am very weary and anxious & my time is cut into most sadly by this continually having to step in between him & the world. Kindest remembrances to Mr. & Mrs. Mason, whose society I hope to enjoy on Sunday (si je peut.) & I look forward to good counsel from you & a happy deliverance from this harrassed existence that has befallen me. Why, Heaven only knows.

Yours truly,
H. TREFFRY DUNN

Please burn when read

P.S. I have a batch of your Books: wh: ought to & shall be returned forth-with If amongst yours you come across 2 vols of the Fr Biographical Dicty I SHALL be glad as I find no traces of them here.

Chelsea, Wednesday, November 1879.

My dear Dunn,

   You wrote on Saturday last leading me to expect you (as you said) *next Monday*. I now judge that you cannot have meant Monday 16th—that is *next Monday now*. Accordingly I will look for your return on that day, as the housekeeper leaves here on the 16th Monday aforesaid to go into the country. I am sorry to hear of your being laid up with cold—as you do not generally succumb in that way I judge it must have been serious, but I trust is now over. I am glad the presentation went off so well, and certainly think the new Cathedral work might benefit you in more than one way.

Ever yours,
D. G. ROSSETTI.

Chelsea, 22 November 1879

My dear Dunn,

   I had understood at the outset from Watts that your business would last for one month. The very prolonged delay was therefore disappointing me, and in minor ways inconvenient but yet I felt no right to raise a question when I got your further letter. However, I was on the point of writing to say that I trusted to see you home after the 24th when I received your 2nd letter. It will certainly be most convenient to me to avoid a month or more of further delay, and I should willingly defray your travelling expenses for the inter-mediate return.

   The Desdemona picture had to be abandoned. I have received a commis-sion to paint the drawing over the mantelpiece (lady in a tree) and to get on to this as to taking measurements, etc. your assistance would be most valuable. Indeed I should have done something towards it already but for your absence. Another thing there is in which you might help at this moment. I have now succeeded in completing Graham's replica (as well as the Predella subjects) with the exception of the figure of Beatrice which I propose to re-design and alter in the replica. This will require studio arrangements, (lay figure, drapery etc.) in which you would be of the utmost service, and it has to be done now at once, as everything else is done, and I have promised to deliver the work speedily. There are other minor matters standing over your return. Several people are rather troublesome about money and I have just given Williams a bill at 6mos.: for his last Xmas A/c £99. 18s. 6d. I suppose this is correct as to former statements.

   It will give me much pleasure to see you again, and I am truly glad that you have made what must be a step in the right professional direction. You will not find me very strong or well, but I am better than I have been a little while ago.

With kind remembrances till I see you.

Yours truly,

D. G. ROSSETTI.

P.S. I am alright with Valpy, but that most easy man is at last getting seriously alarmed about H against whom I judge he is likely to proceed in some way.

P.P.S. You will perceive that Fry's first letter was in answer to a request from me for £500 on further account.

Harry's occasional forays into the world of the freelance artist were mostly brief, if unpredictable. He always returned to Number Sixteen, willing and ready for any assignment. There was the trouble about extending the lease of Tudor House: Harry acted as house agent and "looked over" many houses, including one close to Shepherd's Bush Green.

"Dunn brought round the cat," writes William in April 1887, "which seems well enough inclined to settle down in our house. He says that Gabr. still takes large doses of chloral."

And on January 9, 1879, his diary records: "Dunn called to borrow some books for Gabriel, who has been in a low state of health for some while past. . . . D. strongly insists that it is mere hypochondria and wilfulness."

Chelsea
6 Feb. 1879.

My dear Dunn,

When do you think of returning? I write today to ask you whether you know what has become of the shutter and bar belonging to the door opening into the *back* area? I mean the door under *garden gate*, NOT the one under the small window of my studio. Please let me know by return if you can tell me where they are. I hope you have been prospering with your work.

Yours truly,

D. G. ROSSETTI.

17 February.

My dear Dunn,

In answer to yours I can only say that I shall be very glad now when you *can* return with convenience to yourself, for varying reasons.

I have got the head and hands done in Ionides picture (short of glazing, etc. at a further stage of the work) and am now wanting to set about the drapery as soon as possible. For this purpose it will be necessary to set up a tree or something as substitute to suit the action, and only your genius is equal to this kind of stage machinery; while your help in setting the lay figure would also be most useful. However, before doing the drapery I may probably have to make a study from nature for the position, so this will cause a little delay, nor have I yet quite done all I can do at present to the head and hands; so perhaps our conveniences may meet each other.

There is also a question about a drawing for Graham. I have finished the replica, and the question of the frame has been tackled today. I showed him various drawings he might select from to value of £100 if he would (as offset) pay for such frame. He has chosen three, but they are not such as I much like to issue, and he would evidently have preferred the one which you last hung over the mantelpiece. In this I would much wish to meet his views, but cannot possibly part with the drawing itself which has not yet been painted. However, if you can tell me when you would be likely to be able to commence a replica of it (like the present one, you doing the black work and I the colour) I would make him an offer of such replica instead of the other drawing, which I believe would please him much.

I have had already to sacrifice to him (and it came in very conveniently) the Proserpine you commenced and I carried on, to meet a debt which he proved (to my surprise) of £100 to be met by chalk work, and which had got quite overlooked for years. This Proserpine almost finished and would finish at the same time the replica I now propose for him, if I knew when you could set about the commencement.

I am very glad you are so successful at Truro, and fully feel the importance of the work. I should really think that glass work and even decoration work may most probably result for you in connection with the Cathedral.

Ever yours,

D. G. ROSSETTI

There will almost immediately arise the question of spring flowers and vegetation for my picture, also I think of putting in the hand a large *single* snowdrop if I can get one.

My dear Dunn,

I don't know if you have yet left town. I should like to know the address to which you are going in the country. I am in want of another pair of gloves. I fancy there are several dogskin ones in one of my drawers. Could you send me a pair by post?

Ever yours,

D. G. R.

Saturday 1879

My dear Dunn,

I enclose a letter of Brown's relative to the Percy Cross house. You see, according to him, it might answer but after 6 months dallying, it seems to be an uncertainty now whether it can be had! Such is Fate. I do not lay *great* stress on what you say as to smallness of rooms, nor on the question of the furniture getting in as in my quiet way of living I might probably part with what could not be housed. In *number*, the rooms seem by your firms account to be about as many as at Cheyne Walk.

I am troubled about Valpy who really ought not to choose this moment to trouble me.

I hope to get your answer as to locking all letters in the safe. I remember there is a large number in one of the lower drawers of inlaid cabinet next back door of studio.

Ever yours,

D. G. R.

Another breakdown in Rossetti's health came towards the end of 1879. He was now taking chloral in such quantities that the chemists insisted on limiting his supply.

"Gabriel again very ill—distinctly attributable to his having taken an overdose of chloral on M. night", writes William on October 18, 1879. "Dunn being now away on holiday and no-one else much about the house."

Dec. 1, 1879: Dunn is now back: has been doing some portraiture in his native district, and might perhaps find a good opening there, were he to resolve to do so.

May 31, 1880: G. spoke to me a goodish deal about his money affairs, and the claims wh. Watts & Dunn wd. probably put forward in the event of his decease. He says he has not made any will.

Sept. 27, 1880: Evg. with Gabriel. . . . Dunn has now, after a long absence, returned.

Once again the threads of friendship were taken up again by Gabriel and his art-assistant. Gabriel threw off the gloom which had threatened to overwhelm him, and in 1880 he was writing a great deal of poetry, and painting well, although as he confided to Christina, "with me, sonnets mean insomnia".

Cheyne Walk, 1880 Thursday.

My dear Dunn,

Thanks for the two lots of snowdrops which I judge you most kindly have sent. I painted same in, but have come to the conclusion that I shall probably have to adopt a snowdrop and primrose together. Primroses are not yet to the fore I judge. Tomorrow I begin drapery, but may get on for a few days before it is necessary to fix the lay figure finally with the exact arrangement of tree for support. A fallen tree, in the garden, would probably supply material. It would now be convenient specially to me if you could return the soonest possible. I think I told you of the replica drawing which has to be done for Graham. The Ellis bill has been paid at the Bank and funds are now very low, but I have been so successful with Ionides picture that there is certainly now a full £200 of work on the canvas, and I can write him again.

I hope you are getting on satisfactorily with your work. Miss Asher went away for a week and buried a brother in law, who died, but she is now back.

Ever yours,
D. G. R.

20

Harry regretted to his last hour the circumstances which prevented him from staying by Gabriel's side until the end. As it was, they parted little more than a year before Gabriel's death at Birchington. It was not an irrevocable break. As William puts it, they "remained in communication".

To say the least of it, Rossetti's ideas about the payment of Harry's salary were casual to a degree. Almost peevishly he had written to Fanny in 1877, "Dunn has chosen the present time to begin talking about his arrears of salary. Of course, I cannot be paying him anything now. He has gone out of town . . ." Who, indeed, could blame him?

Then, from Liverpool had come Hall Caine. Harry could hardly be expected to approve of the man who in some ways may be said to have supplanted him. Like Dunn he was a young man from the provinces, who had admired Rossetti's poetry as Harry had admired his painting. When Caine, too, was invited to Cheyne Walk for the first time, he was twenty-five, approximately the age Harry Dunn had been on a similar occasion. He had made no attempt to disguise his hero-worship, and was understandably a welcome guest. But although Caine was more or less constantly at Gabriel's side in the last eighteen months of his life, he could not recall, as Harry could, the long and happy spells when Gabriel had been a gay companion, affable and full of fun. It is not to be wondered at if there was a sour taste in his mouth when he read Hall Caine's *Recollections*, which gave the impression that the two men had been on the most intimate terms for years.

Life at Cheyne Walk had become increasingly difficult for Harry. There is no question that he was hurt by Gabriel's apparent coolness. It is probably that he never realised the extent to which Rossetti's health had deteriorated. He had heard the cry of "Wolf!" too often, and had seen the astonishing power of resilience which had sent Rossetti almost bounding back to what appeared to be reasonably good health. At all events, letters from Gabriel to Harry and from Harry to Gabriel were unanswered. Finally, and in his most petulant mood, Rossetti wrote a letter severing their professional relationship.

Harry had made it clear that if arrears of salary were not forthcoming he would have to find some other means of livelihood. With his letter of dismissal, Gabriel very crossly sent fifty pounds, on account, promising to pay the balance at the rate of three pounds a week. Dunn, stung to a reply, came to London from Truro and the next we hear is when Rossetti breaks the news to Watts-Dunton, saying, "He proposes to remove his goods (or d—d bads) next week." Two days before his curt note to Harry he had told his mother that Hall Caine was coming to stay with him at Cheyne Walk as an "experiment".

Harry felt depressed, grieved by the rift in his friendship with Gabriel and uncertain of his own future. Hall Caine's star was in the ascendant. In a way, it was a relief to be his own master, to be free of Fanny's nagging: but it was hard to break the habits of years. Moodily, he wondered if the past fifteen years had been squandered, precious time frittered away. On the credit side, some good friends—William Michael Rossetti and Wills among them. The trust of a man of vivid character and talent: much laughter: the satisfaction of some good work, at least. Practical results? Well, a modest reputation. But, financially, his position was much the same as when he walked up the steps, past the glowing jasmine to Gabriel's front door, and nervously lifted the dragon-head knocker. He shrugged. It was no use making things out to be worse than they were. He would rent a studio, or share one with a kindred spirit. There was still—all the time in the world. . . .

From William Michael's diary: "Nov. 7, 1881: As I was going round to G.'s I met Dunn: G. parted from him finally 2 or 3 mos. ago, not in the best of humour, and D. is now living in King's Road, Chelsea."

Neither of the two men harboured their grievances for long, and it is pleasant to read William Michael's entry on 23 January 1882: "He (Gabriel) has got on good terms again with Dunn, who is to undertake the laying-in, etc., of those works wh. G. owes to Valpy as equivalents for the Dante's Dream which V. returned to him years ago."

These words were written five or six weeks after a collapse which was the last clear warning that Rossetti was desperately ill, and that there was little, if any, hope for the future. In September 1881 he had made the journey to Cumberland with Caine and Fanny, referred to by Caine as "the nurse".

The change of air seemed to do the invalid good, but he found the late autumn in the northern mountains and valleys dismal and dispiriting, and for the last time Rossetti came home to Chelsea. Except for one more journey he would roam no more.

He was stricken just two weeks before Christmas Day, finding that he could not move his left arm or leg. Dr. Marshall was called and a drastic treatment forbidding the use of chloral was prescribed. For days the sick man lived on morphia, brandy and whisky, suffering from delusions and intermittent spells of violence.

Slowly reason returned and with it, depression. Would he ever walk again? The question nagged. William, remembering how once before, in Scotland, there had been a turning point to recovery when Dunn had been summoned, and came, bringing to Gabriel "the implements of his art", made one more attempt to trace Harry. This time he was successful, and once again was easier in his mind, knowing that he could rely on his old friend to work on paintings which had to be completed, for reasons of honour as well as expedience.

The bungalow in which Gabriel spent the last weeks of his life was a large, rambling place near the cliff face at Birchington-on-Sea. It had been built by an old friend, John P. Seddon, who gladly told him to regard it as his home for as long as he pleased. Possibly only Gabriel himself felt certain it would be his last home.

His companions at first were Hall Caine and his young sister, Lily, and a trained nurse. Old Mrs. Rossetti and Christina joined them early in March. Several friends, among them Watts-Dunton, Shields and his faithful patron, Leyland, went to Birchington to show Gabriel that he was not forgotten.

There have been many accounts of the manner of Dante Gabriel Rossetti's death on Easter Sunday, 1882. These, especially in regard to his last words, vary considerably. The impeccable sources make it plain that almost to the very end he was "calm and clear-headed". These are the words of his sister-in-law, Lucy, who arrived at the bungalow only minutes before he died. Death-bed scenes are harrowing in any circumstances and there is every reason to suppose that Rossetti died with resignation and courage. It is certain that if he had had the advantage of modern medical skills his last years would have been very different. As it was, he suffered with greater fortitude than even those closest to him realised.

The site of the grave near the South Porch of All Saints' Church, with its oak-shingled spire, was chosen by Christina and William and the funeral took place on April 14th. At the committal service were Gabriel's mother, his sister and brother, his Aunt Charlotte and Lucy, William's wife. Present also were Graham, Leyland, Watts-Dunton, Hall Caine, Hueffer and John Seddon. The faithful Stephens attended, and so did Boyce, John Aldam Heaton, Martin Sharp, Philip Marston, Shields and Dr. Harris. These joined the family party of mourners, but Herbert Gilchrist, Judge Vernon Lushington and Murray Marks came unobtrusively to pay their tribute.

The ancient Thanet church was decorated with Easter flowers, and as the mourners looked down into the chalk grave the lid of the coffin was gradually hidden by a mass of blooms. Bunches of azaleas and primroses were dropped into the open grave, with them William's posy of lilies of the valley.

Later in the evening, Charlotte, William, Lucy, Christina and Shields walked sorrowfully to the closed grave and placed on the turf a wreath from Lady Mount-Temple. A wreath of bay had come from Marston, wreaths and "a lovely white cross" from the Leylands. There were more primroses and Mrs. Rossetti bent slowly to place a bunch of flowers, among them woodspurge (recalling Gabriel's poem of that name) and forget-me-nots.

Today, one of the most striking monuments in the churchyard is the Irish cross designed in memory of his friend by Madox Brown. It has three bas-reliefs—the temptation in the garden of Eden, the spiritual marriage of Dante and Beatrice, and the death of the patron saint of artists, Saint Luke. Gabriel's brother, with whom he had enjoyed such an affectionate and unclouded friendship, wrote the inscription. It reads:

> Here sleeps Gabriel Charles Dante Rossetti, honoured, under the name of Dante Gabriel Rossetti, among painters as a painter, and among poets as a poet. Born in London, of parentage mainly Italian, 12 May, 1828. Died at Birchington, 9 April, 1882. This Cruciform Monument, bespoken by Dante Rossetti's mother, was designed by his lifelong friend, Ford Madox Brown, executed by J. and H. Patteson, and erected by his brother William and sister Christina.

Gabriel's mother commissioned a memorial window (the work of Shields) to be placed near the font. The subjects are Gabriel's own design for "The Passover in the Holy Family" and "Christ Healing the Blind Man outside the Gates of Bethsaida".

Death wrote its inevitable tally of personal and financial problems.

The years of illness, the brief bursts of activity, the work commissioned but unfinished—all these factors made William's task a heavy one.

In so many ways, Harry had, in the past fourteen or fifteen years, been closer to Gabriel than anyone outside the family. He had a detailed knowledge of all the work on which Gabriel had been engaged. He had discussed with him so much of his artistic output and knew, from the professional point of view, what had been Rossetti's intentions and wishes.

It was the most natural thing in the world for William to turn to his brother's old friend and companion to bring order into the inevitably tangled affairs. There was, to begin with, the business of making preparations for the sale of Rossetti's pictures and effects.

Harry accepted the melancholy task with sadness. He recalled the many kindnesses he had received from William, and had no hesitation in telling him, "Please rely on me to do everything I possibly can".

Sorrowfully he returned to 16, Cheyne Walk. With infinite care he searched every room for pictures, drawings, sketches, notes. All were examined, and a programme of work was drawn up. In this way he could best honour the memory of the man to whom he had willingly given so many years of his life. In his heart was the sure and certain knowledge that they were his best years. He had been content to live in the shadow of a greater man. He accepted that—and was, in a queer, resigned way, content. He would, indeed, do his best.

One of his first tasks was to work on Rossetti's water-colour "Rosa Triplex". The owner Craven was unhappy about the darkening of certain portions of the flesh, where malachite had been used. Could anything be done, William wanted to know, to remedy this? Harry, examining the picture with his glass, concluded that there was nothing for it but to repaint completely the unsatisfactory part of the picture. When Harry took the picture to William's house William was delighted. "He has succeeded extremely well", he recorded that same day.

And on 25 September 1882, he writes sadly, "Dunn will attend to the job of dispatching the last load of Gabriel's things".

The sale was to be held in the spring, and among the items to be completed were some crayon drawings by Rossetti. He worked on the "Sea Spell" and on the "Rosa Triplex".

William Michael wrote on the evening of 15 August 1882:

> W.(atts) & I looked at G's watercolour Rosa Triplex now in my house;
> whither it was lately sent by the owner Craven, to see whether anything can

be done by Dunn to remedy the darkening of certain portions of the flesh where malachite, I believe was used . . . . D. had lately looked at the work, & I understand he considers the only remedy to be absolute repainting of these portions.

August 22, 1882: In the afternoon I went round to 16 Cheyne Walk, thinking to meet Dunn there, but he was out.

August 30, 1882: Went round to Cheyne Walk, & saw Dunn there.

Sept. 21, 1882: Shields & his wife, Dunn, Cayley, & Christina, dined with us. D. will again take lodgings in The Vale, Chelsea, when he leaves 16 Cheyne Walk at Michaelmas.

Apr. 25, 1883: Dunn called, asking my authority for adding to the sale of Gabriel's works 3 watercolours wh. D. made of rooms in the house at 16 Cheyne Walk. I assented, & gave D. a letter to Christie's. . . . D. understands—but I can't gather that he has any particr. ground for understg. it—that the Nat. Portrait Gallery want to buy of F.(anny) that portrait of G. by Watts.

May 7, 1883: Dunn brought round photographs from his 3 drawings of rooms in G's house: I have consented to specify these in my next (& soon required) list of photographs for sale.

May 24, 1883: Watts called at Somerset Ho. . . . He spoke about the demand wh. Dunn thinks of making upon me in relation to the work wh. he did last year upon certain crayon-drawings &c: I fear the claim will be larger than I am quite prepared to assent to.

Sept. 26, 1883: Dunn at last sent in a detailed account of the sum wh. he considers me to owe him on acct. of G's estate—total £185. odd: this includes £100. wh. was due to him (balance after some payments already made by me) by G. I fancy there is not much to complain of or revise in the total of £185. but must examine the details.

Sept. 27, 1883: Looked thro' Dunn's account. If he charges me for work done last year (as I assume he shd.) at the same rate of pay wh. he recd. from Gabriel, his computation shows that he recd. £312. p.a. from G. As I am not certain about this point & one or two others, I wrote to Watts consulting him.

Oct. 4, 1883: Watts called at Somers. Ho. to talk over a few points affecting Dunn's claim. He agrees with me genery. as to what ought to be the rate of the claim, & the length of time claimed for, & will see D. about it: I daresay however that it may turn out best to pay the amount asked for, without much haggling.

Nov. 29, 1883: Watts called on me at Som. Ho. I gather that of late nothing has been done about the Legacy-duty &c. Dunn was to have sent in some details regarding his claim; Brass can't yet be got to say clearly what his demand amounts to. But, however this may be, W. speaks of sending me very shortly the needful documents to sign, so that we may proceed to wind up the affair.

January 26, 1884: Recd. a further lot of photos., from Hedderly, after the works of Gabriel. Set apart 4 sets of 2 dozen each—as presents for . . . Dunn.

April 3, 1884: Watts called at Som. Ho., & spoke of the outstanding claims Brass, Dunn, &c. I shall have to look up some receipts, & mean to settle at once with D: Watts says that Dunn had an accident lately in slipping downstairs, but may soon be better, & will renew the question of what is due to him from Gabriel's estate—too long left pending.

June 21, 1884: Mamma showed me an oil-head of Gabriel recently painted by Dunn, & presented to her. It seems to me to be mainly founded on that photograph of G., perhaps the best ever taken, done by Dodgson tows. 1864, in wh. G is represented seated, limp hat in hand, on the steps leading down into his garden—the railing of the steps showing conspicuously behind him. D's portrait is really very good—I think the most fairly & fully typical likeness of G. that exists, all things balanced. It makes him handsome, youngish-looking, & with a resolute expression. The flesh is somewhat too sallow, & I think (tho' Christina does not) the eyes of too decidedly blue a grey.

November 21, 1884: Watts called on me at Som. Ho. He explains Dunn's odd letter by saying that D. has taken to drinking of late (wh. is new to me, & I am very sorry to hear it), & that, when D. called upon him the other day, he was in a muddled & fractitious state, & cd. not be got to see matters aright. W. is now seeing after the affidavit wh. I made for extra probate-duty last T. —so as to ascertain whether the sum declared in it ought to be reduced (I fancy it ought) by a sum of money paid to Rowley for frames for the works of art sold at Christies, & by the 2 sums paid to Dunn since Sept. '83.

Dec. 7, 1884: I sent off to Watts, for delivery to Dunn, the extra cheque for £6. 4. wh. I have now consented to pay him, as absolutely final, & a form of receipt for D. to sign.

August 26, 1885: Christina tells me that she learns from 'Geo. Hake that Dunn, who lately had to go into St. Thomas's Hospital will be discharged tomorrow cured. He had got into a frightful state thro' drinking; &, when admitted into the Hospital he was said to be suffering from dropsy, jaundice, &c. The hospital Dr. however called it "alcoholic delirium". What use he will make of his comparative restoration to health remains to be seen: my expectations are not sanguine.

Harry Dunn was forty-four years old when Rossetti died. He lived for another seventeen years, a perfect example of the late Victorian who helped to put the nineteenth century to bed, and was glad to depart before the year 1900 arrived to fulfil its unpredictable destiny.

Almost at once, Harry became an outstanding figure among the Chelsea group of artists. While at Cheyne Walk he had made many friends among the artists who had given Chelsea its reputation. His long association with Rossetti gave him prestige, and a touch of what we might today call glamour. As the years passed, Harry, cloaked and bearded, and wearing his wide-brimmed hat, may well have been the first of Chelsea's Bohemian characters.

For months he worked on his oil painting of Gabriel—an enduring gesture of friendship and admiration.

From time to time he would return to Cornwall, to stay with his cousin Richard Carter. There he would share Carter's studio in the loft of what was once a stable in Barrack Lane: and there he regaled his cousin with tales of Cheyne Walk, pausing now and again to admire Richard's picture of sunset over the Isles of Scilly or of Crinnis Beach, near St. Austell.

He was always welcome in the home of his sister, Edith. She lived in the village of South Harting, which lies at the foot of the South Downs, a mile or two within the county of Sussex. Hampshire is just over the border. Even today the village is in many ways unspoiled. Then it had a fairy, dream-like quality, the result of a subtle harmony in colour of the ochre-washed walls of its houses and the lovely creamy shades of the roads. The surrounding country was an artist's paradise—the chalk of the Downs, the woods of beech, the sands and heather of the lowlands, the bracken and the pine-trees. Here lived Edith Hume and her husband, Gunning King, the *Punch* artist, and Horace Hodges, the actor. Harry climbed the woods to the lovely old house at Uppark, where once lived the peerless Emma— before she became Lady Hamilton and Nelson's charmer. At Uppark, Mrs. Wells was the housekeeper, and here H. G. Wells, her cheeky son, kissed the parlour-maid and had his first love-affair. Here, Harry was relaxed and happy, roaring with laughter as he shared endless jokes with Edith, the brisk, energetic and outspoken companion of his boyhood. They went for long walks, Edith stumping along by his side, planting her square-toed, Pinet-shod feet on the dusty road, her sturdy little figure full of enthusiasm and vigour.

Harry's portrait of Gabriel passed into the keeping of G. F. Watts. Ten years after Harry's death William Michael wrote in his diary:

October 21, 1909: Was much interested in a letter received from Mrs. G. F. Watts. She was recently in Florence and found the Director of the Uffizi very anxious to obtain a portrait of Gabriel to be added to the famous collection of painters' portraits. I will certainly attend to this. Either the posthumous oil-painting by Dunn, or the pastel head by Hunt would have to be given. The former, though the less good work of art, would seem the more suitable. Shall consult Helen about it.

November 9th, 1909: I wrote to the Inspector of the Uffizi Gallery offering the portrait of Gabriel by Dunn.

December 5th: The portrait by Gabriel by Dunn has now been accepted

Q

by the Uffizi Gallery, and by the Minister of Public Instructions in Rome. It lies with me to send the picture off. Today I wrote to Cook & Son in Charing Cross Station, to see whether they would undertake the transmission.

December 7th. Cook & Son will attend to that matter of the portrait by Dunn.

December 11th. Handed over to a porter, Dick—see the portrait of Gabriel by Dunn to be consigned to Cook's, who will deliver it to the Uffizi.

December 12th. Finished up the portrait affair by writing to the Director of the Uffizi stating what I have now done.

The picture shows the upper part of the body, the head slightly inclined to the right side. The picture was painted in 1882, six months after Rossetti's death, and may be regarded as an impressive resemblance.

The portrait was hidden, with others, in the Palatine Gallery in the Palazzo Pitti during the war.

21

Harry's remaining years were far from lonely: if anything, he had too many friends and cronies with whom he idled away the many days and nights. With the sale of Rossetti's effects and of his remaining pictures (which raised a healthy total—considerably exceeding the debts) Harry gradually vanished from the Cheyne Walk circle. A new and precarious life began. For years he rented his own studio, exhibiting at various exhibitions in London.

Fanny, growing older and stouter in her respectable rôle of Mrs. Schott, he never saw again, nor wished to. With Howell he kept up a desultory friendship until that strange and unpredictable character died in 1890—the manner of his dying as melodramatic as any he could have invented. Dying bloodily in a Chelsea gutter with his throat slashed—by whom?—and, grimmest touch of all, the half-sovereign clenched between his teeth. If ever there were an astonishing story to be told, it is surely that of Charles Augustus Howell.

There was much in his colourful personality which was good and it is pleasant to know that the quarrel was forgiven if not forgotten before Rossetti died. He turned up at Birchington one day as spry and cheeky as ever (the adjectives Harry used to describe him) and, by announcing that he was engaged in buying horses for the King of Portugal, gave Gabriel, as Helen Angeli says, "his last hearty laugh on earth".

The last time Harry went deliberately to Cheyne Walk it was to watch Holman Hunt unveil a bronze medallion of Gabriel which had been designed by Madox Brown. Beneath it was a drinking fountain, the work of John Seddon.

He stood on the fringe of the large crowd which had gathered to see the ceremony and wished that he had not come. His own memories were far more poignant than any evoked by the oratory of Mr. Hunt.

Madox Brown was there, with his wife. Harry picked out William's sober figure and noted that Browning had come. He recognised Gabriel's aunt, Hughes and Stephens. He wondered if Whistler would be there but failed to see that small, trim and unmistakable figure. (In fact, Whistler sent a letter regretting that he could not attend.)

He had spent so many days copying another man's creation, copying faithfully—yes, so faithfully that those who should know these things had said many times that it was almost impossible to tell their work apart. But was this the best he could do with the gifts God had given him? How often Harry Dunn had asked himself this question! Perhaps the answer was just that while some men and women are born to blaze with ambition and accomplishment, there are others who feel it is enough to gaze at the starlight without ever trying to catch it.

Well, he could do good work yet. He would devote all his skill to the pictures which lay unfinished in the big studio in Cheyne Walk. He would complete his long-planned portrait in oils of Gabriel. Better, surely, to think of happier things, to dwell in the past, to hear again in his mind the rowdy laughter and the clever talk, to feel the firm hand thumping his shoulder as Gabriel called him "My dear boy".

No use wasting time on things gone forever. Better men than he had found it wiser to compound their destiny. Harry knew his faults. He'd been content to let life take its course, to follow the easiest line, to trick himself into believing that he had all the time in the world. Now, a chapter in his life had ended and he must make some sort of new pattern— meet the right people, obtain some good commissions and—above all— work harder.

He must jot down some of his own recollections of those years of companionship and collaboration. He knew more about Gabriel than Hall Caine ever did and had been infinitely more close to him. William Michael Rossetti could be relied on to tell the truth as he saw it and for the rest, Gabriel must be judged by the appeal court of posterity.

The speakers droned on, and, feeling more depressed and alone since the year of Gabriel's death, he turned and walked slowly along by the river. Someone had told the throng of sightseers that the present occupier of the Queen's House had generously invited those present to look over the house. *The Times* of 16 July 1887 reported that "a considerable number ... availed themselves of the opportunity to visit Rossetti's rooms".

Harry Dunn was not among them.

It would have been pleasant to record that my great-uncle Harry lived out his days in some quiet Cornish fishing village, renting a studio, sharing his memories with fellow-artists and earning enough to keep him in paint, canvas, the art-journals—and tobacco. The truth is sombre: and at times, pitiful.

I can find nothing to explain why he became as much a slave to alcohol as Rossetti had been to chloral. Perhaps it was because Gabriel's death had distressed him. It is also true that his personal ambitions, such as they were, had been unfulfilled. His work was good, but he was no genius— and knew it.

Almost all the members of his family were (within the limits of their period and surroundings) gay and amusing men and women who enjoyed companionship and good talk. They drew friends to them without realising the quality of their charm. People *liked* them.

Harry had this gift for making friends—and one can only conclude that he became less and less discriminating as to his choice of them. Many years ago I talked to two men who knew him in the last years: and, of course, to Mrs. Watts-Dunton. They all described him as a gentle, courteous man, with perfect manners, and a quiet but twinkling sense of fun.

Harry Dunn had a certain stubborn independence, and even when penniless and ill, he refused to seek help from his family. For years the friendly William Michael lost all trace of him. In 1895, Miss Lena Ashwell, the actress, read William's *Memoir* of his brother and noted that he no longer knew what had happened to Dunn.

It struck me [she wrote] that you might possibly care to know where to find him. It is very sad that a man with such talent should have sunk so low, but some three years ago I came across him in a second-hand shop in King's Road, Chelsea. He was painting tables and corner cupboards in the French style. Murray found him in the Workhouse and took pity on him. He is himself a very poor man and I fancy can do little to help Mr. Dunn, and if you would take an interest in him perhaps he might still do good work.

Please forgive my troubling you.

Yours truly,
LENA ASHWELL.

P.S. I think 429 King's Road is the number.

Whether William did indeed trace him is not known. We may be sure he tried to do so: but it is probable that by the time he called at the address furnished by Miss Ashwell, Harry had wandered off. The next we hear of him is when he arrived unexpectedly at the front door of The Pines, weary, homeless and disreputably dressed.

Many unkind things have been said about Watts-Dunton—that he was a fussy little solicitor with literary pretensions, that in his missionary zeal as a reformer he became a nuisance and a bore. But it could never be said that his Christian principles were not given practical expression. He had a passion for helping lame dogs. His treatment of Swinburne and Treffry Dunn was generous and hospitable to a degree.

Harry, in his late fifties, had drifted away from all his old haunts in Chelsea. Deserted even by his most dubious acquaintances he began a long and lonely tramp through England. Even his sister, Edith, had no idea of his whereabouts, or of his plight. Many thought him dead.

In desperation he remembered Watts-Dunton and dragged himself wearily to The Pines. His old friend was out when he called, but Watts-Dunton's sister, Mrs. Charles Mason, recognised in the ragged individual with his mane of unkempt white hair, the once dapper and efficient art-assistant who had been Dante Gabriel Rossetti's companion at Cheyne Walk, and who had painted her portrait. She gave him enough silver to buy food and a night's lodging and asked him to return the following day at an hour when her brother would be at home.

Watts-Dunton, shocked by the change in Harry Dunn's appearance, acted quickly. Harry could stay and repay him by making himself useful in any capacity he could. What in fact happened was that a room at The Pines was fitted up as a studio, and here, with materials supplied by his old friend, he painted away to his heart's content. He took all his meals at The Pines, but his host gave him enough money to pay for a modest bedroom only a short distance away. There was, of course, the inevitable condition —no more alcohol, except for a modest daily glass of ale to be taken at the Green Man. Mrs. Watts-Dunton writes: "Shut up in his studio at The Pines from nine o'clock in the morning until six o'clock in the evening, the reclaimed artist led a sober, even industrious, life." Watts-Dunton would himself suggest subjects, and there is every reason to suppose that Harry, for the first time in many years, felt serene and secure.

Poverty, hunger and physical hardship—to say nothing of those "deplorable" illnesses—had undermined his health. Sitting at his easel one day he collapsed in pain. Watts-Dunton summoned a cab and took Harry to St. George's Hospital, where he died a few days later, in February 1899. With characteristic compassion, Watts-Dunton paid all the expenses of treatment and, in due course, of the funeral.

So passed from the world an unaffected man of more than ordinary gifts, who played a modest but far from negligible rôle in the story of Dante Gabriel Rossetti. He was content to serve a man whose reputation inevitably overshadowed his own. He knew his master's shortcomings— few, indeed, knew them so well—but for him Rossetti remained one of the finest poetic spirits of his century, in whose diction there was magic, and who saw the common things of life and death as though they were illumined by a halo. He watched, as it were, from a chair on the other side of the fireplace the unfolding of a great personal tragedy.

It was Harry Dunn's own tragedy that, deprived of Rossetti's trust and friendship, he sank deeper and deeper into the shadows of his own making.

Index